The Mammoth Book of

POKER

Also available

The Mammoth Book of

POKER

PAUL MENDELSON

RUNNING PRESS
PHILADELPHIA · LONDON

Constable & Robinson Ltd
3 The Lanchesters
162 Fulham Palace Road
London W6 9ER
www.constablerobinson.com

First published in the UK by Robinson,
an imprint of Constable & Robinson, 2008

A copy of the British Library Cataloguing in Publication
Data is available from the British Library

UK ISBN 978-1-84529-807-4

1 3 5 7 9 10 8 6 4 2

First published in the United States in 2008 by Running Press Book Publishers
All rights reserved under the Pan-American and International Copyright Conventions

9 8 7 6 5 4 3 2 1
Digit on the right indicates the number of this printing

US Library of Congress number: 2008923886
US ISBN 978-0-7624-3381-0

Running Press Book Publishers
2300 Chestnut Street
Philadelphia, PA 19103-4371
www.runningpress.com

Visit us on the web!

www.runningpress.com

Printed and bound in the EU

CONTENTS

INTRODUCTION

Nick-the-Greek – Nick Dandalos – one of the biggest gamblers of all time, always said that his favourite thing in life was gambling and winning; the second-best, gambling and losing. Over a lifetime of poker, casino card games and dice, he won and lost several fortunes, reputedly ending his days searching out low-stake poker games just for some action. This book is about gambling and winning . . . a lifetime of winning!

The massive explosion in the popularity of poker at the start of the twenty-first century, ignited by television coverage and the possibilities of endless games online, has made this the gambling game of choice for anyone who wants to enjoy the vertiginous thrills and spills, the adrenalin rushes and sustained high-octane pressure – and to win! Because there are hundreds of millions of people who 'play' poker these days, just for the fun of it, just like on TV, there is now an unparalleled opportunity to play to win: to turn a hobby into a fine source of income, from modest pocket money to full-time serious earnings.

It is no coincidence that the form of poker that has been at the forefront of the game's explosion is Texas Hold 'Em. It's been described as the Cadillac, or Rolls-Royce, of poker variations and it certainly does combine skill and luck and plenty of action. The vast majority of poker hands being dealt right now, as you read this, will be Hold 'Em. This is the form which allows the skilful player to make slow but steady progress up the rankings, be they tournament results or profits in cash games. It is the game the WSOP – World Series of Poker – reserves for the final championship of over a month of poker action. Some experts feel that there is, perhaps, just too much luck in Hold 'Em to ensure that they make the final tables and big payouts regularly. Some think that the game has become too popular; that anyone can play and that the skill element is reduced. They favour HORSE tournaments, which feature five alternating forms of poker, to truly challenge them. The games are Hold 'Em, Omaha, Razz, Stud and Eights or Over. Intriguingly, at the time of writing, all final table action (where the really big payouts are proffered by bikini-clad beauties) is exclusively Texas Hold 'Em, acknowledging that this is the game which you have to master to make it big. The professional players' move away from playing exclusively Hold 'Em is great news for the serious amateurs – there's more chance of hitting it big if some of the pros are staying away. For these reasons we'll be concentrating on Hold 'Em in the Mammoth Book of Poker: it's available everywhere – an international language. If you can play Hold 'Em successfully, given some practice, you'll be able to adapt to any variation of the game to which you put your mind. Play Hold 'Em decently and you'll be a winner. Your hobby will finance itself: meals and hospitality will come your way, trips to Vegas, Europe and Australia, and the opportunity to treat yourself – or a long-suffering loved one – to a gift or two from your profits, be they large or small.

To sum up: the world is full of people who think they can play poker, people who have watched the game on TV, seen it featured in a James Bond movie, but they will be, almost without exception, losers. If you study and master the key elements, know how to recognize the game for you, and you have the patience and discipline to make yourself into a winning player then, with the help of this book, you really will be able to play poker – not just play at playing. You'll win – and win consistently.

I think that Nick-the-Greek was right: gambling and winning is a great feeling. Gambling and losing has its charms too, but it's way down on my list of life's pleasures. Just as the celebrity-obsessed culture of the twenty-first century makes you forget that you have to work to succeed in this world, I'll be reminding you that to become a poker star, you'll have to work – practise and study – and work some more.

One of the world's great poker players, Doyle Brunson, was seen recently saying that winning a poker tournament is a bit like winning the lottery, but that the difference between him and most other players is that he holds more tickets. At the end of this book, you too will hold extra tickets . . . . then, it's just up to you to win.

Paul Mendelson

A BRIEF HISTORY OF POKER

The Chinese are credited with the invention of playing cards and it is from there that the game which has evolved into modern-day poker probably first began. Ranked cards, and the concept of hidden cards, and therefore the ability to 'bluff', have certainly been around for close on a millennium.

In the sixteenth century, a game called 'Primero' was the game to be seen playing in Spain and many believe that this game is the direct relation to modern-day poker. It seems to have involved the dealing of three hidden cards to each player and then a betting structure which allowed for bluffs and double-bluffs.

In the eighteenth century, a French game called 'Poque' made its way with the first settlers from its mother country to Canada and then south to the northern states of America. Many scholars believe that it found its first stronghold in New Orleans, before drifting its way up the Mississippi throughout the country.

In *The Reformed Gambler*, by Jonathan H Green, published in 1858, Green describes his conversion from gambler to exposer-of-cheats and teacher of games. He talks about the 'Cheating Game' which, considering that almost all gambling in those days featured rigging, marking, card-sharping and forceful robbery, was a pretty damning nickname, and how the original game of 3-card 'Primero' or 'Poque' developed into a more 'honest' gambling card game. Green goes on, in later works, to document the rules, such as they were, the correct strategies, as he saw them, and the methodology for swindling the 'Cheating Game'.

Sadly, religion claims Green, after which he travels about the land lecturing on the evils of gambling and the tricksters and shysters that inhabit that world.

When the Wild West came to the fore, dominating not only US history but also folklore, every town in the land boasted a saloon (with the classic swing-doors) and card games being played overtly or in guarded back rooms. Popular during the Civil War, games that we would now recognize as poker have developed consistently into the main games we know today.

Starting with Stud Poker, where cards were dealt and you bet only on your own hand, with no further cards being dealt, the game then developed the facility to exchange cards for new ones – Draw Poker – allowing you to draw to your hand and therefore developing the odds-based considerations which we now take for granted, right up to the modern-day popular variations, featuring shared or community cards, such as Texas Hold 'Em and Omaha.

Indeed, it was the game of 'skilful' Draw Poker (unlike Stud, which was considered a game of pure luck) which led to legalization of gambling in the state of Nevada in 1931 – and look what that led to! During the Second World War, both President Harry S Truman (who popularized a poker phrase with his now famous utterance of 'the buck stops here') – the buck is another name for the dealer button – and President-to-be, Richard Nixon, played poker successfully; indeed, in Nixon's case, his poker winnings were used as his own personal war chest for his political ambitions.

The credit for the extraordinary boom in the popularity of poker must go to those who first thought up the idea of televising poker with beneath-the-table cameras to show players' cards. 'Presentable Productions', a UK-based television company, started it all off with 'Late Night Poker' and, since then, the explosion of poker on television has stoked the online poker revolution with hundreds of millions of players now sitting down at home, in clubs and casinos, and most abundantly, in front of their computer monitors to play.

Of all the games, No-Limit Texas Hold 'Em, often referred to as the 'Cadillac of Poker', is, by far, the most widely played. It is the game of many small competitions within the pre-eminent poker event each year in Las Vegas, the World Series of Poker (WSOP), as well as the format for the 'Big One', the $10,000 buy-in championship, that acts as a finale to the six weeks of world-class poker.

With Texas Hold 'Em offering unlimited thrills and spills, involving a huge percentage of luck, many of the world's top players look to events which offer them a chance to compete against one another at a variety of forms of the game. HORSE events feature Hold 'Em, Omaha, Razz, 7-card Stud, and 7-card Stud Hi/Lo Eights or better. The $50,000 buy-in Championship is now considered by many professionals as the most important event in the world to win.

There will, undoubtedly, be many more forms and variations of poker to come. The professionals will want games of skill and judgment, where luck plays as small a role as possible. The average player will want games which combine both luck and skill so that they can continue to dream that they, one day, might, just might, become World Champion.

POKER SUCCESS: LUCK OR SKILL?

At the beginning of the twenty-first century, Texas Hold 'Em is more widely played than any other variation of poker. Let's see how the game works, take a look at some basic ideas of how to play, and talk about some of the poker language you will encounter.

Poker is a gambling game, which involves skill and judgment, courage and observation, study and luck. There has been a debate raging for as long as poker has been around as to how skilful a game it really is or whether it is just a true gamble enveloped by the mystique of skill. There is no easy answer but I can confidently report that there is, without a doubt, far more luck in all forms of poker than most players would care to admit. Indeed, I would say, as a rough guide, Texas Hold 'Em poker is about 5 per cent skill and about 95 per cent luck.

You may balk at such a figure and, if you can select your game precisely, you may be able to increase the skill factor to, say, 10 per cent. But, at the end of the day, cards *is* cards and poker is gambling.

At this point, you may wonder how it is that, if poker is just so much luck, the famous poker players keep cropping up in the final stages of every tournament they enter. The answer is simple: they don't. What you see on television, certainly in the UK, is coverage from just a few events each year, as well as specially-commissioned events, sponsored by online card rooms and land-based bookmaking companies. In turn, these companies sponsor a group of well-known players to play on their sites, write articles and promote their products, so it is no surprise that the same group of professional players end up on your television screens.

Secondly, back in the 1970s and 1980s, the top pros would always be around at the end of a big tournament. But, back then, there were very few major events and very few serious professionals, so it was inevitable that most would do well playing against a weak field. Added to that, the difference between a professional and an amateur back in those days was enormous, since you needed to play tens of thousands of hands and, in card rooms and casinos, that took years of playing and practising.

These days, there are thousands of people who consider themselves professional players. They have played their tens of thousands of hands online in a fraction of the time it took the old-fashioned pros to gain their experience. Due to this, plus a plethora of decent poker books, widespread television coverage and greatly increased prize money, more and more serious amateur players are devoting much or all of their spare time to creeping up behind the pros, threatening to take them down a peg or two.

The fact is that to reach the final table of a major tournament requires huge quantities of luck, often over a period of several days or a week, but, even with all that luck, you will still need great skill and determination to make it there.

Before you or your friends dismiss poker as just another gambling game, let's take a moment to consider what kind of return a 5 per cent skill factor might provide. Imagine the Las Vegas skyline of multi-billion dollar hotels and developments. Think about the luxurious accommodation you can enjoy there, the free drinks, meals, suites and limousine rides. All these exist and can be yours because the casinos know that they have an edge over you. Played sensibly, many casino games offer the house one or two per cent in their favour and it is on those odds that billions of dollars are made.

If you can make your skill factor count in a poker game, you too can expect, over a period of time, slowly to eke out profits. Play poker for tiny stakes, and your profits will be slow and they will be small. Play for higher stakes, and your profits will increase. Truly master the game and your high-stake play can yield you an income many of the world's population can only dream of. However – and read this carefully – to get decent at poker is hard work, the skill factor will never provide you with a consistent edge, luck will always influence outcomes, sometimes for long periods of time, and you must become a master of your own temperament before there is any hope of mastering the game. Still up for the challenge?

INTRODUCING TEXAS HOLD 'EM

Like all poker games, Texas Hold 'Em involves forming the best five-card hand. The Universal Rankings for Poker Hands shows the order of importance of each type of hand, from the most valuable at the top to the least important at the bottom. This isn't an arbitrary ranking: it is formed strictly on the likelihood of seeing each combination.

The Universal Rankings for Poker Hands

Royal Flush   A♣ K♣ Q♣ J♣ 10♣   5 cards of the same suit in sequence from ace to ten

Straight Flush   9♥ 8♥ 7♥ 6♥ 5♥   5 cards of the same suit in sequence

4-of-a-Kind   K♠ K♥ K♦ K♣   any   4 cards of the same value

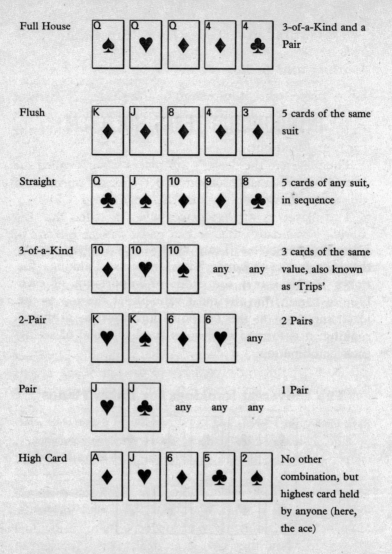

Full House	3-of-a-Kind and a Pair
Flush	5 cards of the same suit
Straight	5 cards of any suit, in sequence
3-of-a-Kind	3 cards of the same value, also known as 'Trips'
2-Pair	2 Pairs
Pair	1 Pair
High Card	No other combination, but highest card held by anyone (here, the ace)

Let's see how Texas Hold 'Em is played and then look at some tips for beginners.

Outline of A Texas Hold 'Em Game

Dealing and Blinds

Every player takes it in turn to be the Dealer. In front of him will be a small, usually white, disk called the 'Dealer Button' (referred to simply as 'The Button'). Before the cards are dealt out:

The player to the dealer's left places what is called the 'Small Blind', a mandatory small bet. (For the purposes of this example, we will say that the small blind is $1.)

The player to his left places what is called the 'Big Blind', a mandatory bigger bet, usually twice the size of the small blind. (For the purposes of this example, we will say that the big blind is $2.)

The reason that these bets are placed is so that there is some money in the pot to be won, even before the cards are dealt out. Once the game starts, if the other players wish to stay in the hand, they will have to match the highest bet that has been made. Currently, this is the big-blind bet placed by the player two places to the left of the dealer. Everyone in the game will take it in turns, as the dealer button moves one place to the left after each hand, to place the small and big blinds.

The dealer now deals one card face down to each player, starting with the player on his left and continuing around the table to himself. Then he deals a second card face down to every player in the same manner. These cards are known as the player's 'Hole Cards' since they are in the hole, or hidden, and only to be looked at by the individual players to whom they have been dealt. It is important to protect your cards from being seen by your opponents.

When he has finished dealing, the dealer places the remaining cards to one side. Some of these will be needed shortly.

The Betting: Folding, Calling and Raising

Everything at the poker table always moves clockwise. Once the deal is finished, the action turns to the player to the left of the big-blind bettor. That player looks at his two cards without showing them to anyone else and decides whether he is prepared to match the big blind's bet of $2 to remain in the hand. The correct strategy for what to decide will be discussed in the section which follows.

If you look at your cards and decide that you do not wish to match the highest bet currently placed, then you push your cards towards the dealer, face down, and you are out of this hand. This is called 'Folding' or 'Passing' and it is an action with which you will quickly become familiar since it is what you do for the majority of the time.

If you do wish to play the cards in front of you, then you place an amount in chips (sometimes called checks) in front of you which matches exactly the biggest bet so far placed (here, the big-blind bet of $2). Before you place your chips, or as you are doing so, you say the word 'Call'. This means that you are matching the bet and wish to continue in this hand.

If you look at your two hole cards and find that they are particularly good (the best two-card hand you can have at this stage would be the highest pair possible, ace – ace), then you might choose to increase the bet that has been made, forcing players who wish to stay in the hand now to match your higher bet. This is called 'Raising'. How much you can raise the bet will depend upon whether you are playing Limit Texas Hold 'Em or No-Limit Texas Hold 'Em. In the former, the amount by which you can raise is limited; in the latter form of the game, you can usually raise any amount you wish, from a minimum of twice the size of the big-blind bet, right up to every chip you have in front of you.

Before you bet, or whilst you are doing so, say the word 'Raise', and push your chips into a small pile in front of you.

By the way, don't throw your bets into the middle of the table straight away. Keep whatever you have bet pushed out in front of you in a little pile. This way, other players can see how much you have bet, so that they know how much they must bet in order to remain in the hand. Only once everyone has had a chance to fold, call, or raise, does everyone's individual bets get pushed into the middle of the table to form 'the pot', for which everyone still in the hand is playing.

To throw your bet into the middle of the table where it mingles with chips already bet is known as 'Splashing the Pot', an action often undertaken by cheats and swindlers who pretended to throw in the correct amount of chips but, in fact, bet less than they stated. Because the chips were all mixed up with other people's chips, no one could really tell what had happened and the cheat got away with it. So, no splashing your chips!

Now that you have raised, let's say to $6, any other player who wishes to remain with you in the hand must match your bet of $6 (or perhaps even raise again – known as a 'Re-Raise'). Only once everyone who wishes to stay in the hand has matched your bet can the action continue.

If no one is prepared to match your bet of $6 – that means that each one will, in turn, opt to fold – then you win the pot without even having to show your cards. In effect, your opponents have given up and conceded the pot to you without playing any further.

Indeed, if, at any time in the hand, one player makes a bet that is not matched by at least one other player, then he wins the pot without having to show his hand. (You should almost never show your hand unless you are required to do so.) This is how you can 'Bluff' other players into thinking that you have the best hand, scaring them away from matching your bet, causing them to fold their cards and concede the pot to you without ever having to reveal what you held.

The Community Cards

Assuming that at least one other player has matched your $6 bet, the game proceeds to the next stage: the first of the 'Community Cards'. In poker, community cards are cards which are dealt, face up, into the middle of the table. Any player still in the hand uses these cards, plus his two secret hole cards, to form the best five-card poker hand.

The first community cards in Texas Hold 'Em are known as 'The Flop'.

The Flop

The dealer discards the next card on the top of the undealt deck and throws it away face down. This is known as 'burning a card'. This is a safety precaution against cheating, or in case any of the players happens to have glimpsed the next card to be dealt.

The dealer then deals the next three cards, face up, in the middle of the table. This is known as 'The Flop'. Every player around the table who is still in the hand now combines his two hole cards with the three on the table and forms the best five-card poker hand he can make.

At this point, there is now another round of betting. Always moving clockwise from the left of the dealer around the table, any player still in the hand must now decide what to do. The first player has the following options:

Checking

He can 'Check'. This means that, since no one has bet anything so far on this round of the betting, this player wishes not to place a bet at this point. You may check only if no one has placed a bet after the community cards are dealt. If someone has made a bet, then you must either match that bet, raise it, or fold your cards.

To check, you can say 'Check' or tap the table (usually twice) to indicate that this is the action you wish to take. The spotlight now moves clockwise to the next player still in the hand. If all players remaining in the hand opt to check, then the dealer will deal the next community card. If one player makes a bet, then any other player who wishes to remain in the hand must match that bet in order to be able to continue. If you do not want to pay further money to remain in the hand, you concede by folding your cards.

Assuming that everyone checks, or at least two players remain in the hand, the next community card is now dealt.

The Turn

The fourth community card to be dealt is known as the turn, or 'Fourth Street'. The dealer burns the top card from the deck and then turns over one more card face up in the middle of the table, placing it next to the three cards already there. There is now another round of betting.

Assuming that all the players still in the hand either check or match any bets that have been made, the fifth and final community card will be dealt. As always, if one player makes a bet that no other player is prepared to match, then he will win the contents of the pot without having to reveal his cards.

The River

The fifth community card dealt is known as the river, or 'Fifth Street'. I think that the name 'river' probably derives from the fact that the last community card to appear often affects the entire game and it is therefore a river down which many a poker player's dreams have ebbed and flowed away.

Anyway, as before, the dealer burns the top card from the deck and then turns over one more card face up in the middle of the table, placing it next to the flop and turn cards already there. There is now a final round of betting.

Once again all players still in the hand may check, bet or raise. As before, if one player makes a bet which no one else is prepared to match, then he wins the hand without having to show his cards. However, if everyone checks, or one player places a bet which at least one other player matches (or calls) then there is a showdown.

The Showdown

The showdown requires all players still in the hand to reveal their hole cards. Everyone then sees who has the best hand and the pot is given to the holder of the highest-value hand.

There are occasions where both players have a similar holding and therefore hold the same hand. If this is the case, the pot is split between those two (or more) winning players.

By the way, there is poker etiquette as to how you should show your cards:

If all the players have checked on the last round of betting, then all those players should reveal their cards more or less simultaneously. The best hand(s) takes the pot.

If one player has bet and another player has called the bet, that second player has, in effect, paid to see the original bettor's cards. Therefore, if you make a bet and you are called, you must reveal your hole cards first. If your opponent cannot beat the hand you now show him, he will probably fold his own cards and not show them to anyone, conceding the pot to you; if he can beat the hand you are declaring, he turns over his cards and reveals his superior hand.

The Slowroll

To slowroll (sorry, it's a nasty poker-world verb) is to turn over your winning cards very slowly, usually after some verbal banter or an exchange of hard stares. This sort of thing happens a lot in the movies and thrillers where the villain makes this move against the good guy. This is a major error of poker etiquette.

If you have won the hand, turn your cards over quickly and claim the pot. Don't milk the moment – at least, not until you have revealed your cards. If you do slowroll, don't expect any sympathy from anyone else if your opponent gets extremely angry; it's just bad form.

Incidentally, if you have lost the pot, you shouldn't really show your cards. However, if you do want to show them, you can take as long as you like (within reason), since provided that your opponent has won the pot, he won't care much how long you take to let him know the good news. Basically, however, keep it simple and, if you are going to reveal your cards, do it quickly.

Information about your Opponents: Tells

The showdown is important, not only for the players still contesting the pot, but also for players who weren't even involved in the hand. Everyone has a chance to see what cards their opponents were holding and remember how that player bet those cards and behaved throughout the hand. It is by observing the actions of your opponents that you learn about them, improve your own game, and build up some information about your opponents which you might be able to use next time you play with them.

As an extreme example, imagine if, throughout this hand, the winning player has been scratching his left ear ferociously. When he shows his cards, you see that he has 'Pocket Rockets' – the nickname for a pair of aces as his hole cards (or 'in the hole') and the best hand he could have picked up. Next time that you see him scratching his ear, you may remember this and work out that when he holds really good cards, he gets nervous and scratches his ear. This is known as a 'Tell', a physical sign, often subconscious, that reveals a player's state of mind.

It is completely obvious to you that he has been doing this, but it may not have been observed by other players, and the player who is doing all the scratching may not realize that he is doing it. If you can spot this tell and remember it the next time you play against him, you have a skill advantage against him because you know something about his behaviour that he doesn't know that you know.

Expert poker players remember just about everything about their opponents: how they behaved with good cards, medium cards, poor cards, how they bet, how their voice altered, how the pulse in their neck started throbbing, or their mouths went dry or their hands shook. You don't need to worry about any of this now, other than to think about constantly observing your opponents to build a picture of their demeanour during the hand.

Now that the pot has been won and the chips gathered up by the winning player, the dealer button moves clockwise one place and the next player becomes the dealer. The next two players place their small and big blinds and the dealer distributes the cards. The next hand has started already.

By the way, poker isn't a genteel game. You can talk to your opponents during a hand and try to unnerve them. You can brag about winning a pot or bluffing someone successfully. You can boast that you are the best player that there is and your opponents are all 'Donkeys', 'Palookas' or any other derogatory term you think of ('Donkey' and 'Palooka' are just two popular ones). Indeed, some players make a profession out of nagging their opponents verbally from the moment that they sit down to the moment they leave. Often, on television, you see players like this and they are often successful.

However, my very strong advice would be not to fall into the trap of talking too much at the poker table during a hand. Talk only between hands, if you must, or when you are not involved in a hand yourself. The moment you do play a hand, whether it is good or bad, then just shut up, hunker down and concentrate. If you do this, you'll give less away and take more in.

So, that's how a hand of Texas Hold 'Em works. You get two, secret, hole cards, and then if the hand runs to the end, there are five community cards (or 'Up-Cards') from which you may use three, four, or even all five, to construct your best five-card poker hand.

However, if you think that your opponents don't have very good hands, you can make a big, bluff bet to try to persuade each of them to throw away their cards, convincing them that you have the best hand. To achieve this is a rare, but particularly sweet, pleasure.

Variations of Texas Hold 'Em

Each variation will have its own chapters to follow but, to start, let's see the three different styles in which Texas Hold 'Em can be played:

Limit

In this style, all bets are limited to specific sums, which cannot alter at that table (except perhaps by the agreement of every player present). Usually, the number of raises permitted per betting round is capped.

Limit Hold 'Em is, these days, considered a little slow and restrictive for most players. However, because pots are always limited to a maximum, players know that their bankroll is protected from catastrophe on any single hand. For players with limited budgets, who do not seek the acutely stressful thrill of No-Limit or, to some extent, Pot-Limit where you know you could go broke on any hand you play, Limit poker is considered relaxing. It is a game for grinders: people who are prepared to work long and hard to grind out a profit. At high enough limits, many poker professionals and semi-professionals make a decent living but, they are the first to admit, it is a job that is anything but glamorous or exciting.

Limit poker is usually played in card clubs and casinos and, at the time of writing, is the pre-eminent form available in the card rooms of Las Vegas. Indeed, whatever style or variation of poker you normally play, this will be the one you find yourself facing when you make your pilgrimage to gambling 'Mecca', Las Vegas.

Pot-Limit

restricts bets and raises to the size of the current pot, but with no upper limit to the size of the pot. These days, with the aggressive style of many players, Pot-Limit may as well be No-Limit when it comes to the overall size of pots. However, because early betting is relatively small – compared to the potential size of the final pot – it is a style which favours those players who like to see a flop. Those who feel they are good at judging how the flop may have helped everyone find that they can reach this stage of the hand cheaply and be in a good position to judge whether they can, once the pot size has grown hugely, make a killing later.

Pot-Limit is predominantly found in European card rooms and, even there, it is slowly becoming a rarer bird.

No-Limit

is the style which most people want to play. Once the blinds have been placed, there is no upper limit as to the size of any bet you care to make at any time. Everything from the minimum permitted bet to an all-in move is on the cards. This means that you can multiply your entire stake on just one hand – or, indeed, lose it. This is what makes No-Limit poker so compelling. It also makes a great money-making activity for those who choose to play it. We'll look at why this is so later on, but one key reason is because it is the style most commonly played in tournaments, be they half-hour, one-table online affairs, or week-long wars of attrition played over hundreds of tables, and players move from a tourney into a cash game and forget to adjust their style. Now, when they play too aggressively or impatiently (styles which are almost always forced on you at some stage or other in tournament poker), they are sitting ducks for a major pot loss.

NO-LIMIT HOLD 'EM

Basic Strategy for NL Hold 'Em Cash Games

For the purposes of these strategy sections, we will assume that you are playing a standard cash game (or 'Ring Game' as it is sometimes called) at home, or in a friendly club, with seven or eight other players. If you have more than nine players at the table, it may prove a bit of a slow game; with six players or fewer, this would be called a 'short-handed' game, as this is fewer than the number of players who would occupy a full table. Short-handed games are best suited to more experienced players who know how to adapt their game to suit different circumstances. We'll learn more about that in the advanced strategy section. Between 7–10 players is ideal for a table of Texas Hold 'Em.

We will also assume that you are playing No-Limit Texas Hold 'Em, which is the most popular variation and form of the game being played globally at the moment. The vast majority of the outlines, tips and strategies suggested also apply to Pot-Limit Hold 'Em so, if this is your local style, simply adapt your betting to fit the limits imposed by the size of the pot.

Elsewhere in this Mammoth book, you will find strategies for Limit Texas Hold 'Em, tournament play, home game tactics, online poker, and other forms of the game.

Beginners' Strategy and Tactics

To play No-Limit Hold 'Em is especially exciting since there are, as the name suggests, no limits to the amount that you can bet at any time. This adds great excitement to the game because it means that on any hand, you might lose all your money, or double it.

Let's imagine that you have exchanged $100 of your money for chips and you take a seat at the table. Stack those chips neatly, so that you can see how much money you have in front of you, and now prepare to be patient. If you follow some basic rules, and remain focused and patient, you can win money even as a beginner in many home and club games.

Starting Hands

The first and, perhaps, most important information with which to become familiar is on what hands you should call or raise to become involved in a poker hand pre-flop (before the flop is dealt).

This is an area where, if you trust the experts and the statistics, you can hugely increase your chances of winning any given session. Quite simply, if you play the wrong hands at the wrong time you will, almost inevitably, lose. All poker players go through losing stages when they begin to play as, like teenagers, they decide to explore and experiment. By all means do this but, if you want to keep hold of your money, come back to the recommended actions as soon as possible. These are tried and tested over billions of hands, and there are players all over the world quietly making money playing poker like this.

Also, remember that everyone goes through a learning stage at poker. The secret of success is not to worry about whether you are winning or losing in any given game, but that you are trying to play correctly without making too many mistakes. This is because, to start with, you will be playing low-stake friendly games, maybe with your mates, or perhaps online. What you win or lose now will be tiny compared to what you may end up winning (or, indeed, losing) once you are more experienced and playing higher-stake games against better opponents. So, get the basics right, and you'll be setting yourself up for a long, successful, poker-playing career.

The good news is that millions of new players have taken up poker, having watched it on television and they are too stupid to realize that to do anything well requires time, patience, dedication, practice and discipline (there will always be the very, very rare exception). This means that there are millions of beatable players, who don't work at their game, think that they are very good, and who are almost offering you their money if you are clever enough to take it.

OK, back to those starting hands:

AA, KK, AK, QQ

If you see a pair of high cards when you look at your hole cards, you have an excellent starting hand. A pair of aces is the strongest possible hand you can get dealt since, with only two cards for each player, no one can hold better than a pair, and you have the highest pair possible. KK and QQ are both very strong hands also.

AK, often known as 'the Big Slick' is also a strong hand but, at the moment, it is only an ace-high hand. However, if amongst the community cards, an ace or king appears, then you will have a highest pair, with a high 'kicker'.

A kicker is a card not directly involved in forming a poker hand, but which may be used if there is a tie. Let's look at an example:

You hold: A♣ K♥
Your opponent holds: K♦ Q♣

You and he stay in the hand until the end, and there is a showdown between you.

The community cards (or 'board') are as follows:

Using the king and the two eights on the board, at the showdown, both you and your opponent claim a poker hand of 2-pair: you both hold a pair of kings and a pair of eights. However, a poker hand always consists of five cards, so there is still one more card to add to each hand. Your next-best card is your A♣; your opponent's next-best card is his Q♣. Therefore you have 2-pair with an ace kicker; your opponent holds the same 2-pair, but with a queen kicker. The kicker plays and you rake in the pot.

When you hold AA, KK, QQ or AK, you should always raise the betting since you are most likely to hold the best hand at the moment and you want to make other players put more money into the pot that you are likely to be winning.

If a player has already raised the pot, you should re-raise him to show him that you believe that you have the better hand. This may force him to fold his cards (conceding the hand to you) or he may call your re-raise and continue with the hand. If he does this, he probably has a strong hand as well, and you must play the rest of the hand with care. What you do once the flop, turn and river cards are dealt, we will discuss a little later.

JJ, 1010, 99, 88

These are good starting hands, but not brilliant. If an ace, king, or queen appears on the flop, anyone with one of those cards in their hands would have a higher pair than you.

My advice would be to raise with all these hands, and call a raise if it is made before you. Ideally, you are hoping for a flop which either contains all cards that are lower than your pair or, better still, gives you a third card to match your pair, making you trips – quite a strong hand to have.

In the case of another good hand, AQ – on which you should also raise pre-flop – you would like to see a queen on the flop, giving you top pair, with the best possible kicker, or an ace on the flop, giving you top pair, with a decently strong kicker.

If the flop does not produce any of these situations, then if an opponent makes a bet, you will probably have to concede by folding your hand.

77, 66, 55, 44, 33, 22, AJs, A10s, KQs, KJs, QJs, J10s

The small 's' next to some of these hands denotes that they are 'suited' cards. This means that they are both the same suit. The advantage of suited cards is that they offer you a small extra chance to make a flush (it is only about a 3 per cent chance). Suited cards are a bonus, but should not be overvalued.

These cards are worth a call pre-flop, provided that no one has made a raise. If they have, the chances are that your cards will not be the best at the table and, even if they are the best hand now, they are unlikely to be so after some community cards have appeared. As you gain in experience, you may wish to play these cards more aggressively but, for now, they should be played carefully.

On the flop, you hope that your low pair will become

trips, that your AJ or A10 is matched by an ace on the flop, or two (or, better still, three cards) of the same suit as yours giving you a draw for a flush, or flush on the flop.

Cards such as QJs and J10s offer the chance of both a flush and also a possible straight. The ideal flop for, say, J♣ 10♣ would be as follows:

This gives you a straight flush draw. That is to say:

if another club appears on the turn or river, you have made a flush if any king or 8 appears, you have made a straight, and if K♣ or 8♣ appears, you have made a straight flush – 'the nuts' (an unbeatable hand on this deal).

So, although you still haven't made a decent poker hand, there are two further chances for you to make a very strong hand if the turn or river cards deliver up something you are looking for. This is what we would call a strong 'drawing hand' – a hand which may well be improved considerably when the last two community cards have been dealt.

Obviously, if you are holding: J♣ 10♣ and the flop comes:

that means that you have no pair, no draw, and no hope of winning the hand unless, by some miracle, the next two cards are both jacks, or both tens, or maybe king and then queen. Never rely on a miracle at poker, never expect one, never put money into a pot hoping for one. *Never!* So, on this flop, the moment anyone else bets, you will fold your cards and hope for better luck next time.

So, play only those starting hands and no others. This

will mean that you are folding a lot of the time (you may do so for hours) and you may become jealous that everyone else is having fun, betting away like maniacs, winning and losing. However, by playing tight this way, you are saving your money for when you do pick up a big hand and then you should be able to win a big pot of money. It's strange, the bigger my stack of chips, especially if I have won them off the other players at my table, the more patient I become. I know that I can win this way.

So, pre-flop, these are the hands you will play:

All thirteen pairs: AA down to 22
AK and AQ
AJs, A10s, KJs, K10s, QJs, J10s

All other hands, however many of them you see, get folded. Resist the temptation to play a hand just because you are bored. The statistics show that you are likely to lose money whenever you play those inferior hands and, in the long run, you will certainly lose money.

Acting on The Flop

If you haven't already folded your cards pre-flop, when the first three community cards appear, this is the time to check that you are still happy to be in the hand and in a position to win money. This is the time when you have to make cold, logical decisions: in the first instance, whether or not the flop has improved your hand. When we move on to intermediate tactics, we will also analyse whether or not the flop cards might have helped your opponents but, for the moment, concentrate on your own hand.

Let's take a look at some examples:

You hold: A♣ A♦. You raised pre-flop and received one caller. The flop comes:

Should you bet or check?

When you first see the flop, it is important to register the texture and make-up of the three community cards. Here, you have a dangerous flop for your hand since, not only are there flush possibilities – there are two clubs showing, but also straight possibilities. If your opponent has called your raise on J10s, he now has an open-ended straight draw.

For these reasons, you should certainly bet here. If your opponent does have a possible draw, you must make him pay to see the next card. I would recommend making a pot-sized bet.

There are other good reasons for betting here also. As you will see, even in the more advanced discussion of tactics, betting when you think you hold the best hand is the right course of action at least 95 per cent of the time and even quite modest poker players can make money in a cash game simply by being disciplined, folding poor cards and betting when they hold good cards.

On this deal, your opponent may hold a king or queen and may continue to call all your bets until you showdown the hand.

What would you do if you bet and then your opponent raised you? This is tougher, because it is possible that you were called on KQ but, as we will see, there are many other hands on which your opponent might raise at this point, and you must certainly call. Personally, I would re-raise again, probably the size of the pot. If that bet is called, you should slow down your betting and hope to reach a showdown without committing too much more to the pot. It is quite possible that you are beaten unless you hit a third ace.

You hold: K♣ J♠. You call and see the flop with three other players. The flop comes:

This means that you hold top pair, with a decent-sized kicker. You almost certainly have the best hand now and you should make a bet at your turn. With three other players still involved, I recommend making a pot-sized bet. In all probability, all the other players will fold but you may find that one calls you holding second pair (he might have A♦ 7♣, and is hoping that another 7 or an ace appears on the turn).

If someone makes a bet before it is your turn to act, I would recommend raising that bet, probably by doubling whatever he bet. If your raise is called by your opponent, then you must consider that you do not have the best hand and you will hesitate before committing any more money to the pot. However, your raise may well frighten your opponent out of the hand and give you the pot before any further cards are dealt.

In both these examples, either you had such a good starting hand that the flop did not really affect you, or the flop gave you the top pair. Far more often, when the flop arrives, you will see that it has not helped your hand very much. That does not mean that your shoulders should slump and that you give up, but you must think clearly about what action, if any, you will now take.

You hold: A♣ K♦ and you raise. You receive one caller and the flop comes:

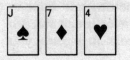

Should you check or bet?

The one good thing about holding AK is that when you miss the flop, it's pretty clear. However, just because you didn't hit, it doesn't mean that your opponent did. Here, you should make what is called a 'follow-up' or 'continuation' bet.

A bet here may well take down the pot for you, since, unless your opponent holds a jack, he has likely missed this flop (not seen anything there to improve his hand) as well. By betting straight out, you force that opponent to guess whether you really do still have the best hand (which you may well do here) or whether it is worth his while calling speculatively. Sensible players will usually opt to fold their cards, leaving you with the pot.

If you are called then, unless a king or ace arrives, you will not make or call another bet. You tried to steal the hand on the flop, it didn't work and now you should concede quietly.

You hold: A♣ J♦. You raise on the button and the big blind calls you.

The flop comes:

| K♣ | Q♦ | 4♥ |

Your opponent bets the pot (makes a bet equal to the total money in the pot so far); what should you do?

You may be tempted to call here because you hold an ace and, if a ten appears on the turn or the river, you would have the 'nut' (best) straight. However, the chances of that ten arriving are very small, so you will be betting hugely against the odds. In the intermediate section, we will look at 'Pot Odds' from which we can tell whether or not it is worth continuing in a hand. My advice to beginners is always this:

Call for a flush or an open-ended straight draw (one which has both a higher card and a lower card which can make your straight), but never call for a gut-shot (or 'belly-buster') straight draw.

You hold: K♣ Q♦

The flop comes:

This is an open-ended straight draw – you can hit either an ace or a nine to make your straight.

You hold: A♣ J♦

The flop comes:

This is a gut-shot or belly-buster draw because only one card – a 10 – will make your straight. There is half the chance of hitting a gut-shot straight draw as making an open-ended straight draw and that is why the gut-shot draws should be discarded and the open-ended draws considered as a decent chance. When you obey these rules, you are giving yourself a chance to make a powerful hand about one time in three.

There are more effective, aggressive ways to play hands when you face this situation, which we will look at when we move on to the Intermediate Strategy.

You hold: 8♥ 8♣ and you raise. You get two callers and the flop arrives as follows:

This is a terrible flop for you since one of the two callers is extremely likely to hold either an ace or a queen. It is probably not worth betting again into this pot. However, if both players check and you are the last to act, you might try a bet about half the size of the pot. If neither opponent holds an ace, they may both fold and you might take the pot. Otherwise, just check and hope that your opponents do also, and perhaps a miracle 8 will appear on the turn or river.

My general rule for mid-sized pairs (66 through to, say JJ) is to play them strongly – by raising and betting – unless there are two overcards (cards higher than your pair) showing on the board. Once that happens, there is too great a chance that you are beaten.

Indeed, the more opponents who are still in the hand against you, the less likely it is that your mid-sized pair will be the best hand after the flop.

If you raise with your 8♥ 8♣ and receive only one caller and the flop comes:

10	9	2
♣	♥	♠

even though there are two overcards on the flop, it is quite possible that your single opponent does not hold a 9 or 10 in his hand and, for that reason, you may still decide to bet – or raise – strongly with your 88 and hope to take the pot on the flop.

With the same hand and the same flop, when you face three other players still in the pot, even that modest flop quite possibly represents too much of a threat and you should proceed carefully, without committing any more money to the pot.

Most new players see the skill in poker as dragging in a big pot when you outplay your opponents. However, that situation is a comparatively rare occurrence. Most of the time, you are folding poor cards before the flop and, if not then, after the flop has appeared. Throwing away cards which are no longer likely to be winning is one of the greatest skills of the game and, over the thousands of hands that you will play, will probably save you more money than you will ever win. To 'get away from' – throw away – hands that turn bad after the flop, is one of the great skills of a good poker player.

Acting on The Turn

If you are still involved in the hand at this stage, you either believe that you have the best hand at the table, or you feel that there is a good chance that a card will arrive on the turn or river which will give you the best hand. You do not want to be here just because you have an ace in your hand or hold the second- or third-highest pair.

Let's take a look at some possibilities:

You hold: A♠ Q♥. You raise pre-flop and receive two callers. The flop comes:

Holding top pair, and not wanting an opponent to be able to draw another club for a possible flush, you make a pot-sized bet and one opponent calls you, the other folding.

The turn is now:

What do you make of that? Your opponent called a pre-flop raise, so you would expect him to hold something reasonable. When he called your bet on the flop, either he held a queen, giving him top pair, or perhaps he held two clubs and hopes to hit a third club on the board, giving him the club flush.

When 5♥ appears on the turn, this card has almost certainly not helped him, so there is every reason to believe that you still hold the best hand. For this reason, you should bet again now, perhaps a bet equal to about half the pot. This way, if your opponent does hold two clubs, he will have to pay too much to see if a club is going to appear on the river (see Pot Odds in the Intermediate Section) and, if he holds a queen, he may well have a smaller kicker than your ace and you may persuade him to put more money into a pot which he is very unlikely to win.

If he calls your bet, he may be a loose player hoping, against the odds, to hit his flush on the river. If a club does appear on the river, you will have to judge whether that was what he was looking for or whether you still hold the best hand.

Whatever you do, don't check, and give him a chance to see the river card for free.

In simple terms, when the turn card arrives, if you still believe that you hold the best hand, you should bet again. If you are unsure whether the turn card has helped your opponent, you can check, and wait to see whether he bets or whether he checks also.

Although there are many opportunities to fool your opponents by betting in a misleading way, the vast majority of the time you will find that players who check are weak; players who bet are strong.

Similarly, players who just call bets are weak and usually hoping that they hit a miracle card on the turn or river; players who raise or re-raise are genuinely strong and do hold the best hand. As you become more experienced, you will learn to judge when it is likely that your opponent is fooling you, and when it is almost certain that his bets represent his hand accurately.

Acting on The River

By the time the final card appears on the board, you should have made a decision in your own mind as to what your opponent has in his hand. This is known as 'putting an opponent on a hand'. As you become more experienced, you will find that your feeling for what cards your opponents hold becomes more and more accurate and your opinion of their cards starts to form earlier and earlier in the hand. Your general knowledge of your opponents' styles of play will help you to make these decisions and we will look at how to classify opponents in the Intermediate Strategy section.

You hold: K♣ Q♦ and, as everyone before you has folded, you decide to raise on the button pre-flop. The big-blind player calls you and the flop appears:

This is a pretty good flop for you, since it gives you top pair, with a king kicker. The big-blind player checks and you decide to bet the pot. The big-blind player calls and the turn comes:

Clearly, this is a very nice card for you and you are almost 100 per cent certain that you have the best hand. Your opponent probably holds either a straight draw (perhaps he has KJ or J9) or a flush draw (he holds two spades in his hand) and possibly even both (say, K♠ J♠), although if he holds the latter, he should have played his hand differently.

The big-blind player checks again, and you, quite rightly, bet again. You do not want to give your opponent a free chance to see the river and perhaps hit his draw. He calls your bet and the river appears:

This is a disastrous card for you! If your opponent was calling to hit a straight or flush, this river card has given him the best hand. He now makes a pot-sized bet. What should you do?

Almost certainly, he has you beaten. Although you have trip queens, you must accept that your opponent has been lucky and throw away your hand. It is a bitter blow (particularly because your opponent really hasn't played the hand very well), but throwing away the second-best hand is one of the most important skills to be developed in poker.

It is tempting to call this final bet, just to see if your opponent has what he says he has but, if you make a habit of this, you will run out of money. It is, of course, possible that he is bluffing and that he has nothing (or very little) but if that is the case, you must just live with it. He has played the hand poorly up to the last bet and, if he has bluffed you, that was a daring and successful move. I would be very doubtful indeed that his final bet was a bluff.

Incidentally, one tip that is worth remembering is what I sometimes describe as the call-call-bet situation. This is where an opponent checks and then calls your bet, checks and then calls your bet and then, on the river, bets out straight away. This is usually a sign that your opponent has hit his hand and is afraid that if he checks again, you may check as well, so he puts in a bet and hopes you will call it. Don't!

General Attitude

As a beginner, or inexperienced player, your attitude should be to treat all the games you play as practice to build up your stock of knowledge about the game and form opinions about your opponents. As a beginner, you are likely to lose, although if you play simply and carefully in the way described, you may lose only a little and sometimes come out a winner. All poker players go through this stage when they begin the game; it is the price of a poker education. The idea here is to make it the cheapest education possible.

Summary of Basic Strategy and Winning Tips

Here's a summary of what we've looked at, and some further tips to improve your game and increase your chances of success. If you follow this strategy and you play in low-stake games, either at home or online, with players of similar experience, you are likely to end up winning. However, more important than winning is to get into the habit of making the correct decisions as often as possible.

1 Raise When you Have A Strong Hand

When you hold one of the premium starting hands: AA, KK, AK, QQ, it is essential that you raise the betting pre-flop. If someone has already raised, then re-raise! Since you almost certainly hold the best hand at this point, the more money you get into the pot now, the more you are likely to win at the end. Ideally, with these hands, you would like to end up playing against just one opponent. In this way, you should find it easier to judge if you are still winning the hand as the community cards appear.

When you have a good starting hand: JJ, 1010, 99, 88, AQ, raise with these cards pre-flop and call a raise if one is made before you (indeed, if you are daring and aggressive by nature, re-raise with these cards also – they are still very good cards).

If you miss the flop, and overcards appear, you may have to let these hands go if there is betting from your opponent(s).

Call with the other starting hands we have discussed. *Fold all other hands.*

You may find that you fold hand after hand after hand. This may go on for fifteen minutes, half an hour, even an hour. If you can resist the temptation to call with substandard hands, you will be saving yourself money. When you become a bit more experienced, you will see that there are times when you can get involved in a hand on poorer cards but for the moment be patient. This is a winning strategy.

2 Bet or Raise When you Think you Hold The Best Hand

Once the flop has appeared, if you believe that you hold the best hand, make a good-sized bet (something between half the size of the pot and the full pot). By betting, you push out players who might have hit miracle cards to overtake you later on, and you also make players who are on a draw, for a flush or straight, pay extra money into a pot that they are still odds-against winning. By betting, you achieve two key aims: you narrow the field against you, as pairs fold; you build a bigger pot when you are the most likely recipient. This is strong, positive play.

3 Fold your Hand When The Betting Tells you That you Are Beaten

Nobody likes to think that they have been bluffed out of a winning hand, but bluffs play a smaller role in poker than many beginners think. You may have seen exciting bluffs and wild plays on television, but this is because you see only about one hand out of every 40 or 50 hands that get played (often even fewer than that), and the producers always save the most unusual hands for broadcast. In the real world, betting with the best hand and folding when you think you have the second-best hand is the way to win at poker.

If you call with K♣ 9♣ and the flop comes:

and you correctly make a bet then, if an opponent re-raises you, you should consider laying down the hand. What can your opponent have? Surely he also holds a king and, quite possibly, he has a better kicker than your nine. If he held a king with a poorer kicker, he might well just have called your bet and waited to see what appeared on the turn and river. He is very unlikely to have any kind of draw, so top pair with a stronger kicker than yours is his most likely hand.

If you must call here – perhaps because you know your opponent is a pretty aggressive character – unless a nine appears on the turn, you should not put any more money into the pot.

4 Bet or Raise; Don't Call

Most beginners find raising very difficult to do. This is because you are not sure whether your hand is the best. Don't worry about this. Even the experts aren't sure when their hand is the best. However, good players use betting to discover whether their hand is good or not and so should you.

Imagine that you hold A♠ J♥. One player raises before you and you decide to call him. The flop comes:

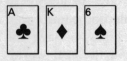

Your opponent makes a pot-sized bet. What should you do?

Firstly, you have to decide what you think your opponent may hold. It is quite possible that he doesn't hold an ace and he is simply making a follow-up bet after his initial raise to test what you have. On the other hand, he may hold an ace, but with a poorer kicker than you. Finally, he may hold AK or AQ. Since you are not sure, this is the time to raise him and see what he does.

When you raise the pot by, say, putting in double the chips your opponent bet, you can then gauge his reaction. We will talk about 'tells', physical reactions, your opponent may make later, but for now, let's see what he does betting-wise.

If he doesn't hold an ace, your raise tells him that you do and so he will probably fold his cards and you will win.

If he does hold an ace, but he doesn't have AK or AQ, he may call. That tells you that you probably have the best hand at the moment.

If he does hold AK or AQ, or even trip aces or kings, he may well re-raise. If he does that, you are probably beaten, and you may well decide to fold your cards.

Of course, your opponent might just be ultra-aggressive and be trying to push you off the pot by making a follow-up bet and he may have none of those hands. If he manages a re-raise in the situation, then he is either mad or brilliant (those two states are fairly close at the poker table) and you are probably outclassed. Otherwise, your raise and your opponent's reaction should help you to sort out where you are – and cheaply. Let me explain:

You hold: A♣ J♥; your opponent holds: A♦ Q♥

He raises 20 and you call 20, and the flop comes:

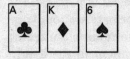

He bets 20, and you call 20. The turn comes:

He bets 40, you call 40. The river comes:

He bets 40; you call 40. He wins; you lose.

Notice that you have called a total of 120 chips and you have lost the pot. You have been unlucky, but you might have done better.

If, on the flop, when your opponent bets 20, you raise 20 (betting 40 chips), and he then re-raises you, say, another 40 chips, you may well be able to judge that you are beaten. You make a great laydown (throw away your cards) and the hand has cost you only 60 chips, instead of 120.

By raising your opponent's bet on the flop, you gained vital information about his hand and came to a decision about your own hand.

On this occasion, you got it absolutely right and saved yourself 60 chips. That is like winning 60 chips! It is not as sexy or as glamorous and you didn't end up pulling a huge pile of chips towards you and gloating over the whole table, but you quietly saved yourself a great deal of money. That is the action of a good player.

So, if you think you have the best hand, bet or raise, don't just call. To call is a weak, passive action. To bet or raise is a strong, positive action and, even if your raise is called or re-raised, you have learnt information about your opponent and his hand. Use that information to decide whether it is worth any further investment in the hand.

5 Pick your Game and Opponents Carefully

Ideally, practise against players slightly better than yourself; it's a great way to learn. However, don't expect to win in the long term and be prepared to lose that money as payment for a decent poker education. Resist the temptation to move up to higher stakes, even if your friends urge you to, until you have gained a lot more experience. Before you play for any significant amount of money, you must be fluent in all the aspects covered by all three sections on strategy in this book (that means this section, the intermediate strategy and the advanced strategy). You may get lucky and win a few sessions early on. If you do, this will be by luck, not skill. You need to recognize that and learn from your good-luck stories as well as your mistakes.

Be careful from whom you take advice. Almost everyone who watches poker on television – and that is hundreds of millions of people – thinks that they can play poker. They can; but, whatever they may tell you, they are almost certainly playing losing poker. Poker players never tell the truth when it comes to how well or badly they are doing, so take boasts from your friends with a pinch of salt. Read books, study the huge number of free tips and articles to be found at reputable online poker sites, and if you play in a friendly club, ask the organizers to point out the best players worth watching. In other words, pick your mentors carefully; there are an awful lot of bad habits that can easily be picked up. The fewer you adopt, the less poor you will be.

Finally, if you find that you are winning a little in a modest game but, when you move up a stake, you find that you are losing, drop back down again quickly. Never mind that your friends may scoff. Your aim is to be a winning player, not yet another losing player who volunteers to be out of his depth just because it looks good to play for higher stakes. Keep your ego out of the game and you will progress more quickly.

6 Don't Bluff

Most weak or inexperienced players hate to feel that they are being bluffed and they will call just to see what you have. Learn quickly that most low-stake, poor-standard games are the wrong place to attempt bluffs as players are just not good enough to be taken in by them. This is one reason why good players should not play against a table of bad players; too many of the game's subtleties are lost when playing weak opposition.

7 Don't Call for Gut-shot Draws or Hope for The Impossible

If you feel that your opponent has a better hand than you, just fold your cards. If you have four cards to a flush or straight, then it will be worth calling a modest bet to see if you can hit your hand. (When we move up to the Intermediate level, you will find that you can also raise in these situations.)

However, don't call if only one card can help your hand: seeking a gut-shot draw, or turning a pair into three-of-a-kind. The chances of hitting your card are so small that, in the long run, you will lose a fortune chasing your dreams. Even if you hit that card occasionally, it won't make up for all the money you have lost on the multitude of other times you have paid out seeking a miracle.

8 Stay Patient

When your cards run bad, and they often do, poker is a boring game. Use the time that you are patiently folding your poor hands to observe your opponents, decide who is strong and who is weak at your table and note the cards that get shown at the end of a hand, remembering how each player bet in that situation. If you identify one strong player at your table, watch how he plays, emulate his style and wait for some good cards to come your way.

Remember this: every time you play poor cards when you should not, you are throwing away money, giving it to your opponents. Resist the urge to play when your cards are bad, and get ready to beat your opponents when they show less self-control and will-power than you. This discipline is how you make money in low- and mid-stake poker games.

9 Never Show your Hand

If you are involved in a showdown, or you are called, obviously you will have to show your hole cards.

However, other than that, never show them. It may be tempting to show that you held the nuts, or even that you have just raised an opponent out of the hand on a complete bluff, but you will do much better never revealing this.

This is because, as you improve at poker, you will learn that observation of your opponents is of vital importance. If your opponent notices that when you bluff, your left eyebrow twitches, he will be able to use that knowledge to judge better what to do the next time you bluff him. However, if you have won the hand without showing your cards, because you made a big bet he wasn't prepared to call, all your opponent knows is that your left eyebrow twitches when you are about to make a big bet. He doesn't know whether this is a genuine, value bet on the best hand, or whether it is a bluff – and that's exactly the information you would prefer to keep secret.

Intermediate Strategy

Now that you have the basic skeleton of the game in your mind, it's time to look at improving your results by learning more about the odds involved, the importance of your position at the table, stealing strategies and pressure bets. As you adopt each of these elements into your game, you will find that your overall style remains simple, patient and aggressive, and these are the characteristics which mark the standard game of the majority of top players.

Position

We start with Position because it is one area where experienced players appreciate its crucial role, whereas beginners either do not understand it, or repeatedly ignore its significance.

Let's take a look at a table:

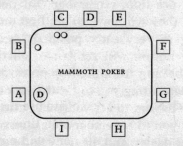

This features a nine-player table of Texas Hold 'Em. You can see the dealer button in front of Player A at the bottom

left of the table, and the small-blind and big-blind bets
placed by opponents on his left – Players B and C. In
poker, the term 'Position' refers to the order in which
players have to act on any given hand.

Pre-flop, the first player who will have to decide
whether to fold, call or raise, will be the player directly
to the left of the big-blind bettor – Player D. This
player is said to be 'under the gun' or in first position.
This player, and the two to his left would be considered
to be sitting in 'early position'. The next two players to
their left will have had an opportunity to see what action
the first three players have taken with their hands
before they themselves have to choose whether or not
to remain in the hand. This 'middle position' – or mid-
position – at least gives those players a chance to have
observed a third of their opponents' actions before
having to act.

The player to their left, one away from the dealer, as
well as the dealer or 'button' himself – Player I – would be
considered to be in 'late position'. This is the best position
in which to find yourself, since you have seen what five or
six players have chosen to do with their hands before you
have to make your decision.

Although the small- and big-blind bettors get the last
chance to act pre-flop, remember that on the flop and
subsequently, they will have to act first and so they will
end up being in very early position. Accordingly, the
player on the button will act last of all the players on
all rounds of betting from the flop onwards.

As well as permitting you to see the actions of the other
players before having to act yourself, sitting in late position can allow you to become more aggressive since there
will be only the dealer, and the two blind bettors who have
not yet declared their hands. As you will see, being on the
button is a big advantage as you are often able to attack the

two blind bettors who have money in the pot already and are, perhaps, looking at pretty poor hands.

To be in early position puts pressure on you since players to act after you may hold better hands than yours. The effect may be that you call with a moderately good hand and subsequently a player in later position raises you. You, probably correctly, decide not to compete any further in the hand, and you fold. However, you have wasted a called bet and, if you continue to do this, you will lose your entire stack by calling and then having to fold when facing a raise.

For this reason, if you call, or raise, when sitting in early position, your hand should be stronger than usual. In mid-position, you will act on your starting hands as described in our basic strategy, and in late position, you will have the freedom to play more hands, more aggressively, to attack players in the blinds and also those who may simply have called in earlier positions.

Let's take a look at a couple of examples:

You hold: A♦ 10♦

What action would you take if you were sitting in the following positions?

a) 1st position
b) 5th position
c) on the button

In 1st position, you might well choose to fold this hand. It's pretty, but you should not overrate the beauty of the suited cards: the suited element will be significant only about 3 per cent of the time. Otherwise, it's just an ace with a mid-kicker and if any player holds AJ, AQ or AK, it could cost you a lot of money.

Players with those latter hands will probably choose to

raise and now you are left with a difficult decision. Having to act first in later rounds is bad news and should probably persuade you to fold.

In 5th position – mid-position – you would probably want to play this hand. Some would raise here but more probably you might just call.

On the button, if no player has raised before you, you may hold the best hand at this point. To find out a little more, and to frighten off the blind bettors, you would raise here – maybe 3–4 times the size of the big-blind bet. The chances of your being re-raised by one of the blind bettors is very small, and players who opted to call originally shouldn't really be tempted to call a raise now; if they do, you will get to act after them on all subsequent rounds of betting, and that puts you in a very strong position, both for maximizing your winnings on the hand, and also being in the best possible position if you choose to bluff.

Notice that, depending upon position, a modest hand like A♦ 10♦ can change from being pretty unplayable in early position, to being worth a call in mid-position, right up to being worth a solid raise in late position. This is one way that your position at the table is so important.

Low pairs, like 22 through to 66, even 77, can be treated in a similar way. Folding in early position, calling in mid-position and raising in late position. Note that if you are sitting at a short-handed table (with 5 players or fewer) you would probably opt to raise with A♦ 10♦ as well as with all the pairs.

Remember that being last to act gives you significant advantages on the later rounds of betting where, if players show weakness by checking on a flop which poses danger, you can sweep in with a bet and probably take the pot. Throughout the hand, late position will give you advantages of information and, potentially, strategic benefit in being able to bluff/semi-bluff your way to an early pot.

Button Raise

This is a well-known, some might say almost routine, play, but nonetheless an effective one.

If you are the dealer and there are no calls around the table to you, or maybe just one, you find yourself in a strong position for a bluff. By raising in this position, you put pressure on the blind bettors since, unless they hold very strong hands, they should probably fold. This is because on subsequent rounds of betting, they will always be the first players who have to decide what to do – and this is an unfavourable position in which to find yourself. Usually, therefore, the blind bettors fold.

Now, you may be left with one early caller. What will he do? He knows that you could be bluffing – because this is the prime spot in which to do so – but he also knows that you could have a genuine hand and that, whatever you hold, you will be 'in position' over him. That is to say, after the flop, he will have to decide what to do before you do – once again, this is an unfavourable position for him to be in, and he may well choose to fold rather than contest a small pot against an opponent of unknown strength, who has position over him.

If both blind bettors and early callers do fold, you have stolen the pot regardless of what your hole cards looked like.

However, always to raise on the button would lay yourself open to being re-raised, firstly by a genuinely strong hand, or by another player who has noticed you repeatedly taking the same action. As ever, at poker, you do best to mix up your actions to disguise your actual hand and intentions. In a cash game, to play genuinely poor cards on the button consistently would be a recipe for disaster. When you hold decent hands with which you would certainly have called in mid- or late position, those are the cards to upgrade into a raise, applying the pressure accorded to you by your position. Hence, with all premium and good hands, you may choose to raise rather than merely call. With decent, but sub-prime hands, you may also choose to raise:

all mid and low pairs
AJ, A10, A9, A8, KQs
QJs, K10s, Q10s
suited connectors*   *see below

would be reasonable hands with which to choose to raise aggressively on the button, rather than merely call.

As you become more experienced, you will encounter players who are confident enough to realize that you may not have a premium hand when you raise on the button and they turn around and re-raise you on a bluff. In turn, you also will gain experience about when to call these re-raises and when to concede quietly.

Suited Connectors

This type of hand contains two cards in sequence of the same suit. High suited connectors, such as Q♣ J♣ or J♥ 10♥ have already been mentioned, but even low cards can form a suited-connectors hand. Cards such as:

7♦ 6♦ or 5♣ 4♣

These hands, though worthless at the start, could become very promising if the right flop hits. Such as:

You hold: 7♦ 6♦ and the flop comes:

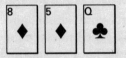

This gives you an open-ended straight draw and, on the flop, a better than 50 per cent chance of ending up with the best hand. These odds allow you to bet heavily on the flop, betting, raising and re-raising your opponent (who might hold AQ or KQ – giving him the best hand now, but slightly less than 50 per cent chance of having it by the time that turn and river have been dealt). Such raising would be considered a semi-bluff, since you do not hold the winning hand now, but have a good chance of over-taking your opponent on the turn and river should he choose to call you down.

You might hold: 5♣ 4♣ and the flop comes:

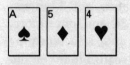

If your opponent holds an ace with a decent kicker, he could well lose a bundle of chips to you with your two-pair. Importantly, if you have called a bet, or even a raise, your opponent is unlikely to imagine that you hold such a hand; this means that your power is well disguised. It is on hands such as these that players can win a lot of chips.

Of course, the ideal flop rarely appears, making betting on such hands pre-flop a bit of a long shot. When, then, might you play suited connectors?

- In late position: where there is little chance of being raised off the hand by a player to act later.
- When there are many callers in a hand: if you have only a tiny chance of hitting the right cards, make sure that there are plenty of people involved in the hand, so that there is a big stack of chips in the pot when you do actually hit your dream flop.

As you will read in the sections on Limit poker, small suited connectors, such as 5♣ 4♣ and 8♦ 7♦ are almost never worth playing. However, at No-Limit Hold 'Em, your chance to win a truly massive pot is that much greater and that makes the risk, in certain chosen situations, worth taking.

5♣ 4♣ is a hand that has both good and bad memories for me. I was playing in a mid-stake tournament at the Mandalay Bay Hotel in Las Vegas a few years back, the chip leader with only about a dozen players remaining. I saw: A♦ A♥ in my hand and raised, to be called by just one opponent.

The flop came: Q♥ 5♦ 4♥ and I made a follow-up bet, called by my opponent. 9♦ fell on the turn, and I bet and was called again. The river produced: 2♣ and, once more, I bet. This time, my opponent raised and, reluctantly by now, I called. He had flopped 2-pair with his 5♣ 4♣ to break my aces.

A few hands later, I picked up: Q♦ Q♥, raised and was called by the same player.

The flop came: J♥ 5♦ 5♥ and following bets and calls, he took another pot from me, holding the exact same 5♣ 4♣ that he had held earlier. Not only was I reduced to scrambling to make it to the final table, but I was psychologically scarred by having the two best hands I'd seen all day being beaten up by the same tiny suited-connector hand.

At the final table, I went all-in with 5♣ 4♣ myself, when I was in the big blind and there had been a small raise and three calls. When the flop came:

I really had to work hard not to laugh out loud. My full house kept me in the tourney for a crucial further twenty minutes and got me a decent third-place payout.

To see 5♣ 4♣ producing monster flops three times within an hour is a very rare occurrence indeed, but whenever I pick up 5♣ 4♣ today, it brings a little smile to my face (metaphorically, I hope). However, it does show that with a big helping of luck, suited connectors can prove utterly crushing, even to very powerful starting hands.

Pot Odds and Potential Pot Odds

As well as all the excitement of bluff and double-bluff, the human desire to gamble, and the fact that, no matter how tough to master, it is just a game, what poker boils down to is being an odds-based gambling game.

If you ignore the odds, the statistics, the percentages, you are denying yourself a proper understanding, not only of your own play, but also that of your opponents. Knowledge of your opponents' tactics and styles is a crucial and absolutely vital weapon at your disposal. Clear, honest self-assessment is almost always essential if you are to improve and, eventually, prosper from the game.

However, it's important here to point out that whilst knowing the odds of a particular play is the barest minimum that is required in order to hope to succeed, winning money is not the sole motivation of many gamblers. If you speak with those who visit Las Vegas, Monte Carlo, or anywhere with enticing casinos, you will find that most gamblers are there for the fun of it. If they win or lose a little bit, that's fine with them. Almost no one will tell you that they have studied and worked and researched the games in which they are going to risk large sums of money because most people simply can't be bothered – they're there for fun.

If you truly do not care whether you win or lose money playing poker, then read no more. You are lucky enough to enjoy the game without any financial consideration. Play it like you want to, how you feel is right, and you will be

welcomed into any poker game you choose. In fact, call me
up and I'll set up a game for you!

However, if you want to win at poker, and most players
do want to win, then take the time to learn the basics well.
Even a thorough understanding of the basics of the game
will provide you with an advantage over those who can't or
won't put in the effort required. As you play more, read
more and experience more, if you use that information,
you will improve your game. That should be the goal of
every poker player.

So, to the odds.

There are many statistics, percentages and charts you
could study (there are a few in the chapter with the highly
original name, 'Statistics, Charts and Percentages', at the
back of this book) but, usually at Texas Hold 'Em, the
odds which really matter are the 'drawing odds' and these
are what we will look at now.

The Right Play at The Right Odds

With the blinds at 10 and 20 chips, there is a raise to 85
chips in 4th position and you, one from the button, decide
to call it with K♣ Q♣. With 85 chips from the raiser and
from you and 30 chips from the small and big blind, the
pot contains 200 chips. The flop comes:

Your opponent now bets 50 chips and you must decide
what to do. As we'll see in the sections to follow, there is a
recommended play here of a raise as a semi-bluff but, for
the moment, let's just imagine you are one of those players
who call a lot. Is it right for you to pay 50 chips to continue
in the hand?

In order to answer that question, you need to know where you stand on the hand, what you think your opponent might hold and what cards you need in order to make the best hand. To illustrate this, we'll keep things simple:

You need to see a club appear on the turn or river to give you the nut (best) flush available. There is a minuscule chance that the turn and river could bring you QQ or KK or KQ, but this is so unlikely we can discount it from our thoughts.

Your opponent may well have an ace and, even if he does not, he is probably beating you at the moment.

There are 250 chips now in the pot.

If you call 50 chips, this will represent an investment of 16 per cent of the pot. If the chance of hitting a club is greater than 16 per cent, then it is definitely worth continuing in the pot; if the likelihood of seeing a club is less than 16 per cent, then you will be betting against the odds to remain in the hand and might well decide to fold.

Hopefully, if you are already playing poker, you know the answer to the above problem but, if you don't, let me show you a quick way of calculating drawing odds.

The way that good poker players consider these situations is to think of all the cards which could help them make their winning hand. They call these cards 'Outs'. In the above example, since any club will give you the best hand and there are nine clubs unaccounted for so far on this deal, there are nine outs to make your hand. Since you can see only 5 cards: the flop and your hole cards, that means that there are 9 chances out of 47 (the remaining unseen cards) to make your flush.

However, since you have both the turn and the river on which you could hit your out, you need to calculate the odds of 9/47 combined with (if a club does not appear on the turn) 9/46. All this is jolly tough to do, even for a trained mathematician. The good news is that there is a really simple, pretty accurate, short cut.

If you have both turn and river cards to come, multiply the number of outs you have by four. This will give you the percentage chance of hitting one of your cards.

If you have only the river to come, multiply the number of outs you have by two. This will give you the percentage chance of hitting one of your cards on the river.

In the example above therefore, the chance of hitting your flush is $9 \times 4 = 36$, about 36 per cent (in fact, it's closer to 35 per cent but a variable range $+/-2$ per cent is as accurate as you will ever need to be).

So, is it worth calling to try to hit your flush? Yes, of course it is. You are contributing only 16 per cent of the pot, for a 35 per cent chance of winning it.

There is, of course, the possibility that if you don't hit a club on the turn, your opponent will bet again and you will have to pay more into the pot to try to hit a club on the river. But, in simple terms, to call for your flush is in line with the odds.

It's also worth noting that there is a chance that if you do hit a club, your opponent will still bet again and now you will be taking even more of his money than you expected and that makes the pot even bigger.

In both the above situations, your calculation of whether or not you should call on the flop has been skewed by future developments. However, good poker players are aware of these situations and can adapt to deal with them. We'll look at that in the sections later on in this chapter.

Let's look at another example in order to ensure that you are happy with the basic odds:

There is a raise to 85 chips in 4th position and you decide to call one from the button with J♥ 10♥. Once again, that makes 200 chips in the pot. The flop comes:

Your opponent bets 100 chips. What should you do?

Firstly, you've hit nothing. Your opponent may not have hit his hand either but the problem for you is that your opponent probably has a bigger nothing than you!

If you hit a 9, you will make a straight and that will probably be the best hand (although your opponent could hold K10 and make a higher straight than you).

There are four nines in the deck. If we use our quick-odds calculation, multiplying the 4 outs by 4 (for turn and river) you can see that we have only a 16 per cent chance of hitting our gut-shot or 'belly-buster' straight. Perhaps, if a jack or a ten hits, this will give us the best hand, but we really can't be sure about that.

If you want to continue in the hand, it will cost you 33 per cent of the pot for a 16 per cent chance of making your straight. And, there is the chance/likelihood that your opponent will bet again on the turn. This looks very bad odds and you should certainly fold.

The only upside of this situation is that it is such poor odds and such a loose play on your part that, if you do hit your nine, you might just get paid quite a lot of money since your opponent is unlikely to think that you called his bet with so little chance of success.

Players who consistently call against the odds are usually known as 'fish' (as in fishing for that magic card). They are usually losing players whose chips slowly bleed away until they do hit their card when they may get paid quite a bit. However, good players will have an excellent idea when they may hit their hand and tend not to contribute any more chips to the pot.

Let's see one more example:

As previously, a raise to 85 chips from the player in 4th position and a call from you on K♥ 9♥ one from the

button. It is just you and one opponent competing. There
are 200 chips in the pot and the flop comes:

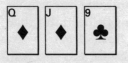

Your opponent bets 100 chips. What should you do?

Firstly, what were you doing calling a mid-position
raise on K9 suited? Next, you did call, so what have
you got? You have made third pair and a gut-shot straight
draw. What does your opponent have? It is tough to tell. If
he holds a queen, he's well ahead of you; if he holds a 10,
he has an open-ended straight draw, and he probably
holds an ace or king to go with it. If he holds a pair in
the hole higher than yours, you are in trouble. Finally, if
he holds two diamonds, he has a flush draw. In fact, it's
quite likely that he holds a combination of all those
features. Say, A♦ J♦ – second pair and the nut flush draw.

I think you can see already, without even calculating the
odds, that this is a hand which you should leave right now.
Fold and say, 'Nice hand' – without sneering.

To say, 'Nice hand', when you fold, or when you find that
you have been beaten, is, typically, said quite sarcastically,
as if to say: you got lucky – this time. Unlike other comments
at the table, it rarely reveals much to your opponents.

As you can't know exactly what your opponent holds,
it's almost impossible to calculate your outs, but let's just
say that you count the four 10s which would give you a
straight, plus the two nines which would make trips for
you. That's 6 outs. I don't really want to count kings as
outs because they make a straight or higher two pair too
likely for your opponent, so six outs it is. Multiply 6 by 4
and you get 24 per cent. You are being asked to contribute
33 per cent to the pot so, even right now, it looks a lousy
bet to call. Naturally, your opponent is likely to bet again

on the turn and then you won't know what to do. Continue in this pot and hitting your card could be the worst thing that happens to you! What do you do if, on the turn, 9♦ appears and your opponent makes a big bet into you? You've made trips, but has he made a flush? I don't want these types of decisions and neither should you.

The key to all of this is realizing that the time to get away from a hand is on the flop. If you haven't made a decent hand by then, or presented yourself with good odds to make a winning hand on the turn or river, then you should throw away your cards quickly. In doing so, you will be losing to bluffs and semi-bluffs from your opponents (which is regrettable) but such discipline will save you from bleeding chips on speculative calls and losing big pots which require close decisions. That kind of stress is one you simply don't need.

Follow-Up, or Continuation, Bets

A follow-up bet is when you raise pre-flop and then, once the flop has appeared, you follow up your previous bet with a further bet. This is used as a possible bluff, a value bet because you have hit a good hand, or simply as an information-gathering bet to see whether your partner has hit anything.

Let's see how they work:

You raise to 85 chips with A♣ Q♦ one from the button and the player on the button calls you. The pot stands at 200 chips. The flop comes:

and you follow up with a further bet of, say, 150 chips (a good follow-up bet will tend to be between 50 per cent and

100 per cent of the pot). You have three ways to gain from this bet:

1) Your opponent may have also missed the flop and, whether he has the same hand as you, better, or worse, he may choose to fold.
2) Your opponent may hold a marginal hand now, such as 77, and decide to pass.
3) Your opponent holds a drawing hand, such as 109, or a made hand, such as AJ. He will now call or raise and you will know that your participation in this deal is now over.

Remembering that it is relatively rare to hit a flop convincingly at Texas Hold 'Em, the first two scenarios are the most likely, and you will pick up many small pots with your aggressive follow-up play. On the occasions that your opponent raises you, or even calls, you probably know that you are beaten.

Note also that, if you choose to check and your opponent bets into you, you have learnt nothing about his hand, since he is likely to bet, when you check, on almost anything in order to try to take you off the hand. If you do decide to call, or raise, his bet, in the long run this is likely to cost you more.

There is a further benefit to the follow-up bet and that is when:

you raise to 85 chips with A♣ Q♦ one from the button and the player on the button calls you. The pot stands at 200 chips. The flop comes:

and you follow up with a further bet of 150 chips. Now, your opponent may think that you are just trying to pressurize him with a follow-up bet, so he calls or raises you on a bluff or semi-bluff, and you are then able to re-raise him again to let him know that you have the best hand. This not only wins you a good-sized pot, but also makes opponents worry that, if they attempt to play back at you after a raise and a follow-up bet, there is a good chance that you will play back over them and cost them dearly. The result of all these plays is to make your opponents less likely to call your raises on speculative hands – since they will fear follow-up bets that will price them out of the hand – and therefore allow you to mix up your play successfully and know that, when your raise is called, it is likely to be on a solid hand. This information will slowly generate a positive playing image for you at the table, and often provide an easier read on the type of hands with which your opponents decide to take you on.

Semi-Bluff Raises into Draws

Let's take a look at a typical situation faced by inexper-ienced players:

The player in 4th position raises to 85 chips and you decide to call, one from the button, with A♣ J♣. There are 200 chips in the pot.

The flop comes:

The raiser now bets 200 chips. What should you do?

At the moment, the raiser may have you well beaten, since his raise could have included a pair in the hole or a king. However, if a third club falls, you will have made the nut flush. You are being asked to put 200 chips into what will be a 600-chip pot, which is 33 per cent of the pot. The chances of hitting the flush are 35 per cent – it seems a decent bet. You call.

The pot is now 600 chips.

The turn comes:

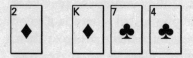

Your opponent now bets 600 chips. What should you do?

You've missed your flush and your opponent is representing the best hand. Now, you are being asked to bet 600 chips into a pot which will be 1,800 chips – costing you 33 per cent of the total pot. However, this time, the chance of hitting a club has fallen to about 20 per cent, so the bet doesn't look so good. However, you know that you'll have the best hand if a club does hit, so you call. The pot is now 1,800 chips.

The river comes:

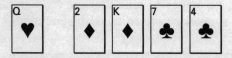

Your opponent bets 1,000 chips. What do you do?

You've missed your draw and the only way you can win the pot is by bluffing. You'll probably have to bet the size of the pot to have any chance of winning: 2,800 chips. Is it worth the risk? Unless you have inside information about your opponent or a reliable tell, almost certainly not. You lay down your hand.

How do you feel about that hand? I hope that you feel that it was played way too passively. Your opponent seemed to decide the bet size every time; you just kept calling, hoping to see your miracle club. If the club had fallen, do you think that your opponent would have paid any extra money into the pot? Probably not, since calling for a flush draw is a classic inexperienced player's move. So, your last call of 600 chips would probably win only that money and not any more (unless your opponents have seen you bluff when you miss draws previously).

Let's replay the hand and see if you can take control.

The player in 4th position raises to 85 chips and you decide to call, one from the button, with A♣ J♣. There are 200 chips in the pot.

The flop comes:

The raiser now bets 150 chips. What should you do?

You should take the role of the aggressor. Firstly, your opponent may simply be making a follow-up raise. He raised before the flop and he wants to test what you have. He may not have hit the flop any better than you. By betting immediately, he hopes to take you off the hand. Secondly, you have a decent chance of making the best hand – any club, plus another couple of aces may make you best. Finally, you want to wrest control of the hand from your opponent. You raise!

I suggest a raise to a total of 350 chips. This play has numerous positive advantages:

Fold equity:	if your opponent does not hold a king, he may well fold, allowing you to win the hand immediately.
Information:	if your opponent calls this raise, then he is likely to have a king in his hand. You know that only a club can really reassure you that you have the best hand (if an ace appears you might worry that he holds AK).

Slow the betting:	if your opponent calls, he may well refrain from betting on the turn, worried that you will raise him again.
	If that is the case, you will get to see the river for free. Notice that when you just called every bet, you ended up spending 750 chips; by raising to the flop, you may well see the river for only 350 chips.
Sets up a bluff:	because you have represented strength on the flop, if you miss your draw, you have a better chance of running a successful bluff at the end.
Disguises hand:	finally, because you raised on the flop, your opponent may well put you on a king and, if he also holds one with a good kicker, he is likely to call a mid-sized bet at the end, allowing you to profit from hitting your flush.

Hopefully, you can see that to take a more aggressive attitude towards draws will prove a profitable strategy in the long run. Not only that, but you also gain vital information from your opponents, and set up a situation where opponents may be afraid to make follow-up bets after raising, knowing your proclivity to raise aggressively.

Bear in mind that, if this were the only time that you raised on the flop, your play would be transparent. However, since you would raise with top pair and a higher kicker, two pair and trips, your opponents can never be certain whether you are on a draw, or value-betting your winning hand.

Potential Pot Odds
(Also Known as 'Implied Pot Odds')

You can see how much is in the pot and, if you can't, ask for the pot to be counted and tidied up. Once you know the size of the pot, you can work out whether, roughly speaking, any bet you have to make is in line with the odds of 'hitting one of your outs' (the odds of seeing the card you need to have the best hand).

If this were the only calculation, poker would be a relatively dull game. Thankfully, one of the pleasures of poker, particularly No-Limit Hold 'Em, is that the pot size can grow enormously at any time. Thus, when considering pot odds, you can also think about the potential size of the pot at the end of the hand. Let's take a look at an extreme example:

The player in 4th seat raises to 85 chips. Sitting one from the button, you decide, strangely, to call the raise with 9♠ 7♠. The pot stands at 200 chips and the flop comes:

Your opponent bets 100 chips. What should you do?

You have missed the flop, other than to leave yourself with a gut-shot straight draw – an 8 would make the nut straight. Since the chance of hitting an 8 is roughly 4 outs × 4 = 16%, to pay 33 per cent of the pot to try to do it seems wrong. However, you decide to call. The pot now stands at 400 chips. The turn card is:

Your opponent now bets 200 chips. What should you do? If you call 200 chips, that will be 33 per cent of the pot, and the chances of your hitting an 8 are 4 outs × 2 = 8%, so clearly this is a bad proposition which, if you keep taking it, will lose you a lot of money in the future – all your money! However, you decide to call. The pot stands at 800 chips, and the river comes:

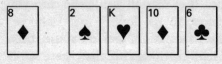

Your opponent bets 500 chips. What should you do now? Stay clam – you've hit your miracle card. Eventually, you will raise, perhaps all-in, perhaps another 1,000 chips, making the bet 1,500. Whatever you do, you want to try to give the impression that you are bluffing. You decide to raise 1,000 and your opponent calls. You show your hand and there is a gasp around the table. Your opponent shows: A♦ A♥ and throws away his cards disdainfully. So, what happened?

You called considerably against the odds at every opportunity and you hit your card, bad-beating (it's a verb in poker) your unlucky opponent. Scores of other times, you would have wasted your chips and, quite soon after, gone broke. However, despite all of that, you could defend yourself by saying that you were calling on the basis of the potential pot odds. After all, when you called your opponent's bet on the flop – 100 chips, you were paying 33 per cent of the pot for a 16 per cent chance of making your hand – not good. But, since your play was so unlikely, and your inside-straight draw so well disguised, you could rationally claim that, if you did hit your hand, you would win a much bigger pot than the one formed on the flop. Indeed, of your final pot, that 100 chips on the flop cost you only 3 per cent of the final pot – making it a great play.

Even the 200 chips on the turn cost you only 6 per cent of the pot, so that too was a great bet.

Hang on! These terrible, loose, passive bets, where you were hoping for miracles, turned out wonderfully this time. Firstly, you hit your hand; secondly, your opponent had a genuinely good hand which caused him to call your substantial raise at the end. In other words, you were doubly lucky on this hand. Let me tell you, even a single bit of luck is rare at poker; to be doubly lucky almost never, ever happens. The fact is, if you play like this consistently, you will lose everything, because there isn't enough luck in the world to keep you afloat.

The point of the example is merely to illustrate that the size of the actual pot need not be your only guiding figure as to whether or not to compete further in a hand. Only if you know that your opponent has a very good hand, that your hand will be the nuts, disguised if you hit it, can you even start to consider potential pot odds. But, those hands do occur and you should take advantage of those improved odds for yourself. Let's take a look at a simpler, more lifelike example:

The player in 4th seat raises to 60 chips. Two other players call him and, sitting one from the button, you decide to call with 9♠ 7♠.

The pot stands at 270 chips and the flop comes:

The initial raiser checks, the next player bets 200 chips. What should you do?

You have an open-ended straight draw and the raiser probably holds an ace. Either of your other opponents may also hold an ace but, even if they both choose to fold, the bettor is likely to bet again, since top pair looks strong here. Even though a bet costs you 40 per cent of the pot, and your chances of making your straight stand at 33 per cent, the bet looks good. Other players may call, and the bettor may well call down bets once you make your hand. A raise is certainly a possibility here, but you might just try to build a pot. You call. The other two players fold. The pot stands at 670 chips and the turn comes:

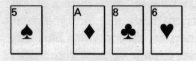

Your opponent bets 300 chips. What do you do?

Everything is going swimmingly. You've made your hand and your opponent may not have noticed. He seems to have aces with a high kicker, maybe even two pair. Should you raise here, or simply call?

Either play may work on the day; you must judge your opponent. A call will often work here against average opposition and, since the board is a rainbow (all different suits), there are no backdoor flushes to concern you. You decide to call. The pot stands at 1,270 chips, and the river comes:

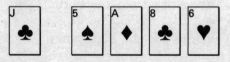

The jack is quite nice for you; your opponent could have AJ in the hole. As it is, he checks. You decide to make a small bet that you hope he will call, and you slide 400 chips into the middle. Your opponent does call, and he mucks his hand when you show him your straight.

When you chose to call the 200 chips on the flop, you were calling slightly against the odds, and you knew that you might have to call again if your opponent bet on the turn. As it was, that 200 chips turned out to be not 40 per cent of the actual pot, but a little less than 10 per cent of the potential pot, as you could reasonably anticipate it. That is how you think about the potential pot odds on a hand.

WARNING NOTE:

Potential pot odds can be used as an excuse to stay in hands when you should fold. Call over and over again against the odds and you will lose your bankroll. You must know that your opponent has a good enough hand to put more money into the pot, that if you make your own hand, it is definitely the nuts, and that there is little danger of an aggressive player betting heavily on subsequent rounds, making the price to remain in the hand far too great.

So, to use pot odds, you must know your opponents' styles, your basic odds of making the hand, your judgment as to how much more the pot is really going to be worth – or whether, if you do hit your hand, your opponents can work it out and therefore bet no more into the pot, making your return a poor one. To adopt an attitude of considering potential pot odds, you must know a lot about the table, and about yourself.

Summary of Intermediate Strategy

Here's a summary of what we've looked at. Add these tips to those in the beginners' section.

1 Position

Be aware of your position at the table in relation to the button.

Early Position: first three players after the big blind
Mid-Position: players 4 and 5 after the big blind
Late Position: one from the button and the button

Small and Big Blinds will be in the earliest position for all rounds of betting from the flop onwards.

The closer to the button you are, the more information you have gained from the actions of your opponents before you have to act. Use this information to judge whether to fold, call or raise – using late position for your most flexible, aggressive actions and early position for the most disciplined and conservative policy.

Note the type of hands on which players in early position opt to call and raise. If you are playing at a tight, good-standard table, you will be likely to see only premium and very good hands being played, and you should note that for the times when you have a decent hand and want to judge whether to play it or not. Weak players will pay no attention to their position at the table and will consistently call on marginal hands in any position. Note this, remain patient, and then raise/re-raise them aggressively when you judge you have a very strong or premium hand. This method requires patience but will win you money reliably and consistently.

2 Button Raises
Since the button offers you the best position of all, use this time to limp in (call) to the deal with hands that offer potential (see suited connectors below) and to raise when you have not only premium and very good hands, but good or modest hands. If there are few callers before you, you have only to persuade the out-of-position blind bettors to fold and you are likely to win the hand pre-flop. If you get callers, you have the best position to pressure them after the flop and on every round of betting.

3 Suited Connectors
Suited connectors (touching cards of the same suit: 9♣ 8♣, 7♦ 6♦, 5♣ 4♣) are cards which are unlikely to win the hand

unless a very suitable flop falls. However, if the right flop does fall, you can often make a very strong hand, well disguised from your opponents, and win a substantial pot. Play these cards only when there are multiple players in the pot. This is so that if you do make your unlikely ultra-strong hand, there will be money in the pot, and the chances of other players making beatable hands is still high. Suited connectors are most safely played in late position, where there is little chance of subsequent raises.

If you hit a draw for a straight, flush, or preferably, straight flush, on the flop, consider using the semi-bluff raise (summarized below) to exert pressure on any opponent who bets into the flop.

4 Follow-Up, or Continuation, Bets

If you raise pre-flop, always consider following up your raise with a bet or a raise on the flop, whether or not you have hit your hand. This aggressive attitude pressurizes your opponents, tests their hand strength and resolve and paints a picture of a player who, when he raises, will play his hand strongly. This image is likely to intimidate loose players into respecting your raises unless they have a very strong hand. In this way, you pick up pots cheaply and gain more information about your opponents' cards when they do choose to play back at you.

This also works well with your default system of play, which is to bet out when you believe you hold the best hand. By making regular (if not continuous) follow-up bets, your opponents may be keener to call you down when you hold the nuts than if your standard play was to raise and then slow-play.

5 Semi-Bluff Raises into Draws

When you hit a straight or flush draw on the flop which you feel that, if you hit, it will certainly be the nuts, consider raising any bet – or indeed betting yourself – to pressurize your opponent(s). The advantages include: representing strength and therefore possibly forcing an immediate fold, setting up a possible bluff at the end, reducing the likelihood of another bet from your opponent on the turn, and, often, allowing you to see the river for a cheaper price than merely calling repeatedly.

6 Pot Odds and Potential Pot Odds

Be aware of the basic odds of any draw you choose to call (or bet, or raise), so that you are not losing chips, hoping for a miracle card when the odds tell you that it simply isn't worth it. Players who consistently make these plays are losing, passive players, and are often described as 'fish' – hoping to catch something.

However, be aware that, if there are multiple players in the pot, or you feel that you know an opponent holds a strong hand, then the pot size is likely to grow bigger by the end of the hand; the size of that potential pot can be used to assess whether a call, or raise, offers a reasonable rate of return. Do not get carried away with pot odds however: often when players call for draws and you hit your card, the opponent knows that you've made your hand, and refuses to pay you any more money.

7 Don't Slow-play Multiple Opponents

In the beginners' section, slow-play of any kind was advised against and, in many games, a simple 'raise with the best hand' policy will win money since most inexperienced players are convinced that everyone is bluffing them all the time, and they are paranoid about throwing away a hand which could have won the pot.

However, there are times when a slow-play is probably a good idea. The advice here is that you should slow-play only against a single opponent and not against several.

This is because, if you leave several players in the pot, there is a much increased chance that you will be outdrawn by an opponent and go on to lose a big pot. For example:

You hold: A♥ A♠ and the player in 4th position raises to 85 chips. There are two further callers to you, one from the button. There are 255 chips in the pot. What should you do? The answer is to re-raise and probably re-raise big. I'd suggest a re-raise of a further 250 chips.

While AA is a big favourite against one player, it is less than 50 per cent on to win against three others. It is therefore vital to reduce the field against you, ideally to just one opponent. However, if your big raise forces everyone to fold, then you have still won a decent-sized pot.

You hold: A♥ A♠ and the player in the 4th seat raises to 85 chips. Everyone else passes to you. What should you do?

You certainly could re-raise; this play will probably work well against many average players. Equally, you can consider just calling, hoping that only you and your opponent are in the hand and he hits top pair on the flop. If this happens, you will probably win a sizeable pot. However, the danger of this slow-play is that when you call, the player on the button and, possibly, even the blind bettors, feel that they now have the odds to enter the action with suited connectors or mid-pairs, hoping to hit a brilliant flop.

So, to conclude: consider a slow-play against one opponent, but raise strongly whenever you need to reduce the field to a heads-up situation between you and the original raiser.

8 Bet with The Best Hand
If in doubt, follow this advice at all times. Though basic and obvious, this style will usually work very effectively in winning you close to the maximum number of chips. Let

me show you a simple example that demonstrates just how this principle works. This came from a social-club tournament, where only five players remained. Player A was short-stacked, down to his last 1,000 chips. Player B was lying in second place with approximately 7,000 chips.

Player A held: 7♠ 7♥
Player B held: A♦ 10♦

Player A raised to 200 chips and Player B just called. These were the only two players in the hand. The flop came:

Player A went all-in and Player B called quickly. Player B missed his flush, but had obviously lost to Player A's four-of-a-kind instantly.

The full board read:

I'm not necessarily advocating going all-in the moment that you hit quads (although it's such an unlikely play, your opponents will certainly not put you on that hand), I am simply showing you that by betting with the best hand at the first opportunity, Player A managed to double through and put himself back in with a chance in the tournament.

Imagine Player A studiously slow-playing this hand.

He checks on the flop and perhaps Player B does so also (in fact, Player B might well bet here, but maybe he is curious that the short-stacked Player A raised and then didn't make a follow-up bet). The turn comes and Player A again checks, hoping Player B might bet. Player B is most suspicious of this slow-playing from Player A, so he checks also. On the river, Player A cannot resist making a bet and Player B, holding nothing, decides to muck his hand.

Note that if Player A goes all-in on turn or river, he gets nothing. By going all-in on the flop, he doubles through.

Naturally, your best style is to mix up your value bets, follow-up bets, bluffs and semi-bluffs, so that your opponents can discern no pattern. However, if in doubt, return to default mode. Bet with the best hand.

9 Be Aware of your Behaviour after Bluffing

Wonderful though it is to win a pot on a complete bluff, especially when you suspect that your opponent had quite a decent hand, one of the greatest skills is concealing what you held in your hand. If you make it clear that you have bluffed your opponent, he will note this for future reference. Many weaker players often go so far as to exhale loudly and blow the tips of their fingers, they are so relieved not to have been called. This revelation of information will be useful for future reference not only to your actual opponent in the hand, but also to everyone else around the table who is paying attention (sadly, that's usually not too many). So, even when you don't show your cards, be careful not to reveal your hand through your reactions.

Advanced Strategy

Before we launch into the next set of ideas to stimulate your poker brains, a quick word about the title of this section. Because you have read and understood the first two sections, this does not make you an intermediate player; nor does reading this section transform you into an expert. These sections are for players who want to know the basic elements of the game, to play them well, and to win some money from the modest games in which they play, making their poker education a profitable one. To become truly above average, you will need to study more, practise more and, maybe most importantly of all, concentrate on developing a poker sense of what is going on around the table. To do this requires patience, determination, and the ability to realize that this is a game which takes many years to master.

Putting Players on a Hand

Good poker players 'put' an opponent on a hand immediately they become involved in a deal with them. Pre-flop, your idea of your opponent's hole cards will be based on your knowledge of their style of play, their position at the table, and any tells, physical or betting, that you may pick up.

On the flop, you will have another chance to modify your opinion of what they hold by observing their reaction to the flop, what they choose to bet and how they react to other factors, such as other players betting into them, raising them, or merely calling them.

On the turn and river, further information will flow your way. Try to come up with the exact hand that they are holding and, when they turn their cards over at a showdown, see how close you were to being right. In this respect, the more you practise, the better you will become. Do this always when you are *not* in the hand, as well as when you are. Be aware, however, that some players are easier to read than others and this is not always linked to ability. In my case, I find very good and very bad players hard to read; average social or club players usually quite transparent.

Table Image: Reading your Opponents' Styles

When you play in a home game or at a club and your table personnel remain reasonably static, this is your chance to form an opinion about the style of each of your opponents. Good players will mix up their styles (or 'change gears') to keep you guessing, but most home games and social club games will feature players who know only one way to play and will remain in character for the entire length of the game. I say the entire length, but actually that may not be true: almost all poker players loosen up in the last hour or so of a game, unless they have won big and they are sitting on their winnings.

The NL Texas Hold 'Em tournament master, Phil Hellmuth Jnr, recommends thinking of opponents like animals: lions and mice and elephants. Other authors apply distinctive personifications to the different characters around the table. Do whatever you have to do in order to help you to remember each player's characteristics. For me, I think of poker players in four different categories:

Tight/Aggressive
Tight/Passive
Loose/Aggressive
Loose/Passive

- A tight player selects his hands carefully, playing only what he considers are the best, using position to his advantage.
- A loose player plays a far wider range of hands, many of which you might consider to be marginal or unplayable. Often, position is not taken into account.
- An aggressive player bets strongly when he has the chance, betting, raising and re-raising in various positions.

- A passive player calls a lot, rarely raises or bets when he need not do so and, when he does bet, it is often at the end when he feels he needs to bluff.

You, of course, are in the first category for most of the time: tight/aggressive. You select your starting hands well, play them differently according to position and then bet with them heavily to ensure maximum payouts when you do hold the best hand, and maximum opportunities to steal hands even when you miss the flop.

Let's see how your opinion of your opponents might affect your play. To begin:

You hold: A♠ J♠. The player in 2nd position raises to 85 chips. The other players pass to you. Sitting one from the button, what should you do?

This is a raise from an early position and should therefore show a hand similar to or better than yours. However, what do you know about this player? If you have rated him as a loose/passive player; seen him play all kinds of hands regardless of his position, seen him raise on marginal hands early on, and tend to fold to raises, then to raise here would probably be the best play.

However, if you have rated this opponent as a tight/passive player, someone who selects his starting hands carefully and rarely raises, then to fold looks a decent decision. Notice the vast difference in your action depending upon how you regard your opponent.

Some of you are marvelling that I should suggest folding here, with A♠ J♠ when you are in position. If you have read your opponent correctly as having a premium hand, then what might he have?

AA, KK, QQ, JJ – any of those would be disastrous for you. AK AQ – equally bad news.

Any mid- or low pair – it is going to be a 50/50 pot and, unless you hit the flop, a further bet from your usually tight opponent will finish your participation in this hand.

Could he have worse? Not if you have read him correctly and he is acting in his usual way. Good players tend not to play predictably, but 99 per cent of the rest of the world's players will – and you must use this to your advantage.

Advertising: your Own Table Image

As a general rule, I strongly recommend not showing any hole cards to your opponents. However, there will be times when it is beneficial to you to do so. You must pick those times carefully and use them to create a table image of yourself in the mind of the other players. Naturally, this should not be an accurate table image.

Let's take a look at some examples:

You are a tight/aggressive player by nature and you have been very patient waiting for some playable hands to come along before committing yourself to a pot. In fact, you've scarcely played a hand all evening. After two hours, you finally see K♥ K♠ in the hole and, in 3rd position, you raise. Everyone folds. This is disappointing, but your ultra-tight image has sunk in to your opponents' minds and they are showing you respect for your raise.

This may be the time to mix things up a little. Perhaps, a little later, you pick up 10♠ 8♠ and you raise with that. If anyone calls, you have a playable hand and you can follow up with a decent bet on the flop. If everyone folds, now may be the time to show your hand. Your opponents will see that you are raising on marginal hands and, now, if you pick up a premium hand in the next few rounds, you are likely to receive action.

My usual style for tournament play is, as you will see, to play tightly for the first few rounds, selecting only the best hands to try to build my chip stack. However, my regular social poker school all know this so, a couple of times a year, I come out raising and betting from the start. Since the only hands that they have seen me show down all year in the early stages are monsters, they all assume I must have what I claim. This allows me, not only to build up a sizeable lead by the half-way stage, having accumulated many of their chips, but also to attract much more action the next time we play since, having had time to reflect upon it, my opponents have decided that I must have been bluffing.

Online, I have noticed several players who adopt the same style of showing down hands when they first join the table and then only showing certain hands subsequently. It doesn't really matter that I have noticed this since there are enough tables online to make sure that you can play against different opponents for most of the time. Their style is to pitch up and start raising immediately in most positions at a high frequency. This usually wins them a few blinds and scares other players into folding when they might have called or raised. Next, the loose call, or the hyper-aggressive raise, works and they show down their poor cards which have been hit by the flop perfectly. This may win them a decent pot also. Finally – and this may be after as little time as half an hour – they tighten up. They need hit only one really good hand in the next hour or so, and the likelihood is that they will get called, and called and called some more before picking up a substantial pot. Then they leave the table!

In this last example, the showing of their sub-standard cards is clear advertising with the intention of loosening the other players sufficiently to induce them to call later when they should not be doing so. Because it is an aggressive strategy, they can lose several heavy pots but, in the long run, they will pick up blinds, steal some small pots, and look to cash in on one or two enormous pots when opponents think they are bluffing when they are not.

Each of these examples of either deliberately, or perforce, showing your cards, demonstrates how you can create a false image over a few hands or many sessions, allowing you to mix up your play to great effect at the crucial moment.

Take note: any play which requires your opponents to be paying attention assumes that they will be of decent standard. Weak players pay no attention to their opponents and misinterpret what they do notice. These advertising plays will not work against poor players, in the same way that bluffing them is unlikely to work either. So, pick your audiences carefully.

Re-raising to Smoke Out The Stealers

In most games, there are players whom I term 'chancers'. These are the players who always raise when there have been checks to them, always make button raises, and always try raising in the blinds. You can let them go quietly, but they will affect the way that you wish to play and the best way to deal with them is to observe them carefully, pick your moment and then attack them with a re-raise. Do this several times, until your opponent is worried that any attempt to raise will result in your taking even more aggressive action. Once this chancer is convinced that he'll get nowhere when you are in the hand, you will find that he frequently passes when you are involved and continues his aggressive stealing against other players.

This is what, in a ring game, we might call 'taking a stand'. If you don't hold your ground, you will be bullied out of your usual style and into a more defensive, passive one and that is bad news for you.

Incidentally, if you find that your opponent will not back down and that he routinely re-re-raises you or calls you down on marginal hands, then you should consider moving seat or moving table. Do not allow your ego and a desire for revenge to cloud your sound judgment. You are not here to beat any single player (who may simply be enjoying a run of good cards and find that his timing is on song), but instead, you seek to record regular overall winning sessions in order, slowly, to grow your bankroll. Stand up and leave. The aggressor may take no pleasure from your departure. He is happy to have you there when all is going well and he will be sad to see you leave. Indeed, far from giving him victory by leaving or moving, you are taking exactly the correct action: a considered retreat in preparation for a new attack.

Betting, Raising and Re-raising on Paired and Suited Flops

Two kinds of flop which inexperienced players dread are the paired flop where, immediately, they fear you may have trips, and the suited flop (all one suit) when flushes and flush draws abound.

In both these situations, my instinct is to bet out, raise and even re-raise whatever I have. This bluff style works far more often than is statistically necessary for it to be the correct play, and sets up excellent positions for when you really do hold trips or a full house, allowing you to value bet such flopped hands and expect callers.

This aggressive stance on such flops often forces your opponents into revealing what they have, and allows you a chance to bluff them later if they show any hesitation in betting back at you.

This is not an automatic play on every occasion, and certainly one to be used with care against good opponents. However, online and in home and social club games, to play these flops aggressively usually leads to substantial winnings over time.

Layers of Understanding

One of the most important elements of improving your own game and playing against better opponents is that both you and those opponents will have a better idea of your general style of game and a repository of information about you and how you played certain hands in the past. This will lead to plays which, earlier in your poker-playing career, you would not have considered. These advanced plays based on player knowledge can be described as 'layers'. Let me explain why:

You play in a regular game of a decent standard. You have noticed that one of your friends in the game – we'll call him Al – raises regularly one from the button and on the button and, on the rare occasions that he shows down his hand at the end (when he has hit the perfect flop) you notice that these raises have been made on very poor hands. As a result, you decide to re-raise on marginal hands to try to take him off the hand pre-flop. This works a few times, and you have established your image for not being bullied.

This is the first layer: you have identified an opportunity to play back at a player, and your reading of him and how to counter his play has worked.

You continue to play in the game and when Al raises close to the button, you are ready to play back at him. However, after a few weeks, you find that, rather than folding meekly when you re-raise, Al comes back over the top of you and re-raises himself. At first, you fold but, on a hand where you call and there is a showdown, you notice that he raised originally on J9s, called your re-raise, and then played the hand out to the end, winning the pot. What does this mean?

It means that a further layer of understanding has been added to your poker relationship. You know that he raises on poor hands when in position, and he knows that you know that, because you have started to re-raise him. He has now taken the battle between you to the next layer – or level – by calling, or re-raising your bets. Since you have folded a few times, he now knows that you are re-raising strategically rather than simply on hand strength and, with that knowledge, he has played right back at you. This is the next layer.

For poker experts and professionals, these layers can run into many bluffs and double bluffs when the cards held are almost irrelevant to the higher-mental battle being fought in the betting.

For you, as the improving player, your task is to analyse what you know about your opponents and to use that information to pressurize them. However, you must also remain aware that those opponents will be noting your actions and, when they feel confident that they have a decent read on your actions, they will play back at you. If you are aware of both elements: your own reading of them, and their reading of you, you will find it easier to judge what to do when the pressure turns back to you.

Through all of this, your self-knowledge – of how you appear as a poker player – must be candid and honest, so that you can adjust errors of predictability, stem leakages, and regroup your thoughts to take on those chosen opponents about whom you know the most, at the next level. So, be aware of how your play paints a picture of your overall style, try to mix up your playing styles to keep that picture occluded, and be prepared to change styles if you feel that your current play has become too predictable.

Check-Raising

You will see players of just about every standard undertaking the satisfying manoeuvre of a check-raise. To act weak and then, when your opponent dares to stick his toe into the betting and you come over the top of him with a hefty raise, is extremely gratifying. Let's see an example:

In 4th seat, you hold: J♠ J♥ and you raise to 85 chips. An opponent on the button calls you. There are 200 chips in the pot, and the flop comes:

You check and your opponent bets 150 chips. What do you do? Well, naturally, you are going to call: slow-playing the hand, or raise: completing the check-raise. Personally, I'd raise substantially now and hope to take the pot, unless my opponent is on top pair or two pair. Naturally, then, I'm happy for him to call me down. My problem is that I'm not quite sure what my opponent is holding. He has called my raise originally (and I will have a range of hands in my head based on his favourable position and his known style of play) but his bet after my check could have been made on anything at all – a complete bluff or a decent hand. If the hand continues, I'll have to hope that I have him well beaten, but there are many hands which he could hold where the turn and river cards could destroy me and cost me a big pot.

So, when you check-raise, you learn less about your opponents' hands. But it could be even worse:

In 4th seat, you hold: J♠ J♥ and you raise to 85 chips. An opponent on the button calls you. There are 200 chips in the pot, and the flop comes:

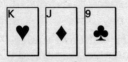

You check – and your opponent checks after you.

The turn comes:

This is a catastrophic card for you, since your opponent may now have made a straight, and may have developed a flush draw also. Even if it hasn't improved his hand, the thought that it may have made your hand will frighten him sufficiently to dissuade him from contributing any further to the pot.

In other words, either he may have you beaten and it may cost you money to find out, or you were winning all the time but your excellent hand was well disguised. Now that the board is straightening, your opponent will become fearful that his top pair or two-pair is well beaten and you gain no further money from him.

The bottom line is that a check-raise is a dangerous option for players to take, unless they have a pretty good read on their opponents' hands. It is, in effect, a slow-play manoeuvre – and slow-playing is not generally recommended, except against a single opponent in a situation where your position in the hand is easy to read.

Let's replay the hand and, on the flop, put in a decent-sized raise. If your opponent has hit nothing, he will fold. That's fine – you were almost certainly not getting any further action on the pot. Incidentally, if he just holds a hand such as AQ or A10, he'll almost certainly fold too, making the gut-shot straight draw something that you won't need to worry about.

If he calls you, then he may suspect that you have simply made a follow-up bet. He may have called you with Q10 and now be slow-playing you to bleed you of chips, but this can happen on any hand at any time and it's just very bad luck.

If he raises you, then he is either trying to take you off the hand if he suspects a follow-up bet from you on not much, or he may have top pair or two-pair and want to find out where he stands. I'd re-raise him promptly and make it a pot-sized raise at that. Now, you'll find out who was trying to steal from whom.

One further argument against the check-raise being used regularly is that quite often you would have generated a bigger pot had you simply bet your hand for value at every opportunity. In their quest to be seen as creative and special, players of all standards forget that betting with the best hand is often the best way to play it.

In short, consider a check-raise a rare play to be made probably against a single opponent in a slow-play situation; be aware that a check-raise which ends up resulting in a free card for your opponent(s) can lead to a big pot for you, but also a huge loss if your opponent subsequently hits his card for a serious draw. Use sparingly.

Incidentally, I like to use a check-raise against weak or average players as a bluff manoeuvre whenever I suspect that someone may be trying to steal a pot from me. This often forces an early lay-down.

Semi-bluff check-raises when you are out of position can buy you the river card more cheaply than checking and calling, or even, sometimes, betting out directly. To flop a flush or open-ended straight draw, check and then raise, will sometimes buy the pot then and there and, at other times, allow you to check the turn and see your opponent check also, giving you two chances for the price of one to hit your hand. Following all of that action, a hefty bet at the end can often seem very strong and force a lay-down from your opponent.

So, in brief, check-raises are pretty good for most things except, ironically, a really good hand!

Summary of Advanced Strategy and Extra Tips

1 Putting Opponents on A Hand

Use time when you are not involved in a hand to observe your opponents and, from their betting style and any physical tell, try to put them on a hand: guess exactly which two cards they hold.

The more that you practise this, the more accurate you will become so that, when you are in the hand, and your money is in the pot, you will have a better chance of judging your actions correctly to win you that pot, or save you further investment.

Hands that must be revealed in showdowns or calling situations must be shown to all at the table. Notice that expert players who may appear to be relaxing between hands are actually observing all the action, reaction, betting styles, physical tells and atmosphere at the table so that they can use that information when they come up against these same opponents later in the session, the next day, or a few months down the line.

2 Advertising and Changing Styles

If you are playing against unobservant, weaker opposition, stick to your default tight/aggressive style and vary it little, maximizing the potential of the good hands, and sitting back on marginal hands.

Against stronger opposition, be prepared to mix up your style of play more. If you are trying to present a looser, free-wheeling style, then show some weaker hands on which you've raised pre-flop and after which everyone has folded. You can also call down small bets hoping to catch a miracle card to give you trips or a straight/flush draw. If you hit it, you win a good-sized pot and show that you are prepared to call for long-shot draws; if you miss the draw, you can still casually flip your cards so that some opponents see them. You will find that the comments follow rapidly around the table after that. Having advertised your loose style, you'll hope to hit some decent cards, or some excellent flops, before milking your eager opponents.

Conversely, if you play tight for the first ninety minutes and find that no cards are coming your way, you can switch your style for the next half-hour and play many more hands with bets and raises; you can expect to win many of these hands simply because your opponents will expect you to have some decent cards for all your sudden action.

In the excitement of a poker game, with so much else to consider, it is hard to remember not only your opponents' styles, but also to analyse and be aware of your own style and how that is presented to your opponents. Against good opponents – at least, those who are truly observing all the action – the ability to mix up your style of play will be paramount to your continued success in the game.

3 Re-Raising Blind Stealers and Chancers
Identify aggressive positional play and, when the time is right, start to play back at those players. If you do not, you are likely to be dominated by those opponents.

For example, you notice that one player always bets when there have been some checks to him post-flop, or turn. He may make unnecessarily large bets, predominantly designed to scare away players, but also to set up a big pot when he does hit what he needs. You will probably find that, if you raise him, he will assume that you are slow-playing a powerful hand, and he will fold quietly.

Repeated raisers on the button, or one before the button, can also be smoked out by re-raising. Even if this requires you to take aggressive action in poor position of small blind or big blind, such action may well prove worthwhile if it serves to cut down the amount of aggressive button action you have to counter in the future at this table.

If you do not feel able to make a stand, or you feel intimidated by the aggression being shown in the betting, then be prepared to leave the table and seek less stressful hunting grounds elsewhere. Remember that, at a table of six or eight or ten players, there should not be a personal battle occurring between two players. This is because, if you concentrate too deeply on one opponent, the others will simply wait for their moment and pick you off when you are not fully focused on the entire table.

Feel bullied, outclassed, unlucky? Get up, leave the table, grab a drink, a snack, take a walk – and join another table.

4 Playing Suited or Paired Flops Aggressively

Attacking players of a modest standard when the board pairs or comes down suited is often an effective way of picking up a few chips on hands where the flop appears too worrying for others to wish to compete. Bet, raise, or even re-raise into such situations. A small raise or re-raise often works better here than a big one: the small bet looks like you are trying to milk the opponents and usually players resist that immediately, thinking that they have smelt a rat.

Be aware that these plays are unlikely to be successful against very weak players, since they will call you down on any hand at all.

5 Layers of Understanding

Remain alert to what you know about your opponents and what they know about you. Realize that as good players become familiar with your style of play and your tactics, they will alter theirs to counter your plays. Once you have read that their plays are a direct counter to your own tactics, you can then seek to counter these plays . . . and so the layers of deception and aggression grow.

Incidentally, a simple way to counter these plays without committing further chips to the pot is to change your style of play dramatically for a few rounds so that your opponent is no longer certain that his counter is the right one for the style you have now adopted. Having made your aggressive opponent uneasy, return to your default tight/aggressive style and remain unmolested for a while as your opponents adjust to your new strategy.

6 Check-Raises

Use sparingly against single opponents, on hands where your relative strengths can be measured accurately against the board cards. Be aware that the effect of a check-raise is often to slow-play the hand. Two pair and trips are both good hands which remain highly susceptible to draws throughout the hand, but which remain tough to lay down to a big bet at the end.

Consider the use of a check-raise as a bluff manoeuvre. Against weak and average players, this is likely to work well, since a check-raise usually carries an aura of great strength about it and you can trade on that reputation to take down pots on which otherwise you might have folded to a bet. Use it as both a complete bluff and as a semi-bluff into straight and flush draws.

Hand Examples for All Levels of Students

Let's assume the blinds are 10/20 and you have bought in for 2,000 chips.

Pre-Flop

1) You hold: A♣ 10♣. In the 4th seat, a player raises to 85 chips and the player in 6th seat re-raises to 170 chips. You are one from the button, what action should you take?

2) You hold: A♣ 8♣. In the 2nd seat, a player raises to 85 chips. There are several folds to you. What action should you, one from the button, decide to take?

3) Sitting one from the button, you hold: 10♦ 9♦. What action would you take if:
   a) there is one raiser in 2nd position and no other callers?
   b) there is a raise and there are two further callers before you?
   c) there is no raise, but there are five callers to you?

4) Sitting one from the button, there are three callers to you and you hold: A♦ Q♣. What action should you take?

5) You hold: K♠ 10♠. What action would you take with this starting hand in the following positions:
   a) in 2nd seat?
   b) on the button?
   c) in the small blind?

6) You have been folding patiently for the last hour. You pick up: K♥ 7♣ one from the button. What action do you take?

7) On the button, you hold: A♥ Q♦. You raise to 85 chips and the big blind re-raises you to 200 chips. What should you do?

On The Flop

8) In 6th seat, you hold: A♣ K♦ and you raise to 85 chips. You receive one call from the player on the button. The pot stands at 200 chips and the flop comes:

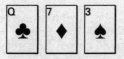

What action do you take?

9) In 6th seat, you hold: A♣ K♦ and you raise to 85 chips. You receive one call from the player on the button. The pot stands at 200 chips and the flop comes:

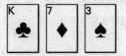

What action do you take?

10) There are three callers to you on the button. You hold: 10♣ 9♣. You decide to call. The small blind folds and the big blind checks. There are 110 chips in the pot. The flop comes:

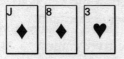

a) after two checks, the player on your right bets 100 chips. What action do you take?

b) what are the odds of your hitting your straight draw?

11) There are two calls to you and, holding Q♣ 4♥, you call on the button. The small blind folds and the big blind checks. There are 90 chips in the pot. The flop comes:

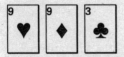

There are now three checks to you. What action do you take?

On The Turn

12) You hold: K♣ Q♣. There are two calls to you and, on the button, you decide to raise to 85 chips. You get one caller. The pot stands at 200 chips and the flop comes:

You bet 150 chips and your opponent calls. The pot stands at 500 chips, and the turn comes:

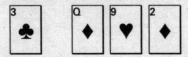

Your opponent checks again. What action should you take now?

On The River

13) Continuing with the hand above, whatever you decided to do on the turn, the river comes:

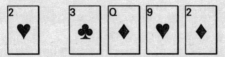

Your opponent checks. What action should you take?

Answers to Hand Examples
for All Levels of Students

Pre-Flop

1) Fold. Your A10 is a marginal hand when there has been an early raise, and it becomes virtually unplayable once there has been a re-raise. Do not be seduced by the suited nature of your hand – that will help only 3 per cent of the time. If you are up against another ace with a higher kicker than yours, or a high pair, you could lose a lot of chips on this deal.

2) Fold. I know that A8 looks nice when you have been staring at J3, 74 and 62 the entire session, but you are unlikely to get rich with these cards. Ace and a low or mid-sized kicker is a very dangerous hand in No-Limit, since you will need to hit 2-pair, or find a flush draw to feel confident you know where you are on the hand. If an ace does appear on the flop, if your opponent doesn't hold one, you may well not get paid; if he does, his kicker is likely to be better than yours.

3) You are in a good position one from the button and 10♦ 9♦ is a playable hand here. However, because you will need a very suitable flop for your hand to improve, you need money in the pot – or the potential for lots of money. So,
   a) With only one other player in the pot, to call the raise is decidedly speculative. As exciting as that sounds, to call here will be a losing action in the middle to long run.
   b) With three other players in the hand, this looks a reasonable time to enter the fray. If you pick up trips, 2-pair or a straight/flush draw, you may be in position to win a big pot. One pair will almost certainly not be enough for you.

    c) With five other players in the hand, this is perfect to limp in with a call and see the flop cheaply. Some experts might raise with this hand, but on highly speculative hands such as suited connectors, you ought to see the flop as cheaply as possible.

4) Raise. There are three callers to you holding A♦ Q♣. Ask yourself: is my hand likely to be the best now? If you believe that it is – and it probably is – then you should raise now. What you would like is for one player to call you on a hand not as strong as yours. What you do not want is for there to be three other players in the pot all with hands which have not been defined. This situation increases the likelihood that you will be outdrawn and provides no information with which to work. Raise here to reduce the field or win the pot outright.

5) a) Fold. This looks very passive but to call or raise with this hand in early position leaves you open to a re-raise which you should not call. Again, the suited hand looks much better than it is.

    b) Call – if there have been two or three callers, you might choose to see a cheap flop, or even raise to bring the hand down to a heads-up with one other opponent.

    c) Fold. This looks a very tempting bet. You need to put in only half the big blind to compete. However, remember that you will be in the worst possible position for the rest of the betting and K10 is still very susceptible to numerous other hands and could cost you dearly if someone else holds KJ or KQ – both hands on which they might have called but not raised. Save yourself huge sums of money in the long run by not calling in the small blind.

6) Fold. Just because your cards have been dreadful does not mean that you should lessen your starting-hand requirements.

   Every starting hand has an expected win or loss rate in each different position. Anything marginal (such as K7) has a negative expectation of profit in any position. This means that the more often that you choose to play marginal hands, the greater the likelihood of your losing money. Simple as that. Stay disciplined.

7) Re-raise. Your action may depend on your style to date. If this is your first raise on the button, or your first for a while, then the re-raise should be shown more respect. Indeed, if you have scarcely raised at all in the game, you might just call.

   However, if you have been raising reasonably often, especially on the button, then the big blind's re-raise is likely to be trying to smoke out a button steal. Here, you are not stealing, but making a genuine value raise, and you must re-raise now to test your opponent's strength.

On The Flop

8) Bet 150 chips. The amount you choose to bet is up to you, but the standard follow-up bet on the flop is usually between 50 per cent and 100 per cent of the pot. Here, you have missed the flop but hope that your opponent has done so also. By betting first, you put the pressure onto him and, unless he has a promising draw, or he has indeed hit the flop, he is likely to fold now.

9) Bet 150 chips. Whatever you would have bet when making a follow-up bet, having missed the flop, should be similar (or identical) to the amount that

you bet when you do hit the flop. In this way, you increase the chance of receiving action from loose, weak players. By keeping a similar style for when you miss the flop and when you hit it, you make your play harder to read whilst optimizing your chances of taking down pots – that is an enviable combination.

10) a) You have a choice here of simply calling or opting to make a semi-bluff raise. The advantage of calling is that it may persuade other players to remain in the pot, so building you a bigger pot should you hit your straight draw.

However, the disadvantages of a passive call are far greater: you are likely to have to call again on the turn if you miss your draw; if you hit your draw and then bet, it may look so obvious that your opponent folds; with two diamonds on the board, you would prefer not to have to worry unduly about a flush if another diamond hits on the turn or river. Ideally, you should almost always prefer playing heads-up from the flop onwards, making your reading of your opponent's likely hand much easier.

The two main advantages of raising now are:

i) your opponent may fold and you take down the pot immediately.

ii) your opponent calls but checks on the turn, providing you with a chance to check also and see the river for free.

Finally, this classic semi-bluff raise reinforces the image of you as a tight/aggressive player who, once he is in the hand, will play it hard and aggressively throughout, and not a player who is a calling station, simply hoping to hit the right card at the right moment.

I would raise to 240 chips or thereabouts.

   b) The odds of your hitting your straight draw are
      roughly:
      8 outs × 4 (since you have both turn and river to
      come) = 32%
      The actual percentage is 31.5%
      Once you have missed your draw on the turn, the
      chances of your hitting it on the river are roughly 8
      outs × 2 = 16%
      The actual percentage is 17.4%

11) If there are checks around to you, your natural in-
    stinct should be to want to bet. Here, with a paired
    flop, a bet may well take the pot. If you get raised, you
    should probably fold quietly. However, if your op-
    ponent is known for trying to smoke out stealing bets,
    then re-raise him. This will come down to your
    knowledge of your opponents and the number of
    layers you believe to be operating in your confronta-
    tion with him.

On The Turn

12) Bet. Your opponent has not re-raised, which suggests
    that he might be on a draw, or perhaps a loose second-
    pair call. Either way, the turn cannot have helped him
    and you mustn't give him a free look at the river.
        If he is on a straight draw, with say, 109, then he has
    less than a 20 per cent chance of hitting; with top pair/
    poorer kicker, or second pair, he has even less chance
    of making a winning hand. Whatever he has, make
    him pay for the draw. Since there are 500 chips in the
    pot now, bet about 200–250 chips to make him pay far
    too high odds for his draw, but a small enough amount
    for him to wonder what to do with, say, QJ.

On The River

13) Bet. It looks tempting to check here but, either your opponent has missed his draw, or he is holding a queen with a lower kicker than yours. It is always possible, especially online, that you are playing against a madman who called you twice with a 2 in his hand but these characters usually bet out on the river, so you can discount that possibility. If your opponent is holding QJ or Q10, then a small bet here at the end will probably persuade him to call you down, maximizing your winning potential on the hand. Into a pot of, say, 900 chips, I would bet 200 chips.

TOURNAMENTS

Tournament poker is a fantastic way to play the game without committing substantial sums of money. The basic principle is that you pay a fixed entry fee and that is all you can lose. If you make the top fraction of the field you can win a decent return on your entry fee. Make it as far as the Final Table and the payouts will be much higher; end up in a medal position and you could win a life-changing sum of money. Above all perhaps, plenty of tournament action provides a massive amount of play, practice and experience which, in the old days of slow cash games, could take you years to amass. Better still, the aggressive style which you must adopt for tournament success is a great way on which to base your game, whatever variation of poker you choose to play.

A poker tournament works in a very simple way. In exchange for their entry fee, each player is given the same number of chips at the start, say, 1,500, and the blinds start low, say, 5/10. If you lose your chips at any time, you are out of the event and, to win it, you will have to acquire every chip in play. At the start of a tournament, I often look around the room and think to myself: the winner of this event is going to have everyone's chips – every last one – in front of him at the end. It's a weird feeling, especially as you start to work out how that person is going to be you!

If the blinds stayed static as with a cash game, it would take forever to whittle down the field, but in a tournament the blind bets are raised regularly at set intervals (anything from 20 minutes to two hours). This has the effect of forcing competitors to play more hands since, if they just wait for the premium starting hands, their stacks would get whittled away just by the blinds.

After the blinds have gone up six or seven times, and maybe stand at 400/800, you can see that only players who have built up a significant stack will still be sitting around the tables. There may even be, at some events, ante-bets which must be placed by every player, every hand, further eating away at your stack. Everyone else will have been knocked out. As players leave, tables close down and amalgamate until, eventually, the remaining players meet at the apex of the poker tournament – the Final Table. Here, the blinds (and ante-bets) continue to rise, until finally, one player has accumulated all the chips and is crowned the winner.

The first time you win a poker tournament, be it one containing thirty players or one with a field of thousands, you will experience the most fantastic feeling of euphoria. You will be exhausted too, because to win a tournament requires great reserves of concentration, stamina, luck and determination. In this chapter we'll look at some of the basic principles of good tournament play to give you the best chance of reaching the Final Table and, perhaps, holding aloft that trophy.

Nowadays, with both an explosion of poker clubs and casinos offering poker, as well as the twenty-four online action, you can play in a serious poker tournament twenty-four hours a day, seven days a week.

In the Online Poker Chapters, we'll take a look at Sit & Go tournaments and satellites. Here, we'll look at the best strategy for multi-table tournaments, from your local card club to the World Series of Poker.

Types of Tournament

Before entering an event, it is important to know that not all tournaments are the same. Because there is quite a marked variation between some of the styles on offer, the style of play required to succeed in them varies quite considerably. Let's take a look at some of the styles of tournament you are likely to encounter, and how best to tackle each one:

Freezeout

A standard Freezeout event is one in which you pay a single entry fee – let's say $100 – and that is your entire financial commitment. You will be given a set number of chips, often 1,500, and, when you lose those chips, you are out of the event.

At random, you will be allocated a starting table and number. You take your place, meet the opponents at your table, and then the organiser will call for you to begin. You are on a poker thrill-ride now and there is no way to get off without losing all your chips and being eliminated.

The blinds will rise at regular intervals and ante-bets may also be added towards the end. As other competitors are eliminated, the number of tables will dwindle; new players may join you, or your table may be disbanded with your being moved to another table.

Eventually, only one table remains – the Final Table – and, if you are there, you have done very well. The blinds (and ante-bets) continue to rise until one player holds all the chips. He is the winner.

There are two extra important factors to appreciate when entering a poker tournament:

1) How many big blinds is my starting stack?
2) For how long is the tournament expected to last; how long is the interval between blind levels?

Your starting stack, in relation to the size of the blinds, tells you how much skill level will be involved in an event, and to what extent luck is likely to play an increased role.

In simple terms, the smaller your starting stack, the more action you will have to see in order to avoid being blinded away. This will have the effect of creating more play on marginal hands and a greater tendency for opponents to go all-in against you, in order to increase pressure. This style of play is more open to the slings and arrows of misfortune and is therefore considered a better format for less experienced players who might get lucky a few times and find themselves in a strong chip position.

Better players prefer a bigger starting stack and slower blind raises, leaving more time to form opinions about opponents, to wait for profitable situations and cash in on any loose, weak plays made by less experienced players.

So, a player who saw that he started with 1,000 chips, but that the blinds would start at 25/50 would realize that he was starting with only 20 times the big blind – an incredibly low factor. This is a tournament for inexperienced players who do not mind that luck will probably be the deciding factor.

An average tournament might offer you 1,500 chips and the first-round blinds would be 10/20. This is offering you 75 times the big blind – a fair factor for a poker tournament.

The WSOP Big One, the $10,000 buy-in finale to the event, provides 10,000 chips and the first-round blind level of 25/50 – giving you 200 times your big blind. And, since this event is played over sometimes nine days, the blind levels tend to move very slowly, rising once every two hours.

Even this is not considered by the elite players to be enough time and enough hands to weed out the merely lucky from the truly expert and some tournaments with even bigger buy-ins are offering a double stack of chips, providing 25,000 chips with slow-rising blind levels and a starting value of just 25/50 – or 500 times the big blind.

The more skilful you want the event to be, the higher the factor of starting chips against initial big blind should be.

The longer a poker tournament is scheduled to last, the more skill is likely to rise to the top and the lucky run out of good fortune and sink without trace.

The longer the blind levels, the longer the event is likely to last.

So, a two-hour event at your local club, with a few chips against a relatively high initial big blind is just a sociable couple of hours where everyone stands a chance of winning. A two-day event at a casino, with slow blind increases and an expectation of, maybe, twenty hours' play, is a good deal more serious and the better players are more likely to win (it is, by no means, guaranteed) than the average palooka.

Re-buys

A tournament which offers re-buys is one in which there is a get-out-of-jail clause available during the first period of play (usually one hour, sometimes longer). This is called the Re-buy Period. If you lose all your chips, you have the chance to re-enter the tournament by re-buying into it. The cost of the re-buy will vary: it may be the same as the initial entry fee; it may be more than the entry fee; or it may cost less than the original entry fee. You need to know which of those three options is in operation, even if you don't re-buy yourself. This is because:

the chance to re-buy your entry fee for a cheap price will encourage loose and aggressive play from players who enjoy to gamble early on, knowing that they can re-buy into the event cheaply and still be in a good spot, even if they have busted out half a dozen times during the re-buy period. In this format, you can expect bluffing, over-raising, all-in moves and aggressive raising and re-raising action from the off. It will be difficult to play a patient tight/aggressive style when you are so likely to receive multiple raisers and callers.

To re-buy into the event at the same price as the entry fee will ensure that there is a little more discipline and respect early on as, unless the buy-in was very cheap, players should not be so keen to re-buy unless they are forced to do so.

To re-buy into the event at a price higher than the initial entry fee sounds a little prohibitive since, as more people buy in, the effect of all the extra chips in play is inflation: their re-buy will be worth less to them than their initial chip stack at the outset. Since they are required to pay more for it, they will not be keen to re-buy unless forced out of the tournament on an unlucky or close hand.

Whenever there is the opportunity to re-buy, whatever the cost of that re-buy, there will be players who are prepared to be ultra-aggressive early on in an attempt to build a substantial, even dominating, chip stack before the event returns to the Freezeout format at the end of the re-buy period. For that reason, all re-buy events must be considered at the outset to offer a lower-than-usual factor of chip stack versus big blind – this is because there will be many more chips in play after all the re-buys and your own stack is therefore devalued.

Recently I was invited to play in a tournament at Sun City in South Africa. I asked about the format. There was the buy-in and an extra long re-buy period. The re-buys would cost much less than the initial entry fee. There would then be an add-on (see below) and that would be only a fraction of the price of the entry fee. Even though I was assured that it was a very mixed field, I didn't really fancy this event.

This format ensured that there would be a massive amount of aggressive action early on with players almost forced to gamble wildly to build up a substantial stack. It would be necessary to play in a similar vein if you were not to fall too far behind the chip leaders. Then, you would have to purchase the add-on since it was so cheap that everyone would do so and, as a basic rule, you should always want as many chips as possible at the table.

All this has one major positive effect on the event: it boosts the prize pot massively. Not only do you have the entry fees, you have multiple re-buys and the cost of adding on to your chips too. For me though, it reduces the skill level and leaves too much to chance. The amount of time following the mad, ultra-aggressive gamblers' period was not enough to sit back and pick off the weak players. They would have big chip stacks and needed to get lucky only once against you to knock you out. A good friend of mine placed well at this event and made good money but he did admit to me that it was a bit of a turkey shoot. I'm not knocking it – those events can be hugely entertaining – it's just not my particular style.

A re-buy can vary in size. Sometimes you may be able to buy up to only 50 per cent of the original starting stacks. Also, a re-buy may be available to you before you lose all your chips. Some events offer a re-buy the moment you fall below the starting stack; others when you have less than 50 per cent of your starting stack . . . and so on. Whenever you go to a professionally arranged event, all these details will be explained to you and now you will, at least, know what they mean.

Whatever type of re-buy is offered to you, they all have one thing in common: they are available only during the re-buy period. When that ends, the event changes to a Freezeout and, once you've lost your stack, you're out.

By the way, when should you decide to purchase a re-buy?

You have to consider that you have just been knocked out of the event. Was it because you were outclassed at your table and that the going there is very tough? If so, you should probably resist the temptation to re-buy since you will stay at your table and face the same opponents and with a smaller stack than most of them.

Maybe you just suffered a bad beat and you feel furious and frustrated at your bad luck (I don't blame you – these amateurs drive me mad). You know if you get back into that game, you'll get revenge on that lucky SOB and beat him good, humiliate him in front of everyone else and that'll feel real good. Don't re-buy into the event! You are on tilt and your game will be affected and your skills diminished. Don't get me wrong, remember every detail about the play of that little guy who bad beat you on the river. Stare hard at him, smile sardonically, nod knowingly, and then leave the table. You can get him next time.

If you went out because your opponent hit a marginal draw and you had become a little short-stacked because you lost a decent-sized pot on a kicker early on; and you

think that you are amongst the best players at your table
and that your opponents' chips can genuinely be picked up
smartly if you stay in the game, then re-buy. In fact, if the
game is really promising for you, then re-buy more than
once if you want to. Just don't do it for the wrong reason.

I saw an ultra-glamorous Hollywood blonde playing in a
qualifying event at the WSOP a few years back. She went
all-in on QQ and some guy called her with AJ and hit his
ace on the board. She re-bought at the table (it was $150)
and the next hand, she re-raised an opponent with AK. He
called and turned over 88. The eights held up and the
bombshell bought in for another $150. The very next hand
– the very next one – she re-raised all-in with AA and got a
caller. He had AQ. The flop came QQ4 and she was calling
for a re-buy even before the turn and river appeared. I
watched her re-buy three times more before the re-buy
period ended and she was out within a few moments. She
must have spent $1,500 in entry fees to play in a qualifying
event where the entry fee was $1,500. Several of the guys
came over to sympathize with her, telling her how unlucky
she was. She stood up and beamed at the table.

'It's okay,' she told them, 'I won $180,000 on the slots
yesterday.'

I tell you this story because when you play poker you
learn that no sooner do the gods shine on you, you find
that they are defecating all over you the next minute.

So, finally, don't re-buy if nothing is going right for
you. There are so many opportunities to play poker; if one
isn't working, take a quick break, and start somewhere
new.

Add-ons

An add-on is a chance to purchase more chips to add to
your stack. Usually, there is only one chance to do this,

and that is at the end of the re-buy period, when the opportunity is offered to you. You don't have to take it – you may have big enough stacks to reject the investment, but you'll find that most players do buy the add-on.

The size of the add-on may vary from tournament to tournament. In most social and club events, it will be the same size as your initial stack; sometimes, it is less.

The cost of an add-on may vary also. Again, generally, it will cost the same (or pro rata) as the initial buy-in.

Listen to announcements or consult rules to ensure that you know what any re-buy or add-on will cost you.

As a general rule, if I play in a tournament, I assume that I will purchase the add-on and I add that to the entry fee as my investment in the tournament. If you want to play in an event, but you cannot afford the add-on, my advice would be not to play in that event. Find a lower-priced entry fee for another event and make sure you have the cash for the add-on if necessary.

If you are a player who wants a full evening/weekend's entertainment, then be prepared to bring sufficient money for at least one re-buy and the add-on. Never play poker with a limited bankroll because, if you are worrying about money, you can't concentrate on the cards. Moreover, good players at your table will pick up on your money worries and use your anxiety to bully and pressurize you.

One final factor must be that, when you are offered an add-on, how many current big blinds will it provide you with? For example, the blind levels stand at 75/150 and you have the opportunity to add-on 1,000 chips. Would you add-on?

I'm not sure that I would. The blinds are about to rise – they usually do at the end of the re-buy period when the add-ons are offered – so they'll stand at 100/200. I am adding only five big blinds with my add-on – that equates to little over three rounds. If I have sufficient chips to play my usual game at this stage, I'll probably not add-on unless the chips come for a very cheap price.

Let's imagine now that the blinds are at 25/50 and the add-on is 1,500. The blinds will then rise to 50/100 probably, but that still gives me 15 big-blind bets for my add-on – or ten rounds of betting. That is offering me far more time to find my good cards in a good position and become aggressive. I'll take this add-on for sure, unless it is prohibitively priced. Even then, I may take it, since I shouldn't have entered the tournament if I couldn't afford the add-on which I imagine most players will take.

Don't add-on if any of the factors which prohibited you from re-buying are in place – just to remind you:

- you are outclassed by the opposition;
- your seat is very unfavourable at this table;
- you have suffered bad beats and you are steaming;
- everything you've touched today has gone wrong;
- you are angry, depressed, paranoid, desperate, hungry, sexually frustrated, or broke. (I added a few extra ones – but they are all valid.)

So, for rewarding skilful play, look for: long period of play, small blinds rising slowly, no re-buys, no add-ons. Ideally, start with Double Stacks.

A tournament offering Double Stacks means that everyone will start with stacks double the usual size. For example, many tournaments offer 1,500 chips as your starting stack; a Double-Stack event would give you 3,000 chips. The effect of this is to provide more time early on to get to know the styles of your opponents, and, as a result, good players tend to fare better over the longer playing time.

For fun, sociable, luck-heavy poker, seek out: short play time, blinds starting high, rising quickly, re-buys, add-ons, small starting stack.

These definitions apply equally to land-based games as well as online. Indeed, online poker sites tend to offer a far wider range of tournaments from which to choose. It's up to you to find the games which suit your style, your bankroll, the amount of time you have available and your skill level. That choice is unique to online poker; land-based casinos will give you a limited selection of games.

Entry Fee

In live games, the higher the entry fee, the tighter the game usually starts. Players have invested a significant sum in the event and they don't wish to be knocked out early on, or made into a short-stack when there are still many sessions to follow. Raises and re-raises will be shown respect.

If you are confident, you can use this information to play more loosely and far more aggressively than usual during the early stages. It is not my preferred style, but it can work very well.

Incidentally, online, for the most part, the size of the entry fee seems to make little difference to the attitude of the majority of the players. The overwhelming attitude of most online players is that it doesn't matter much what happens – there'll be another tournament along in a moment. This often leads to very aggressive play early on. (See more in the online poker section.)

Prize Pot

If you are even a little serious about poker, the size of the prize pot should be of interest to you. Especially when playing social games, check that all entry fees go into that pot and that the organiser isn't taking most of what should be your prize fund.

In a professionally arranged event, the moment the game starts, you should be able to find out how many people are playing. As soon as the re-buy/add-on period ends, the total prize fund should be publicized, along with the amounts paid to each position. This is vital information for you because, later on, you will have to decide whether to play to reach the low-level money or whether you are going to attack aggressively the top spots (and risk leaving the event out of the money).

In the UK, many casinos have installed monitors which display all those facts to competitors and which can show you at a glance what the average chip count stands at; how may players remain in the event; what the blind levels are and how soon they will rise. This is great information to have at your fingertips because you are then in a position to decide whether to play all-out to try to win the event, or merely remain patient and try to sneak into the money. Similarly, when your chip stack falls below the average in the tournament, you know that it is time for you to become a little more aggressive and, when your stacks are healthy, you can afford to be a little more selective in the hands that you choose to play.

The Bubble

The Bubble is the one position in which no poker player wants to finish. It is the place one off the money. So, if the tournament pays the top-ten finishers, to be 'out on the bubble' means that you finished eleventh. However, there is a significant tactical advantage to the positive player when the bubble approaches: so many players are transfixed by this break-off point that they will do anything to avoid it. I have seen players lay down hands where they must be ahead, simply to avoid the ignominy of being eliminated on the bubble. This is a situation that you must turn to your advantage. As the bubble approaches, you should become more aggressive, not less. For you, as a successful player, reaching the bottom of the pay-out list should be of little concern to you (unless it is a very high payout structure). You should be interested in not only making it into the money, but also challenging for the top spots which, inevitably, pay proportionally much higher sums.

Usually, the first few pay-out places are particularly low, often refunding only the entrance fee. Once you have made it so far into a tournament, with a genuine chance of winning or placing in the top three, it should be in your mentality to shrug off fears about the bubble and go for the higher position.

Certainly, when I first started playing, I was happy just to reach the money but, once you've been there a few times and then found yourself with so few chips at the Final Table, you soon learn that it is better to be out on the bubble a few times than at the Final Table with some big stacks getting ready to win big: economically, it makes sense.

Tournament Strategy

There are many different approaches to tournament play and you may find that you prefer one over others, or that you are happy to mix up your styles depending upon whom you find yourself playing at any given time. That would be the ideal but, because most tournaments move very quickly, it is often tough to read your new opponents sufficiently well to mix up your play. The longer the duration of the event, and therefore the gaps between blind rises, the more time you have to assess your opponents and determine which style best suits each opponent.

Assuming that you are playing in a freezeout event – or that you have passed the end of the re-buy and add-on period – here's a suggested strategy for keeping you in the event and with sufficient chips to make a decent play for the money places.

Table Awareness

At the start of a tournament everyone is a little nervous. Do not be keen to play any hands early on, unless they are monsters. Whenever you become involved in a complicated hand, involving betting manoeuvres, you want to have the best possible information about your opponents; if you play hands early on, you simply won't have that information available to you. Even at a regular home-game table – many now play tournaments – you may know your friends, but have you yet managed to determine which style of play they have brought to the game on this particular occasion?

So, relax, watch how the action unfolds and mark each player with a basic tag of how they are playing and their general approach to the event: I like the tight/aggressive; tight/passive; loose/aggressive; loose/passive demarcations; but if you prefer other ones, use those – but do use them. You will also want to note the frequency with which certain players raise, their awareness of positional advantage, their desire to steal, chase or relinquish pots, as well as the physical tells that they may be displaying during these early minutes when nerves are still affecting them.

The result of this discipline on your part will be to create a table image of being very tight. This will allow you to steal some pots in the short term, unless your cards improve, and then loosen later playing some hands as semi-bluffs from the outset. Your tight image will work for you in the early stages of a tournament.

Throw away any marginal hands, or if you feel you must call because you are receiving good odds, then be decisive in mucking those cards unless the flop hits perfectly for you.

During this time, also obtain information on the total chips in play (and therefore how you stand in relation to the average chip count), how the prize pool breaks down, at how long the blind intervals are set. All this information, updated regularly, is important to know when playing in an event. This is another reason why playing ultra-tight at the outset is such a good idea, particularly if you are nervous or playing in a big event for the first time.

One final advantage such a strategy imparts is that you will seem quite relaxed and therefore confident. This is, of course, because you won't play any hands other than premium cards in good position (and therefore, probably, no hands at all). This allows you to settle your nerves, assess your table and your own position at it.

Now is the time to divide the event into different sections and use those to guide you as to the correct style of basic play you should be adopting. For me, unless it is a tournament which spans several days, I like to divide an event into four sections – or quartiles – and use those to guide me through the changing styles required to succeed. Within these templates, there is still plenty of room for you to mix up your play, introduce your own style of game, and target specific opponents for particular attention. However, as a fall-back position, if all else fails, this strategy is more likely to keep you in the hunt than many others.

First Quartile

At the beginning of this first quartile, you are assessing your table, your position and your standing, whilst developing a table image of being ultra-tight. The simple fact is that a tight image at the outset will almost always serve you well in the later stages of a tournament, particularly if you are playing at a single table, or if opponents against whom you played early on pop up again at a Final Table.

On top of this, a tight start is sensible as many players, even very good ones, often like to be aggressive early on to intimidate nervous competitors. You won't be intimidated, because you won't be in the hand and, when you are, your hand will be so strong that you can play back at the bullies and immediately assert your strength. Those advantages are very great.

Be aware, at every table at which you find yourself, that your position in relation to other players is of paramount importance.

If you find yourself with tight/passive players to your left, players who are likely to fold to a raise unless they hold a premium hand, increase your raise frequency by lowering your raise requirements and pressurize them.

If you find loose/passive players to your left, who call on sub-standard hands, be prepared to increase the size of your raises (the standard pre-flop raise is three to four times the big blind – an increase might mean raising four to six times the big blind) to dissuade this loose-calling attitude and to gain a better read on the type of hand that they may be holding if they do call.

If you find yourself with tight/aggressive players to your left, those who call or re-raise only with good hands or speculative hands with good pot odds, remain aggressive in your style with good hands.

With loose/aggressive players to your left, who raise regularly on a wide range of hands, consider more calling and less raising. When you do raise, consider smaller raises, allowing you to fold to a re-raise or keep a pot reasonably small if other players pile into the pot.

This last category is really the worst for you, since these opponents can raise on all kinds of hands, leaving you with little information on them and a creeping tendency not to raise as often as you might like. You may choose to tighten up dramatically and wait for these players to get knocked out or disperse to other tables. Certainly, when you do hit the flop well, mix up a check-raise (these aggressive players will bet and bet and bet, doing your work for you) or a strong follow-up bet, which may tempt them to re-raise you, allowing you to move all-in.

There is a further downside to having these players at your table and, especially, to your left. If you do raise with a premium hand, and you are called by two loose players to your left, any further players still to act now have excellent pot odds to enter the hand with suited connectors, ace-small suited hands and other speculative hands. Remember that AA against one player is at least 80 per cent on to win; that same AA against four callers is odds-*against* to win. That is why one or two loose callers to your left can invite the rest of the table in and devalue even your very strong hands. If you do hold a high overpair to the board, and you have multiple callers, consider a pot-sized follow-up bet following the appearance of the flop – consider betting even more if necessary. Such overbets might be poor play in a cash game but, in a tournament, they have their place in driving out players from multi-player pots.

Players to your right are also of importance, since much of your profit often emanates from the players over whom you are sitting.

Tight/aggressive players are, at least, reasonably easy to read pre-flop. Good players will mix up their style, making it hard for you to know when they have their advertised strength and when they are stealing.

Tight/passive players will call frequently, increasing pot odds for callers. If you notice a lot of calling ahead of you, enter hands with a raise, or consider staying out of them, however tempting it may be to play 6♦ 5♦ when there have been five other callers.

Loose/aggressive players can be a real pain, since their style is to raise on a wide range of hands. This, in turn, makes it far harder for you to limp cheaply into hands in late position on speculative cards. Prepare to re-raise with premium hands and, if you notice a very high frequency of raising by your opponents, re-raise on merely good hands also. Somewhere along the line, if you are stuck with these same players for any length of time, you must make a stand against this aggressive play, or you will find yourself falling into a reactive mode, instead of a proactive one. You seek to set the agenda; you do not want to be at the beck and call of your opponents, especially those sitting in front of you.

Loose/passive players will simply call a lot. They really don't change your strategy at all, other than to boost the size of the pot when you raise pre-flop and take the pot down then. Ideally, you would like as many as possible of these loose/passive players calling on your right. Raise when you feel it is right to do so; otherwise, maintain a disciplined selective style.

I like to stick to only premium hands in early or mid-position and add in a few good starting hands and some speculative ones also when I have good, late position.

AA, KK, QQ
are worth a raise (or re-raise) in any position almost all the time (I wouldn't do anything all the time at a poker table, but to slow-play these hands is, fundamentally, a mistake).

JJ, 1010, 99, 88
I recommend a mixture of raising with these hands – more when in late position, and limping in with them. Later in

the tournament, you will probably choose to raise with these hands most of the time.

Low pairs

I find low pairs very tough to play in tournaments and, early on, these hands should be played conservatively, unless there have been no callers to your late position, when you would want to raise with them.

AK, AQ

To raise with these cards in any position is pretty standard tournament play. With AK, I would raise and re-raise pretty freely pre-flop. However, during this early stage, I would not want to call an early raise with AQ, nor raise with it other than if there are very few callers. You can get far more aggressive with this hand in the later stages.

AJs, A10s, KQs, KJs, suited connectors, ace-low suited

These are all worth calls and, sometimes, raises in late position. If you know that the players to your left are very conservative, you can choose to raise with AJs or A10s in mid-position also.

KQ and KJ suited, as well as ace-suited, are drawing hands and, early on, should be played as such, limping in late position.

Unsuited variations of these hands, I would be tempted to pass most of the time pre-flop during the first quartile of an event.

Don't play on if your ace-low suited hits an ace on the flop – only when you make a straight flush draw or 2-pair should you continue. Playing low aces early on in a tournament is an almost certain way of being eliminated even before you've settled into your seat.

Back up pre-flop raises with follow-up bets whether you

hit the flop or miss it completely. Remember that to slow-play more than one opponent is madness unless you hold the 100 per cent nuts (and even then, betting out often results in a bigger pot than a crafty slow-play).

If you hit trips or top two-pair, bet it strongly – both these hands are very susceptible to draws.

If you hit a nut flush draw, this might be a good time merely to call rather than to raise if it means cheap cards on the turn and river. Otherwise, make the semi-bluff raise and attack your opponents.

Keep the pots small and avoid bluffing at any time. This should not be difficult to do since, if you follow the very tight strategy, you should not be involved in any large pots.

By the end of the first quartile, you should find yourself about even since you will probably win a few small pots but otherwise you will have played very quietly. This may not sound very impressive but there will be plenty of players who have become short-stacked during this period and it is they who will become your prime targets during the next quartile.

On occasion, you will find yourself well ahead of the average chip stack. This is because there are many players who opt for a very aggressive, busy, action-filled early section. The experts do this very well, but less experienced players often misjudge big bets and bluffs and this allows you to pick them off in relative safety. I have certainly found myself with three, even four or five times the average chip stack having just played a few hands in the early stages. So much of poker is about ego and, for some players, that ego can be reinforced only by the stealing of pots and repeated bluffing, even right up to their entire starting stack. Remain aware of these aggressive players and wait your turn to have a good crack at them.

Let's take a look at some examples, all assuming a full nine-player table with blinds at 10/20:

1) You are sitting in the fourth seat holding: A♣ J♦. There is one caller from the second seat. Do you call, raise or fold?

During the early stages of a multi-table tournament, I would fold these cards in this position. If any other player holds an ace, you may lose a substantial pot; if a player in later position raises, you certainly won't want to call that raise. You are unlikely to win a big pot, but you may lose a big one.

2) You are sitting one from the button holding: A♣ J♦. No one else has called yet, and you decide to raise to 85 chips (this isn't in our strategy for the first quartile). You are raised by the button to 200 chips. Do you call, re-raise or pass?

At this point in the event, you were a little aggressive with AJ. However, now that you have been raised by a player with good position over you, you should almost certainly pass. If you know that your opponent is super-aggressive, then you may decide otherwise but if you hadn't been in this deal with a marginal hand, then you wouldn't have to make this decision.

3) You are sitting one from the button. You hold: A♥ 7♥. There is a raise from the second seat to 85 chips and two further callers. Do you call, raise or pass?

You are being asked to contribute 85 chips into a pot that is currently 285 chips, so you are paying about 30 per cent of the pot to play. Since you will not be happy if an ace falls – unless it comes with a seven – and you are hoping only for hearts, it doesn't seem worth the bet now. If the flop hits the initial raiser, you are likely to get caught up in raising and re-raising situations. This is a hand to stay out of during the early stages of an event.

Had there been three callers to you, then for only 20 chips (even though it represents a similar percentage contribution) you should almost certainly call. You have a slim chance of hitting the nut flush draw and, with plenty of players already in the pot, you may get rewarded handsomely should you make your flush.

4) You are sitting on the button with A♣ K♠. There is a raise from the player on your right to 110 chips. Should you call, raise or pass?

This is a premium hand in an excellent position. It is quite possible that your opponent was trying to steal the blinds or holds a marginal hand and a decent-sized raise here may push him out. He may also hold the kind of hand many players think is an automatic raise in this position: AQ, AJ, mid- or low pair, even KQs or KJs. Against any of those hands, you have an excellent chance of picking up a good-sized pot and you are in position to control the size of the pot if you simply choose to call it down. At this early stage of the event, if your opponent calls your raise and then bets into you on a flop which misses you, just muck your cards and wait for a better opportunity.

Incidentally, notice the size of your opponent's raise. If he is nervous or inexperienced, he may be slightly over-betting (the big blind is 20, the normal raise × 3.5) to protect a mid- or low pair, or a marginal raising hand, so it will be good to test out his reaction to the re-raise.

5) You hold: Q♣ J♣ on the button. There has been a raise to 85 chips from the player two seats to your right and a call from the player in between you. You decide, perhaps

rashly, to call and see a flop. The pot contains 285 chips and the flop comes:

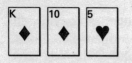

The two players before you both check. You decide not to risk a bet here and you check also. The turn comes:

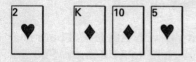

The initial raiser bets 150 chips and the next player passes. What should you do?

Tempting though it may be to you to call for the open-ended straight, you should definitely resist. Odds-wise, it's the wrong bet. You have only a 17.4 per cent chance of making your straight and, if you do, your opponent may not pay you any more.

Let's say that you do hit your straight, but the card with which you make it is a heart or a diamond. Are you certain that your opponent hasn't made the flush?

The fact is that the initial raiser may well have been attempting a check-raise on the flop and, when he got no action, he decided to bet out his king-high hand on the turn. He may have nothing of course but, then, neither do you!

The moral is probably not to call. Raise pre-flop (which I don't like at all); bet on the flop – which could easily cost you; or fish for a magic card at the end. I dislike all of those and, for that reason, it's clear that if we are going to present a tight/aggressive image, we should definitely have passed pre-flop.

Drawing and bluffing are poor plays during this early section of play and should, generally, be avoided.

6) You hold: 9♥ 9♣ on the button. There is a raise from seat one to 85 chips and two further callers. Do you call, raise or fold?

There is plenty to be said for raising here, although I am worried by the raise under the gun, and that two other players have been prepared to call. Much later in the event, to raise might work but, here, you do not want to risk your stack. Call and await the flop. The pot stands at 370 chips and the flop comes:

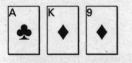

The initial raiser bets 150 chips and one of the next two players calls and the other folds. Do you call or raise?

This could be the time for a slow-play and hope that the chips continue to be ploughed into the centre of the table. However, the initial raiser could have AA or KK (although the arrival of both on the table seems to make that less likely), but what is the guy in the middle of you calling on? A speculative flush draw, perhaps with a gut-shot straight in there too? This is the right time to play your hand strongly. If you lose this hand to trip aces or kings, or indeed a flush, that will be very bad luck, but you must try to find out where you are right now. Raise. Let's see: there are 670 chips in the pot now – let's raise to 600 and see what reaction you get.

A flush draw will likely fold here (although if player one calls, player two might just think it worth the risk of a further call). I think that both players will recognize that they have represented good hands and that your raise is not a bluff. If one or both call, you will want to check this hand down; if only one calls, you may feel similarly pessimistic. However, both may well pass, especially if player one was on an ace with a mid-kicker, and player two was, indeed, on some kind of a draw. If you receive a huge re-raise from player one . . .? I don't even like to think. You will have to judge his style to see if that is how he would play trip kings or aces, or whether he is pushing far too hard.

Even though I think you will take this pot down now if you are winning, you can see just how dangerous, early on in an event, it is to play marginal hands – even when they hit! Maybe you should have re-raised pre-flop after all.

Second Quartile

You have presented a tight/aggressive image to the table and now it is time to cash in on this by raising a little more freely in late position, pressurizing the blinds. Remain aware of your relative chip position to the average and be prepared to change gears rapidly if you start to head towards being short-stacked. It is much better to play as if you were short-stacked when you are on the way to that position than to wait until you really are. This is because whilst you retain sufficient chips to make a meaningful re-raise (if necessary, all-in), your bets will still have fold equity (the added chance of your opponent folding to your bet) and that is something denied to the truly short-stacked player, who must rely on good cards or luck to double through.

Assuming that you are still around the average mark, look for the short-stacks, and seek to attack them as they become ever more desperate to double through. To this end, when you do take on a short-stack, you may choose to lower your raise (from the standard three-and-a-half times big blind, down to maybe two-and-a-half times) so that, if you are re-raised all-in by a short-stack, you can still choose to let the hand go without feeling pot-committed.

Pick the opponents against whom you will steal or bluff based on the knowledge of them which you have gained by observing during the first quartile.

Keep starting-hand quality up for early position plays and reduce it slightly for mid- and late position action. Continue to play good hands very strongly, raising and re-raising to gain information and maximize pot size.

Remain aware, at all times, of the changing faces at your table. By the time the second quartile is in full flow, you may well have lost two or three players from your table or even had your table dispersed to others. Remember that the dynamics of a poker table can change dramatically with the introduction, or elimination, of just one player. Watch the newcomers at your table with an eagle eye to ensure that you can rate them as soon as possible.

If you have breaks scheduled – and this can apply just as well to online events as for land-based clubs and casinos – ensure that you use that time to escape the pressured atmosphere of the playing space. If you can take a stroll outside for a few moments, or escape to a quiet room where there are no other players, this will be a great advantage. If you do nothing but talk poker without ceasing, eventually your brain will try to resist. If you give it a break for a while, it can make a huge difference. Also, try not to dwell on big successes or disasters which may have occurred during the most recent session. Unless they concern the particular play of an individual still at your table, push these thoughts to the back of your mind; you will have plenty of time to learn from these situations later.

Finally, as players begin to drop out of the event more quickly, you must be aware of three key elements:

1) What is the average chip count?
Are you ahead, with it, or behind this total?

Incidentally, if you have no information about the average stack size, you can always multiply the starting stack by the number of entrants and then divide by the number of players still sitting at the tables.

If you are ahead or with it, continue to play tight and aggressively, still selecting hands carefully before committing chips to any large pots. If you are behind in the chip count, become more aggressive – especially when in position – and be prepared to play bigger pots. Because you still have the table image of an aggressive but tight player, some of your raises may well be given greater respect than they deserve.

2) Because the blinds will be so much bigger, expect more blind stealing to occur from players in late position. If, when you hold position over them (they are sitting to your right), you can re-raise, you may well find yourself taking down several decent-sized pots without competition. This is the moment to cash in your carefully constructed image, stealing blinds and re-raising mid- and late raisers whom you suspect of blind stealing. Aim to steal more blinds yourself, especially when players to your left are short-stacked.

3) Consider raising pre-flop whenever you decide to play a hand. This adds to your aggressive image, whilst playing on the fact that you may not have played a very high frequency of hands previously. Your plan is to win pots without even seeing a flop. If you do have to see one, don't automatically make a follow-up bet; you can still get away from a hand where the flop does not fit, without crippling your stack.

Above all, throughout an event, you need to have the mindset to accumulate chips. Never sit back after winning a big pot and relax for a while; you will have lost vital momentum. Equally, don't play extra pots simply because you have won big; it would be foolhardy to dribble away your chips cheaply just because you loosen your style.

So, stay focused, remain aware of all the factors and prepare for the third quartile of the event.

Third Quartile

By this time, many of the weaker players will have been eliminated from the tournament, and there may be one or more runaway leaders with big chip stacks. Do not worry about these chip leaders now. They will probably choose to continue attacking short-stacked players and, eventually, one or more of them will double through against these players. The effect of this will be the levelling out of the overall chip position by the time the end of this quartile approaches.

If you are still sitting with many of your original opponents, take note, not only of their styles, but also reflect upon the image that you have projected. If it remains a tight/aggressive image, your raises will be taken more seriously than if you've had a run of hands where you have been entering the pot. How you behave in the future, in relation to your actions so far, will influence the way other players regard your bets and how easily you will be able to read their reaction to you.

For example, if you have been playing only premium and very good hands, and have shown down little else, and then there has been half an hour since you last raised, when you do raise, anyone who has been observing you should know that you hold a good hand. If they choose to call or raise your bet, they will be doing so knowing that you are strong. Presumably, therefore, they are stronger than usual. On the other hand, if you have shown a loose gambling style, a player who re-raises you may be doing so on a complete bluff, expecting you to lay down a marginal or sub-standard hand to their big bet.

How your opponents perceive you and your style of play will therefore directly influence their own game, and the way you read what they might be holding.

Let's look at an example. Imagine that you have been playing a tight/aggressive style throughout the tournament. You raise and re-raise, make follow-up bets and generally value bet. You find yourself sitting one from the button and you pick up: A♠ A♥. You decide to raise and the player on the button calls you. This is great news. The flop comes:

K♠ 7♣ 2♦

This is also very good for you, because there are no annoying draws out there to worry you, and your opponent may have made top pair. What should you do now? The key here is that, if you check, planning a check-raise subsequently – or even a slow-call – your opponent may wonder what you are holding to have made you change your perceived style of play; indeed, he may become very suspicious. Instead, simply make the follow-up bet of around half the pot that your opponent was expecting and hope that he makes a move on you.

In other words, be aware of your own image and, to avoid drawing attention to yourself, don't divert from it.

In this third quartile, you may find the introduction of ante-bets as well as the endlessly increasing blind levels. This added pressure on your stack must be met with a strong, positive and aggressive strategy. Never allow yourself to be blinded away. Even if you have lousy cards one from the button and on the button, ensure that you raise or re-raise at least once every two rounds, preferably more often than that. You may be called and find yourself in a coin-toss situation or in a 60–40 type hand. If you have become short-stacked, it is essential that you realize that for 99 per cent of the time, your only way back into the tournament is to play aggressively and get lucky whilst you still have sufficient chips to make a double through worthwhile. For one per cent of the time you might suddenly pick up huge cards, but don't rely on it.

So, if you are short-stacked, you are looking for all-in, double-through opportunities, whereas, if you are middle-stacked, you seek to play smaller pots and commit a sizeable proportion of your chips only with the nuts. Bear in mind that short-stacked players often call raises on marginal hands, happy to have any chance of doubling through: your fold equity when raising them strangely reduces at this stage of the event. The mid-stacks and those just below average chip count are more susceptible to a big raise since they still consider themselves well in the event and with a good chance of placing in the money.

If you are a big stack, you still cannot afford to relax, although you will have a little more time during which you will hope to see some decent hands. With a big stack, there is no excuse for not stealing blinds regularly.

Some years ago, expert poker author David Sklansky introduced an important concept which has come to be considered standard thinking, especially at these later stages in tournament play. It is called the 'gap concept' and, in simple terms, explains that you have to be stronger to call a raise than you need to be to make one. This supports our desire always to raise when entering a pot – or re-raise – and to show reluctance to join a pot merely by calling (unless you are trapping with, say, AA or KK).

The bubble is now approaching – the point at which the payouts begin – and you must use this to your advantage. Most mid- and short-stack players will be hanging on, hoping to place in the money. You must be fearless about going out just short of a payout, since the lowest prizes are hardly worth having. Instead, use this time to pressurize short- and mid-stacks with big pre-flop raises, designed to commit them to make the big decision which could knock them out of the event. Don't let them take the initiative and make raises before you.

At this stage, calling for draws should become less important to you than the quality of your starting hand. Let's see our attitude to starting hands at this stage:

AA KK AK QQ

These are still the premium hands; consider trapping with AA or KK if there are only one or two callers to you in late position (or the blinds). Otherwise, raise and re-raise aggressively with these cards.

JJ 1010 99 88 AQ AJs

These cards gain in value at this stage, since mid- and short-stacked players will raise and call with hands such as A10, A9, A8, KQ, etc. – putting you in a dominating position over them. Raise with these cards in any position and re-raise with all but AJs, which should still be handled with care (it's really not a great hand).

77 66 55 44 33 22

Personally, my record with twos, threes and fours in the latter stages of tournaments is not good, but most experts feel that all pairs gain in strength as the tournament progresses. The argument would be that, if you raise strongly with all these hands, unless you are up against a higher pair, you are unlikely to be much worse than 50 per cent on to win the hand. Add to this the fold equity (the chances of your opponents folding) and it makes it a good odds-on bet to make in these late stages.

Ace-small suited; suited connectors
These hands have devalued. For a start, at this stage of the
event, you are likely to be facing a pre-flop raise on most
hands. These hands are for quietly limping into the action,
not for calling a raise. Secondly, free cards on the board
are most unlikely at this stage as players will be keener to
take down pots before the board is complete. Since these
hands almost never make a completed hand on the flop
(but sometimes provide decent draws), you will have to
pay a great deal more money to see if your draw actually
makes.

Finally, these hands should not appeal to your strategic brain at this stage; your instinct should be to be
raising each time you enter a pot, not calling on speculative hands.

Even if you have been moved from your original table,
your previous tight/aggressive form will still be known by
one or more players at your table and it may cause an
opponent to fold on a hand where he was ahead of you.

Remember, to double up at this stage of an event is of
far greater importance than to double through early on.
That is why you are prepared to take some risks now to
knock out short-stacks and any remaining weak players,
whereas earlier, you were protecting your stack.

There are some further key thoughts to have in mind at
this point:

1) As the end of this quartile approaches, the Final Table
   will come into view. Many inexperienced players – or
   even better ones who have been having a bad time at
   the tables recently – will be set on just making the Final
   Table. It's an ego thing. Resist this, increase your
   aggression and do not fret if you get knocked out before
   the Final Table. You want to be there with a chip stack
   worth playing, otherwise, making the Final Table is

somewhat pointless, other than as a story to tell your friends.

2) Once the bubble has passed and all remaining players know that they are in the money, you will find that there is a short period where everyone relaxes following the intense concentration to get into the money. Players who seem relieved to have made it may become looser now, feeling that they have achieved their prime objective – to make the money. Note these players and avoid bluffing them – they are too likely to call you down. More serious competitors will remain focused.

3) The amount of chips required to call a bet (or, preferably, to raise) will seem enormous. Where you may have started off raising three-and-a-half times the big blind for 90 chips, you may have to make the same play with 3,500 chips, or even 35,000 chips. Try to remember that almost all players will be feeling the effects of fewer players all with more chips, and you must not be scared to make the correct bet, however much it seems to be costing you.

4) This is not a television event. There are no cameras (and, if there are, ignore them as much as you can). There will be many hands where everyone folds to the big blind, or where there is one raise and everyone folds. This stage of the event is a war of attrition as players wait for some kind of hand to make a play. Remain patient, but assess your strategy in relation to the style of the players remaining. If everyone seems patient, try raising a little more aggressively than you might; if there are one or two consistent raisers, wait patiently and then take a stand, in position and with a decent hand – you may well find that they fold to your re-raise.

5) Remember that you cannot win a tournament (indeed, even make it to the final stages) without a good deal of

luck. Tournament poker always involves more luck than a cash game. The longer the event, the more skill comes into the reckoning but, even then, you are going to need to win some 50–50 hands, maybe bad beat a chip leader, and certainly pick up some decent hands at the right time. If you don't, there's not much anyone can do. So, don't freeze up waiting for a premium hand; be prepared to gamble because, to win, you will have to do this.

If you now make the Final Table, congratulations. Reaching the last six or eight, nine or ten players, is a real achievement, especially in an event over several days. Savour the moment – but not for long. This is a big chance for you, and you want to fight hard, and sensibly, to give yourself a shot at the top prize.

Final Quartile

Just as there is a bubble for the prize money, so there is also for the Final Table. Everyone wants to reach this apex of the tournament, but fear of being knocked out before that moment may provide greater fold equity for your pre-flop raises than you might expect. Try to remain fearless.

Unless your table is ultra-aggressive, when a tight, disciplined approach may see you safely through to the Final Table, your default attitude at this stage must be one of great aggression. Many players will be raising with marginal hands and you must be prepared to re-raise them if you pick up any tell from them that they might be sub-standard. Remember that good players will be pushing with low pairs as well as any ace in late position. This gives you an opportunity, not to call, but to raise and apply pressure immediately.

Unless you are a play-on-the-flop specialist (which usually only the world's best can claim to be), then you want most of your pots decided pre-flop.

While I would normally recommend a mixture of size-able raises and trapping calls should you hit some premium or good hands, my experience is that to continue to bet and raise your hands in a traditional value-betting style will work in all but the most expert company. The simple fact is: at this point in a tournament, everyone is playing sub-standard hands most of the time and they will assume that you are too. You are just as likely to get paid by betting out your winning hand as by being clever and attempting to slow-play it.

Continue to attempt blind steals on all possible occasions.

Final Table

You've made it. Don't relax and enjoy it too much. Set your goals now:

If you are short-stacked:

Note differences in prize money and aim for the highest you can realistically make. If you get very lucky and double through a couple of times, you can change your plan. However, if eighth, seventh and sixth places pay, say, $1,500 up to $2,500 and fifth place pays $4,000 – that would be a good target to aim for, using a mixture of tight play and attack at any time others seem weak. Here, your plan is to survive.

If you are mid-stacked or close to the chip lead, survival should not be in your vocabulary. You must seek to accumulate more chips the whole time. Most action will be pre-flop, involving different-sized raises, according to hand, position and relative chip strength. As in the third quartile, be aware that short-stacks may be prepared to gamble all-in more readily than mid-stacks, so adjust your raises accordingly: maybe three to four times the big blind against mid-stacks and wealthy players; two to two-and-a-half times the big blind against shorter-stacks. You must also judge your raise in relation to the size of the short-stack in terms of what may happen subsequently: does an all-in re-raise commit you to call; does your raise really mean that the short-stack will have to go all-in to play the hand; does your raise leave the short-stack with sufficient chips to fold the hand later on? All these factors must be considered.

Ultimately, aggression and luck must be on your side. Without the aggression, you will require too much luck, and without the luck, your aggression can end badly. However, since you can choose to be aggressive, but you have no control over luck, that is on what you should be focused.

Almost always, first place pays considerably more than second, and second much more than third. After that, different tournaments offer different pay-outs but they all usually drop off considerably. You will already be aware of these pay-outs at the start of each quartile of the event and, of course, before you take your seat at the Final Table.

If you reach the final stages of the Final Table and the table becomes short-handed (five players or fewer), then the hand values become inflated still more.

By the time you reach three-handed or a heads-up situation:

all the following hands are considered to be premium hands:

    any pair, even low ones
    any ace
    any two face cards
    mid-suited connectors

You must adjust to these new ultra-aggressive hand values and betting styles if you want to prosper in these short-handed situations. The best way to prepare for these situations is to play as many Sit & Go events as possible. These are one-table events, which take the form of a Final Table. One-table events are available in card clubs, casinos and home games but, for a lot of experience quickly, nothing beats playing a few dozen online Sit & Go events. See the Online section for full details.

Summary of Tournament Strategy

Before Event and during Opening Blind Level
- Play ultra-tight.
- Ascertain average chip count, blind-level frequency and prize-payout schedule.
- Be aware of re-buy options and add-on opportunities. Ensure that you have sufficient funds to pay for an add-on since most players will do so. Remember that when re-buys and add-ons are cheap, players tend to be extremely loose and gamble regularly in an attempt to build a very big chip stack before the end of the re-buy period. Where the re-buys are expensive, compared to the initial buy-in, or the re-buy is limited to one occasion only, play will be more disciplined.

  If you choose to be ultra-aggressive during the re-buy period, prepare to re-buy several times if required.
- Assess opponents at your table, rate them, and decide which players you wish to attack, and against whom you wish to avoid major confrontation.

  This establishes strong table image, allows you to relax into the event, and to be well informed about the style of any player with whom you subsequently become embroiled.

- Note styles of your opponents sitting both to your right and left. How you rate them will directly affect the way you will have to play at this table. The longer you will be with these opponents, the more important your position, and the way you react to it, becomes.

First Quartile of Event
- Stick to ultra-tight hand selection, especially in early and mid-positions.
- Play big cards very strongly. Do not semi-bluff or call for draws unless the price is very cheap. Avoid bluffing.
- Establish tight/aggressive credentials.
- Fold more readily in marginal situations.

Your intentions for this section are to gain information, protect your stack, move aggressively when holding the best hand and keep the pots small (unless you have the nuts yourself).

Second Quartile of Event
- Remain tight/aggressive in your style, loosening hand requirements for mid- and late positions.
- Attack short-stacked players, or those who seem over-eager to attack. Consider reducing standard pre-flop raises of three-and-a-half times the big blind, to two-and-a-half times or double the big blind. This is so that, if a short-stack re-raises you all-in, you can choose to fold rather than doubling him through.
- Remain aware of your chip stack size in relation to the average, and be prepared to change gears to a much more aggressive style when you feel that your chips are dwindling.
- Take advantage of breaks to stretch legs and take some fresh air; do not focus too much on previous errors.

- Stay alert to changes of table personnel; one new player can change the whole atmosphere of a table.
- Do not relax. Keep pushing to gain chips at all times.

Third Quartile of Event

Players will be dropping out of the event rapidly at this stage. Remain aware of relative chip counts and become markedly more aggressive as soon as you fall below average chip count.

- Be fearless of the bubble. If you get knocked out just before the money, especially if you were odds-on to win the hand, that is no shame, since you should really want to be building your stack to aim for a high finish. In any case, raising aggressively in the period as the bubble approaches will work well, as many players subconsciously are really hoping only to make it into the money. Use that reticence and fear to your advantage and push on.
- Attack mid-stacks even more aggressively than short-stacks at this time; they are more likely to fold than a very short-stacked player who may be happy to gamble even for an odds-against chance of survival.
- Do not fear the size of bet required. Everyone has to bet proportionally more throughout an event.
- Remember that you will need to be lucky. You cannot win an event on luck alone and, as the blinds rise and players are pressurized, your fate may well be down to increasing your odds a little, not playing only nut hands.

Final Quartile and Final Table

Aggression throughout the latter stages of a tournament is essential. You will require both to exert pressure and to get lucky. Only you can influence the aggression you display in the betting, so that is down to you. Luck is down to the poker gods.

- Most action occurs pre-flop; if blinds are relatively low compared to everyone's stacks, expect a period of tight play from all, as players adjust to one another. There will be passing to the big-blind player, and one raise followed by all passes. Blind stealing is the best way to keep up with the chip leaders and to slowly build your stack. This will be a slow, meditative period (you never see this on television, because it's dull).

- When the first bubble has passed – the one that gets you into the money – a second one will appear – the one that means a place at the Final Table. Attack both bubbles aggressively and fearlessly, paying particular attention to the mid-stacks who will be seeking to preserve their place more than the really short-stacked players, who will be happy to gamble.

- As the number of players at the table diminishes, so the hand values grow proportionately. Do not feel intimidated by the size of bets, calls and raises that are required (everyone is playing at much higher stakes) nor by the aggression all good players will exert as the table becomes short-handed (five or fewer).

- Heads-up, you may find that any two cards are played. Loosen up your style; increase your aggression.

Hand Examples for Multi-Table Tournaments

For these examples, assume that you are playing in a day-long multi-table tournament. The standard is about average for a club game, with one or two good players, many inexperienced players and the rest still learning the game. The entry fee is $150 (for 1,500 chips) and there are no re-buys or add-ons. There are 120 entrants, with blinds rising every half-hour. The top fifteen players get into the money, with the main prizes awarded to the Final Table of nine players. First, second and third all pay particularly well.

There are dozens and dozens of hands on which you pass quietly, and a few where you bluff unsuccessfully because weak players keep calling you down. We'll look at a few hands where your decisions provide a revision of some key standard elements.

Hand One – blinds $5/10

It is the first hand of the tournament. You are fifth to act – in mid-position – and the player to your right raises to $40. You hold: A♥ J♠. What action do you take?

You know nothing about your opponent's style of play and your hand is a marginal one anyway. Fold quietly and hope to see the type of hand this opponent is raising on in mid-position so early in the event.

You don't want to play marginal hands unless you are forced into doing so when you are short-stacked. During the opening blind level, sit back, play only premium cards, and observe the actions of your opponents.

Hand Two – blinds $5/10

You are one from the button, with only one call from the player directly on your right. You hold: A♠ Q♠. What action do you take?

You probably have the best hand at the table and you should protect it against the button and blinds limping in. You correctly decide to raise to $40. Everyone folds to the caller on your right, who calls. There is $95 in the pot, and the flop comes:

Your opponent checks; what action do you take?

There are no draws and, you can assume, only the king is significant. You should make a follow-up bet of about half the pot. You bet $50, and your opponent folds.

Your opponent didn't hold a king and his call was, perhaps, rather loose considering that he had not raised in late mid-position and that he was out of position to your raise. This may seem an unusual situation but, in fact, in many tournaments players routinely call, then call a raise out of position, and then go quietly to a bet. If you check here and your opponent hits second pair on the turn, he may decide to call you down, so the follow-up bet sorts out the loose call of your raise.

Hand Three – blinds $5/10
Even though it is still early in the tournament, you note that the player to your right is raising regularly. You are in fifth position to act and, after a call from seat three, this same opponent in seat four raises again to $40. You hold: K♣ Q♣. What action should you take?

It seems as if the opponent on your right is set on an aggressive start to his tournament, and he intends to pressure you by raising repeatedly. You could sit back and wait for a monster hand to take him on, or you could make a stand now in an attempt to dissuade him from this aggressive course of action. Don't be tempted to call. If you want to make a stand, re-raise him, and see his reaction. You decide to do this, and you raise the bet to $80. Everyone else passes, but your opponent calls. There is $185 in the pot, and the flop comes:

Your opponent bets $85. What action should you take?

This is a good flop for you. You are likely to be behind only if your opponent holds: KJ or AK. Since he might have re-raised you initially with AK, KJ seems more possible but, with that holding, he might choose to check-raise to you. More likely is that he does not hold top pair, and he is making a follow-up bet to test your re-raise, in case you have a mid- or low pair. You could just call here but, to confirm your read, you might re-raise. You decide to make the bet $200. Your opponent raises his eyebrows and passes.

This play worked well for you. You hit a good flop for your hand and continued to lay on the pressure. Since your real ambition on this hand was to lay down a marker that you were not going to be bullied, there was no need to slow-play – you re-raised and then raised his follow-up bet and that was enough to show him that you would not be bullied. Expect a stronger hand from your opponent the next time he raises.

Hand Four – blinds $10/20
You are in the small-blind seat. There are two calls to the player one from the button who raises to $80. You hold: A♠ K♦. What action do you take?

Even though you are out of position, it is definitely worth raising here. A raise from the small-blind position is about as strong as a raise under the gun, and is the strongest representation of a good hand that there is. You decide to make it $200 to go. The callers fold, but the player one from the button calls you. There is $440 in the pot, and the flop comes:

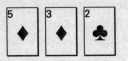

What action do you take?

The flop is not a disaster for you since, although it has missed you, it is likely to have missed your opponent also. You have also picked up a gut-shot straight draw, and a runner-runner second-nut flush draw. You could approach this hand now in two ways: you could bet straight out, or you could check-raise – your opponent is likely to make a play for the flop if you check. I probably favour the slightly more conservative action of betting straight away. You decide to bet $180.

Your opponent considers for some time, and then mucks his hand.

All you have done so far is to bet out your good hands, taking a stand against any player before you who seems over-aggressive and wanting to bully your table. Note that you have done no calling so far – only betting and raising. This is the profile that you want to pursue.

Two hours have gone by and there is a short break. You take a walk, grab some fresh air, drink (preferably a thirst-quenching soft drink), and return to your table. Whilst everybody is reassembling, you find out how many players remain in the event. You discover that there are 101 players still in. Originally, there were 120 players each with 1,500 chips at the start, that makes $180,000 in play. Now that there are only 101 players, the average chip stack is about $1,780. You have $2,020, so you are a little ahead of average.

You then glance at each player in turn, remembering what information about their styles of play you have gleaned during the early stages of the event. What elevates the truly great players from the average poker player is the ability to remember every last move made by each opponent, store that information away, and bring it out to good use at a crucial moment. Who calls a lot of hands, but folds to raises? Who calls raises, but never re-raises? How often does a particular player become involved when he is sitting in an early position? If you can remember the answers to these types of questions then, when the action becomes forced, you will have a greater insight into what players might have for any action they take. That advantage translates into crucial timing later on for your own plays: bluffs, re-raises, slow-plays, check-raises, etc.

Hand Five – blinds $50/100
You are sitting one from the button. There are two calls to you from the player in second seat and also from your aggressive opponent to your right. You hold: A♣ 7♠. What action do you take?

Fold. You have a poor hand, in mid-position. If any other player holds an ace, it will probably be with a higher kicker. These hands can cost you your tournament, and I avoid them like the plague, until the table becomes short-handed. Even AJ and A10 are dangerous hands in all but late position and should be considered marginal. Early on, avoid all marginal hands.

Hand Six – blinds $50/100
You are sitting two from the button. There is one call to you. You look down to see: K♦ J♣. You should probably fold, because two unpaired picture cards are not nearly as good as they first seem when you see all that paint in the hole. However, you decide to call. The button folds, but the small blind raises to $250. The big blind calls this raise, the early caller also calls. The pot stands at $900. Do you call or fold?

This is a classic situation many less experienced players encounter. They enter a hand with marginal cards hoping to see a flop. They get raised and see others calling, and they decide that they shouldn't bet good money after bad, and so they now fold.

The key is to realize that the $100 call you made earlier is irrelevant. What you face now is a completely separate decision. Should you bet $150 to remain in the pot?

The answer is a resolute yes! You are being offered 6–1 odds to call here and, although KJ is not a nice hand, it won't be 6–1 behind anyone else at the table. So, you call. The pot is now $1,050 and the flop comes:

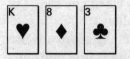

The small blind, big blind and early caller all check. What action will you take?

This is a fine flop for you, lacking threatening draws but, as a multi-way pot, it is no time to slow-play. Make a good-sized bet here, because you think you have the best of it and, if someone is slow-playing (however unlikely) AA or KK, or even AK, you want to try to gain information. You bet $400. The small blind calls you, but the other two players fold. There is now $1,850 in the pot, and the turn comes:

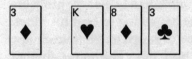

The small blind checks. What action do you take?

It seems very unlikely that your opponent has a truly premium hand. If he has, and he's played it like that, he's very brave. Since the second three hasn't had any effect and the only draw out against you is a possible diamond flush, you can consider both checking and betting. If your opponent is now short-stacked, this may be the moment for you to move all-in and persuade him to part with his last chips. If the stacks are more balanced, a check here is unlikely to lead to trouble for you. You decide to check. The river comes:

Your opponent checks. What do you do?

It looks like your opponent simply wants to check down the hand. Since you rate to have the best hand now, don't allow him that luxury; tournaments are too pressured to miss out on grabbing some extra chips when you can. Try a small value bet and hope that he calls.

You bet $500. Your opponent calls. You show down your K♦ J♣ and he flashes 9♥ 9♣ at you, before mucking.

You are grateful for that information, because it lets you know that whilst he was prepared to raise in the small blind, even one overcard on the board put him off from betting further. He was indeed wanting to call you down cheaply, and at least you made a further $400 from him at the end. If he had raised more pre-flop, both big blind and early caller might have passed – and then you would not have had the pot odds to call him with your KJ. He would have won the pot, instead of losing over half his stack.

On the flop, if he bets out immediately, he will probably be able to work out if anyone has a king to beat his nines. As it is, you would have called or raised and he can choose to fold, saving himself valuable chips. This is yet another example of when calling costs more and gains you no information. After all, you were the last to act each time and you could have been bluffing having missed the flop yourself.

Hand Seven – blinds $50/100
On the button, with two callers directly on your right, you hold: 8♣ 7♣. Do you call, raise or pass?

Much of this will depend on your own style and how big your stacks seem. You have been doing well so far and, with two callers already in, and with the likelihood of the

small blind also calling, you will probably find that you are
getting good pot odds to hit a great flop. You call. (You
could raise occasionally to mix things up a bit, but,
basically, suited connectors were born to be limped with!)
The small blind calls, but the big blind raises to $600. The
early callers fold to you. What do you do?

There is $1,000 in the pot, and you are being asked to
bet $500 more to call. The pot is offering you 2–1 to
enter the fray. This doesn't sound good. Getting 4–1 or
5–1 pre-flop is one thing; 2–1 is much poorer. Fold your
hand quickly and get out of there. The small blind folds
also and the big blind takes the pot. It's hard to know
what he might have since, with all the weak-sounding
calls, he might just have been applying pressure. Whatever he had, it worked.

Hand Eight – blinds $150/300
You are in second position, with the player under the gun
having passed. You hold: JJ. What action do you take?

The correct textbook action is to make a decent-sized
raise, as you do not really want to see a flop since any
overcard will scare you. At most, you would like to be
heads-up with one other contender. The usual raise here is
slightly bigger than the usual three to three-and-a-half
times the big blind, maybe four or five times the big blind.
However, to raise bigger like this in early position somewhat signposts your mid-pair, and you should seek to vary
your bets. In early position, a small-ish raise can sometimes seem bigger than a big one. Most of the time, then,
raise to $1,200 or $1,500, but once in a while, settle for a
raise twice the big blind – you may find that opponents
think you have AA or KK and that you are trying to lure in
the unobservant.

You raise to $1,400 and everyone folds. That's fine.
You've picked up the blinds – a not inconsequential $450 –

and avoided undue stress. Since that is about to come, it is best to delay its onset for as long as possible.

There is now another break. Eat, drink, relax, stroll. Avoid chatting too much to friends and opponents about poker since you need a rest to clear your mind. You are still in the event, and the pressure starts building on you from now on: one mistake, and you're out.

You find that you are at a new table for the next round and you know little or nothing about any of your opponents. Hopefully, they are in a similar position.

There are 42 players remaining, making the average chip stack $4,285. You have $5,500, so you are a little bit ahead, but not nearly comfortable enough to rest on your laurels. You note that the chip leader at your table is sitting two places to your right – this is good – he will have to act before you. There is an average stack to your left, followed by two fairly short stacks. They may become desperate soon, and you must be prepared to keep them under pressure, especially when you are in position over them.

Hand Nine – blinds $200/400

This is the fourth hand at your new table and you have learnt nothing concrete about your opponents, except that, based on a very limited sample, the table seems pretty tight. You are on the button, holding: K♥ 9♣. There has been one caller to your right. What action do you take?

This isn't a bad hand on the button and now is the time to begin applying pressure to those short-stacks. Remain aware that short-stacked players seek opportunities to double through, so there is no need to raise too much here. The fact that you are in position, an unknown quantity, and have a decent stack size will dissuade them from taking any rash decisions early on. Raise two-and-a-half times the big blind to $1,000.

Everyone folds.

If you find yourself making this play quite a few times in late position, with everyone folding before you have to show down a hand, don't be surprised if your opponents become suspicious and plan to take a stand. Players who consistently show down good hands create real fear in opponents when they subsequently bet. Players who keep winning pots without showing hands increase their opponents' curiosity until, eventually, it gets the better of them. You want to vary your play sufficiently that your opponents don't, en masse, come to believe that you are stealing every time you raise.

Hand Ten – blinds $200/400
You are in third position, after two passes, holding: 4♠ 4♦. These low-pair hands are always tough to judge, especially in early positions, and particularly when there are short-stacks who might come over the top of you. However, you decide that there has not been much raising, so you call. The player one from the button calls also and the big blind makes it $1,300 all-in. The pot stands at $2,300. Do you call, raise or pass?

It's no use regretting your call now, you have only one decision to make. Do you bet $900 to call this raise? The pot is offering you 2.5/1 or thereabouts and, if your opponent has an overpair, you will be 4.5/1 behind. But there's more. If you just call, the player on the button may call also, and you definitely don't want to be in a three-way pot with 44 – there could even be more betting.

Despite the fact that the short-stack all-in could have any two high cards, your position makes it very unwise to continue and you should just fold.

The button calls, and your opponents' cards are revealed. The button holds: A♥ J♠; the short-stack K♣ Q♦. This is great news for you because, although you would have been ahead pre-flop, your two opponents have masses of outs to overtake you. The board produces both a queen and an ace – without a four – and the button eliminates the short-stack.

Calling with a low pair in early position feels bad and is bad. Note that it is one of the very few hands where you did not raise. Not only did you get knocked out of the pot even before the flop, but you also appear weak. Your early calls are less likely to be respected now.

Hand Eleven – blinds $200/400

You are one from the button and hold: A♣ Q♠. After one call from the player in fifth seat, you decide to raise three times the big blind to $1,200. The player in the big blind, who is now a short-stack with only $2,300 chips, calls. You are slightly perplexed that he didn't raise all-in, but he doesn't seem a great player. The initial caller passes. The pot stands at $2,600.

The flop comes:

Your opponent goes all-in for his last $1,100. What do you do?

This seems like a lot of money and your opponent may just have slow-played a big or mid-sized pair. However, less experienced players would probably have gone all-in pre-flop rather than attempt any kind of slow-play. Here, you are short-stacked and see a premium hand, you are usually reaching to push all your chips in without even being aware of it. Here, you are being asked to pay $1,100 into a pot of $3,700, so you are getting better than 3–1 odds. The flop is most unlikely to have hit his hand in any way and, importantly, he may think the same about your hand, hence his all-in bet.

You call and he turns over: A♦ 10♥. It hasn't made any difference whether he re-raised pre-flop or bet after it – all the chips were likely to be going in. No ten appears on the turn or river, so you knock him out.

Your table now disperses and a new table is formed. You note that there are now only 18 players remaining. Three will end up without a cash prize, and you know that for some of these players, that will be a major blow, so you plan to pressurize them as much as you can.

The average chip stack is now $10,000 and you have dropped to only $8,500. You must remain aggressive and positive or risk being blinded away until you make the bottom of the prize list. That isn't worth the bother; you are aiming for at least the Final Table.

Hand Twelve – blinds $300/600
You have big chip stacks either side of you and you seem to be at the table with the majority of the chips in play. If you want merely to survive past the bubble, then play slowly, fold every hand, and hope that others crash out. I hope you don't play like that.

You are one from the button and the chip leader at your table, sitting one place to your right, makes the first bet of the deal, raising to $2,400. You look down to find: J♠ J♥ in the hole. What action will you take?

If you merely call to see a flop, you risk the other big stack at the table (on the button) also calling. You may be faced with a 50–50 chance if you get called but, equally, your opponent may simply be trying to bully the table. As a low-ish mid-stack, you are perfect prey for him. You decide to re-raise all-in to $8,500. Everyone folds to the raiser who stares hard at you, looks at his hand a few times and then folds with a big sigh. That sounds like he had nothing much, but just wanted to let everyone know that he's made a great lay-down.

This was a great hand for you: you picked up $3,300 ($2,400 from the raiser and $900 from the blinds); you showed the chip leaders that you won't be bullied; and you have now got above-average chips and lessened the stack of one of the chip leaders. A fine hand's work.

Hand Thirteen – blinds $300/600

The table has become seven-handed and the tournament director has announced that you are all in the money, there being only fifteen players remaining. Do not pause for one moment in your attempt to grab other players' chips. You've really not achieved much yet.

You are second to act and, once the player under the gun has folded, you look down to see: 9♦ 9♣. This is a nice hand anyway, but at a table with only seven players, rather than nine, it is a little bit better. You want to raise to eliminate all but, perhaps, one opponent; and you certainly don't mind if everyone folds and you pick up $900 of blinds. How much do you raise?

Three to four times the big blind is, as usual, the right amount. Betting $2,400 seems a huge amount, but everyone's bets have got very substantial. If you raise less, you risk the hand becoming a multi-way pot, and that makes 99 look weak. Everyone folds except the player on the button who calls. The pot contains $5,700.

Instead of watching the flop appear, you correctly watch your opponent's reaction and, at the same time, ascertain how many chips he has left. He has a few more than you, so you are unlikely to be able to bully him off the hand. The flop comes:

This is a great flop for you as you have hit trips. How good is it for your opponent? It's OK. If he holds a queen in his hand, you will get paid handsomely; if he has J10 or 108 (both somewhat unlikely in an average-standard tournament), he has a draw. Two clubs also give him a flush draw. If you have picked up that your opponent likes the flop, you might consider going all-in, but it is better to try to maximize your fantastic position by more intelligent betting. It is rare that you hit such a good hand late on in a tournament and you do not want to squander this chance.

To check here could lead to a check from your opponent too, and that would be weak and dangerous play. To make a standard follow-up bet here of approximately half the pot will look normal and may even be considered as a bet to attack. You bet $3,000.

Your opponent calls. The pot stands at $11,700. The turn card is:

What action do you take?

You are never laying down trips here, whatever he bets, so you should take the initiative and bet yourself. Half the pot should suffice, although if he raises, you will have to call, so to go all-in here seems reasonable. He may have a straight draw or still a flush draw and, if you put in your last $6,000 or so, he may be tempted to pass and still have some chips to play with.

You go all-in, and your opponent folds.

Perhaps you could have bet less on the turn; it's not clear what your opponent had, but he might have had a flush draw and simply lacked the guts to raise you all-in (probably just as well here). He might also have held KQ and feared AQ in your hand. Who knows? But, you made a vital extra $3,000 from your thoughtful bet on the flop, and that is important money to you.

Hand Fourteen – blinds $400/800
You are on the button, with no callers to you. You see: 5♥ 5♠ in the hole. What action do you take?

You note who is sitting to your left in the blinds. The player in the small blind is the chip leader at your table; the player in the big blind is short-stacked, holding only $6,200 after placing his blind bet.

You want to ensure that you either steal the blinds, denuding the short-stack of even more of his equity, or that you set the short-stack all-in, without the additional interference of the chip leader being involved. Since you should be exerting pressure, you should raise here but by how much? If you raise too much, you risk a big re-raise from the small blind to which you will have to fold; if you raise too little, you may get two callers and find your fives in severe jeopardy.

You raise three times the big blind to $2,400. The small blind folds and the big blind goes all-in. What do you do?

You are now being asked to contribute $3,800 into a pot of $9,000. Unless your opponent holds a higher pair, you are getting almost 3–1 odds for what is likely to be a 50–50 race. Since the short-stack must take a stand about now, he could have any two picture cards or a low ace. These races are inevitable as the Final Table looms and you will need to get lucky a few times to succeed. You call. Your opponent turns over K♣ J♣.

The flop brings no help, the turn provides a flush draw, but the river is a harmless red six. Your fives have held up.

A few hands later, another player leaves your table and suddenly the tournament director announces that you have made the Final Table. There will now be a short break.

There are nine players remaining. The average chip stack is therefore $20,000. You have $31,500. This is good but, with blinds at $500/1000, the stacks will increase and decrease at great speed. Since you have noted that the top three places pay substantially more than the next six, your target is to win the event, placing second or third if the luck doesn't hold out for you.

You take your seat. Both the chip leaders are to your left now, which is disappointing. A couple of players from your first table are there also. Search your brain for the information that you stored on them; it could prove crucial.

You see no cards for the first two rounds, and they have cost you $3,000 in blinds alone. Then, one player goes all-in and loses to one of the chip leaders. You are down to eight players.

Hand Fifteen – blinds $500/1000

You are on the button. Everyone has passed to you, and you hold: 10♣ 8♦. You have passed the previous two rounds on the button and the blinds should have noticed this. You decide to raise, attempting to steal the blinds. You bet $3,500. Both blinds pass.

You will not be able to do this every time, but you had to show that you were here to win and not just to wait for a good hand. If you had been called, 108 is a playable hand and, in position, you wouldn't have been too unhappy to see a flop.

Hand Sixteen – blinds $500/1000

You are one from the button on the next round. You pick up: A♠ J♦ and decide to raise the uncalled pot to $3,500. The chip leader to your left re-raises to $6,000, everyone else folding. What action do you take?

AJ is not a bad hand, eight-handed and one from the button. The question you must ask yourself is this? Does my opponent think I'm stealing and he is testing me, or does he truly have a superior hand?

The former is much more likely, especially because you have pegged him to be an aggressive player. With a big chip stack, he can afford to try to bully his opponents and drain them of chips. You may not see as good a hand again at this Final Table and I think you should refuse to be bullied. You could fold, but it sets a dangerous precedent: what will you have to have to call a re-raise from this player? As you will be out of position from now on, calling presents dangers. Re-raise him, possibly even all-in, but certainly a significant amount. You have approximately $26,000 remaining. Make it $12,000 to go, putting in a further $8,500. If he goes all-in himself, you can choose to believe him and pass, and still have sufficient chips to play with.

After a long pause, he passes, flashing an ace at you. He probably had ace-small and was pressurizing you. He made a good fold but you are relieved also because you have reinforced your strong image and, with you both holding aces, an ace on the board was unlikely and you would have had a torrid time if he had called you.

Several rounds pass. Two other players are eliminated. There are six of you remaining. There are two chip leaders, two mid-stacks, and two short-stacks.

Hand Seventeen – blinds $750/1500
You are the big blind, holding: K♠ Q♦. The first three players all fold and the button, a short-stack, raises to $4,000. The small blind folds. What action do you take?

Your opponent is, quite rightly, attacking you, in an attempt to pick up some chips to bolster his dwindling stack. However, KQ is well above average here and you must defend your big blind when short-handed and in high-pressure situations. You could raise here but, if your opponent is in the mood to try to bully you, you may decide to let him do the betting. Calling to see the flop seems reasonable. The pot stands at $8,000, and the flop comes:

It's a great flop for you. Despite the risk of the club flush, to check here is likely to work well since your opponent will surely bet at you, whether or not he has actually hit a hand. The best time to slow-play is when you know that your opponent will be betting for you. You check, and your opponent bets $7,000. What do you do?

This is quite a big bet and, if you are beaten, it's extremely unlucky. Since both the straight and the flush draw are out there, to call is risky and may result in your winning less at the end. A raise is called for. You raise to $18,000. Your opponent folds.

Nice work. You defended your blinds, hit a good flop and, since your opponent presumably missed the flop, you elicited a further $7,000 from him, further shortening him and increasing your stack.

Two further players are eliminated. You are down to the last four, but you are now the shortest stack at the table.

Hand Eighteen – blinds $1,500/3,000
You are on the button. The first player passes and you hold: J♠ J♥. With queens, you might consider a limp, but jacks are just too vulnerable. Besides, everyone is expecting you to raise on the button, so go ahead. You raise to $7,000. The small blind folds and the big blind re-raises you to $20,000. What do you do?

With the blinds costing $4,500 every four hands and the aggression levels at full power, your opponent could have anything, reckoning you are on the steal. To call might leave you with a tough decision later and you are almost pot-committed anyway. You re-raise all-in and your opponent calls you.

You show your: J♠ J♥; he shows: A♠ 10♣. You have got your money in at the right moment. You are close to 3–1 on to win and, if your hand holds up, you'll be right back in the event and in a position to win it.

The flop comes:

That's fine for you. The turn comes:

That provides your opponent with eight more outs – any ace, any club beats you. The river is:

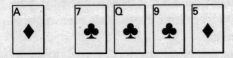

Damn!

You shake everyone by the hand, smile as best you can, and stumble away from the table, exhausted and very disappointed.

You ran your luck up to the end, but then it deserted you. You had the best of it going into the crucial hand but, although it was extremely unlucky that you lost on the river, your opponent had about a one-in-four chance of beating you on the last card, and it seems like his day.

Relax now. You've done well. You finished 4th out of 120 entrants, playing conservative, disciplined poker, matched with aggressive stealing and defiant stands against bullies. The hands you played, you entered most of the time with raises and re-raises and that is a good profile to project. You didn't sit around hoping for miracle cards or try to run big bluffs to win insignificant pots. You waited and played your good hands strongly. As your skill increases, your chances of going all the way will increase also but, always remember, there is a huge amount of luck in tournaments and, to win, you need a lot of it.

These hands illustrate some of the elements that have been discussed in this chapter. These are only the basics required to survive in a social, club, or casino tournament. To compete with the experts and professionals, you will require many more moves, much more experience and nerves of steel. However, if you follow the guidelines here, you will do well in modest tournaments, where most of the players are almost dead money (they have zero chance of winning).

Finally, please note that I advocate a disciplined, aggressive approach to hand selection. No single style is preeminent in the game; both hyper-aggressive, and supertight players have won major events. Pick the style you are happy with but, if you are starting out, the tight/aggressive style is easiest to play, gives you maximum chances to remain in the event and get lucky, and is much easier to play once the board has started to appear. Play on the flop, turn and river is where the experts really gain their edge. If you are up against exceptionally tough players, take solid decisions pre-flop and put the pressure on them right from the start.

PLAYING POKER ONLINE

If there is one characteristic that defines the average online poker player it is this: they are loose. Sometimes, they are so loose that they will call at the end of the pot when they have nothing but a queen or jack-high hand, knowing that you have better. Impossible? If you've played a bit on numerous sites, you'll know that it isn't. This play occurs and it is not nearly as infrequent as you would think.

The online poker world is also awash with players who have watched poker on television but have never learnt the game, never read a book, never want to. They think that they know how to play and they are there to play – never mind that most of the time they end up losing. It doesn't matter what form of the game they try: Hold 'Em, Omaha, 7-card Stud – cash games or tournaments, the Internet is awash with terrible poker players.

Of course, this presents you with a golden opportunity. There are already many professional and semi-professional players out there making anything from a really handsome living through to generous pocket money. And you can join them . . . if you know how. However, be careful: online poker sites are pretty much agreed that for over 90 per cent of their players, poker is a losing game. In this chapter, we'll look at how you should adapt your style for the online game, how your multi-table tournament strategy differs online from in a live game, how to streamline your cash-game play and focus on the winning strategy for Sit & Go events, which are single-table tournaments. For those players who have time to play only five or six hours per week, the Sit & Go events provide not only the best possible practice for all tournament play (especially for final-table action) but also a nice, reasonably steady, income to reward your studies and time.

As throughout this book, the game in the spotlight is No-Limit Texas Hold 'Em but, if your favourite variation is another form of the game, you will find it easy to adapt the advice herein to your own style of play.

Additionally, it is worth discussing a recurring concern for online poker players: is the game honest?

Over the years, there have been hundreds of thousands of complaints of suspicious actions from online players, of doubtful dealing, and rigged situations. Can you trust online poker?

I have spent many years investigating the honesty and fairness of online gaming sites. I have certainly ruffled a few feathers and received a few disturbing responses to my inquiries. However, after all of that, I can report that, for the vast majority of online poker sites, I believe their service to be honest and their performance to be pretty impressive.

When playing online, every hand and every action of every player is recorded and can be checked upon. This is not possible in a live game. All the leading sites have departments which investigate claims of malpractice or suspicious behaviour. Again, casinos and card clubs simply cannot monitor their games that closely. Finally, the online poker business is vast: it is worth hundreds of millions of dollars. One proven accusation of malfeasance against a well-known company could destroy their reputation and their business. It simply doesn't make sense that any site would knowingly take that risk to swindle their customers. So, to conclude, the majority of online poker sites seem on the level and are trustworthy in their actions.

However, there have been documented and publicized instances of fraud from within the companies perpetrated by employees. There is, without doubt, the danger of collusion between players who may be communicating on the phone or by e-mail what cards they are holding and, both now and in the future, there is a real opportunity for computer experts to create programs which play perfect textbook poker all day long – these are popularly referred to as 'bots'. With all these threats comes increased surveillance from the poker sites, good customer service in responding to queries and complaints and, generally, an improving reputation amongst experienced players that the online game is safe.

Computers have long sought to create genuinely random numbers, usually relying upon massive algorithms. Even though these are not technically entirely random, they are as good as random numbers and there has been no suggestion by any experts that these numbers lead to unrealistic poker distributions. If you play poker for long enough, you still learn that, as unlikely as it may seem, a four-handed game can still throw up a hand where two players have AA and KK between them and all the chips go in the pot.

One of the most common complaints is the length of time it takes some online casinos and card rooms to pay out winnings when players withdraw money from their accounts. Since you are aiming to be withdrawing money more often than depositing it, this is of importance to you. Using an online transfer and payment account, such as

PayPal or NeTeller, will usually speed up payments but, even if you want winnings paid back to credit cards or sent to you as a cheque, all the leading sites manage this efficiently. So, talk to your friends, ask them which sites they prefer and then join several sites – they will all offer you joining bonuses – and see which one performs best for you.

Finally, please take note of this warning. Many poker sites now offer casino games – especially Blackjack – at the click of an on-screen button. This was clever thinking by the poker sites since many are owned and operated by online casino companies anyway and, when you are enduring a lengthy run of folding hand after hand of very poor cards, your attention does wander somewhat, and it is easy to be lulled into a casino gambling game. Unlike poker where, if you play decently, you will have a positive expectation of winning, casino games have a built-in negative expectation for the player – the house edge – so, however well you do at poker, you will inevitably lose at the casino games. Therefore, do not be tempted to play them.

Furthermore, in my opinion, there is at least one Blackjack software operation that is not fair and honest and which I believe (backed up by the study of many thousands of hands) is rigged against the player, both in terms of the random nature of the cards dealt and the reaction of the software to stake-size changes. Since this appears as an option on one of my favourite poker sites, this is a real danger. I've always believed that, if you are going to gamble, you should be able to trust the outfit providing that opportunity and that you should be able to influence – through your own developed skills – the outcome of the situation. Poker provides that opportunity and that is why, whilst it remains a gambling game, it is certainly one that can be consistently beaten through the application of expertise, time and patience.

Online Poker: Starting Out

Even if you have played poker online for a few years and you are certain that you know all the ins and outs, don't skip this section and move right on. Within this section, we talk about table selection, game plans, bankrolls and most of the crucial stuff. If you think you know it all, then just speed-read it, but please do take a look because, in my experience, the vast majority of online players are unaware of much that is contained here, and it will give you a significant edge over those who simply don't bother to improve their games.

If you have never played poker online, I highly recommend it. You can play briefly or all day long; you are in your own home, able to sit comfortably, eat and drink what you like, and even consult friends, books and computer programs as to how best to play. Above all, you play, on average, four times as many hands per hour online as you do in a live game, and it therefore provides a brilliant opportunity to practise and hone your game far more quickly than was possible in the old days.

Picking a Site and First Steps

Check that you are legally permitted to play online gambling games where you live. If you are, ask your poker-playing friends which sites they like and ask them to recommend you. This way, you will benefit from your mates' experience of different sites immediately and, not only will you receive a sign-up bonus for joining the site (usually released slowly as you play hands, or hours, on the site), but the friend who recommended you will also receive a bonus. Since all bankroll contributions should be welcomed with open arms, these offers should be exploited.

Once you have decided on your site or sites, download the software on to your computer, ensuring that you have an up-to-date firewall and virus protection, since you will be employing online transactions. The proverbial six-year-old child will be able to arrange all this for you if you are not a computer whizz-kid yourself.

Explore the site and check that you are happy with the look of it and the ease of understanding its various features. There are dozens of different styles of online card room operating software provided by as many different companies. You may find one which, to you, looks easier on the eye than others. You can practise your game and try out the software using 'play money' which is a feature offered by almost every site. Although the poker itself will be appalling (since no one cares whether they win or lose play money) you will, at least, gain a good feel for the way that you play online. Above all, you will be introduced to the high-speed nature of online poker.

As soon as you are ready to play for real, register your name, address and personal details with the site, arrange a method of paying in some money – a credit card is easiest, but online payment options suit many players better – and download some cash. You can easily start off with as little as $50 but if you plan to play regularly for a decent stake, download the maximum amount in order to take full advantage of sign-up offers. At the time of writing, this is usually in the $200–$600 range. As you will see oft repeated, it is also a very good idea to have a good-sized bankroll so that, if you encounter a few days, weeks, or even months of poker turbulence – and you *will* – your bankroll still contains sufficient funds for you to continue the battle.

Having done this, you will select a screen name for yourself and, sometimes, pick an 'avatar' – which is a cartoon character, downloaded photograph, or picture –

which appears in your seat whenever you play. Personally, I'm not into jokey little items like this, so I just have a screen name for each site I play on. Remember that playing poker involves a bit of acting and, online, you can choose to be whoever you like. If you want to pretend to be the Dalai Lama or Sharon Stone, a surfing dude or a ditsy blonde, that's fine. Just be aware that most people pick misleading names in order to create a false impression of themselves – so don't be taken in by 'Little Old Lady Beginner', because he's probably a seriously well-practised teenaged poker semi-pro who's saving up tens of thousands of dollars for a comfortable retirement in ten years' time.

The Lobby

This is the most important part of a poker site as it provides crucial information which, if you are to succeed, you must be able to interpret and apply to help you make your game and table selection. It is called a lobby because, as in a real-life poker club, it is the area where players wait to see who is playing at which table; where you sign on for tournaments and special events; where you see how many tables are in play at each different stake and variation of the game. All sites vary a little, but the basic layout of a lobby page looks like this:

HOLD 'EM	OMAHA	STUD		RAZZ	HORSE	SIT & GO	MTTs
table	stakes	type	players	waiting	av.pot	plyrs/flop	hands p/h
alleycat	$1/2	NL	8/9	1	$55.86	21%	77
norman	$1/2	NL	8/9	0	$51.01	34%	58
sands	$1/2	NL	7/9	0	$33.16	26%	61
jaguar	$1/2	NL	4/9	0	$11.44	55%	78
orchard	$2/4	NL	6/9	0	$121.17	51%	65
nimby	$2/4	NL	3/9	0	$76	44%	76
krakatoa	$2/4	NL	0/9	0			
clocktower	$5/10	NL	4/6	0	$277.50	66%	97
kindling	$5/10	NL	2/6	0	$90.54	79%	134

hide full tables ☐

At the top, or along the side, of the lobby page, you will see the different variations of poker game available, including the option to move to the tournament part of the lobby to see which games are available there. In this example, we want to play a Texas Hold 'Em cash game. We click on the Texas Hold 'Em button and a list of tables available – usually in order of stake size – will appear. You will often be presented with a box to tick if you want only tables with places available at them to be shown. If you do not check this box, all tables will be displayed whether or not there is a seat available. Sometimes, you can specify which stake range you are looking to play in. Whatever you do, you'll end up with a screen that looks like the diagram. Let's take a quick look at what each of these columns is representing:

table: Online poker sites almost always call their poker tables by name. Often players decide that one table is luckier for them than others and stick to that one. We will have a far more important set of criteria to consider before selecting our table(s).

stakes: This shows the blind size. In tournaments, the figure shown will often be the starting blind level, which will rise throughout the game. For cash games, the figures shown are the small blind and big blind, which remain constant throughout. $2/4 means that the big and small blinds are $2 and $4 respectively.

type: This shows whether the game is Limit, Pot-Limit, or No-Limit Texas Hold 'Em: (Limit), (PL), (NL).

players: This indicates how many players are sitting at a table, and how many seats are available at that table. The figure 7/9 indicates that there are seven players seated at the table, and a total of nine seats available.

Most sites offer full-table games of nine or ten players and short-handed tables of five or six players. The latter requires a much more aggressive style and should be attempted only once you are fluent at your general default style of play, and you are ready to expand your horizons.

waiting: How many players are on a waiting list for this table. If there are many, perhaps there is a well-known loose player spewing his chips to everyone else and there is a feeding frenzy of other players wanting to cash in on this one player's largesse.

average pot size: The average size of each pot at the point at which it is won. This provides some indication of how aggressive this table might be in terms of raises and calls and pot-building.

percentage of players seeing flop: This figure indicates what percentage of players get to see the flop on each hand. On average, you would expect a maximum of 33 per cent of players to see a flop at a nine-player table. If the figure is higher than this, it suggests that the table is full of loose, calling, passive players, whereas a lower figure suggests that there is a raiser and, perhaps, one caller and the table is tighter and more aggressive.

hands per hour: This is, perhaps, the least informative statistic available. A low figure suggests a slow game, with people taking the maximum time to make decisions. A high figure suggests an experienced, confident table where decisions are made quickly and hands end prematurely due to big raises or good decision-making.

To choose to play at a particular table, you usually double-click on the table name and you are taken there immediately. If all the seats are actually taken by the time you arrive, you will be offered the opportunity to join a waiting list for that precise table or for any table with similar characteristics in terms of style of game, stake and number of players. If you don't want to do this, just close that table, return to the lobby and seek out a new table. We'll look at how to select the right table for you – a crucial decision – a little later on.

Once you are there, if there is a choice of seats available, you select which one you want by clicking on the free seat, transfer some funds from your poker site account into your stack at that table, and begin to play. Which seat you pick, how much your buy-in should be, and how you should begin your campaign is discussed below. The table will probably be displayed something like this:

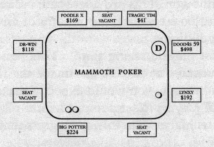

Most sites offer you the chance to rotate your view of the table so that you are sitting in whatever position you like (keeping everyone else in order). Usually people opt to sit at the bottom centre of the screen so that they can watch everything happen in a clockwise motion around them.

The screen will usually offer you a set of options from which you can select (by checking or unchecking boxes).

These are the ones I would check – or have switched on:

- result of each hand – summary
- auto-post blind bets (switch this on – it saves everyone time and trouble)
- auto-muck losing hands (you don't want to show losing hands to anyone)

These are the ones I would uncheck – or have switched off:

- online chat with your opponents and even with spectators (I would turn this option off and keep it off)
- dealer chat – the program explains whose turn it is to deal, who has placed blinds and what each player opts to do
- sounds: from dealer voice, to background noise, to chip sounds (although the last is quite fun, especially if you are winning pots regularly)
- fold to any bet (you never want this box checked – you want to make all decisions in your own time)
- check/fold auto-button (again, you want to make your decision in your own time)

Then, there will be buttons for non-poker actions, such as:

- stand up, or leave table
- re-buy chips
- go to cashier

These you will click only if and when you wish to take these particular actions.

If you need help with what to do at any time, there will be a 'help' button which will connect you, either with help pages under topic headings, or a live-chat box allowing you to speak with a representative from the site. You can also choose to switch on chat at your table and ask your fellow players how to achieve a particular change or effect at your table. I wouldn't recommend this last option because, if you ask these questions, the players at your table will quickly realize that you are a new player and, as a result, they may choose to try to bully you.

Preparing to Play

The single most important way to improve your game online – to increase your winnings or reduce your losses – is to prepare properly every time you sit down to play. These actions will take between five and ten minutes – a long time in poker terms, I know, especially when you are eager to start playing. However, considering that you are about to start gambling, whether it be with a few dollars, hundreds, thousands or tens of thousands of dollars, that time will make you money. If you don't want to make money, skip the rest of this chapter (in fact, skip the rest of this book, because one of the core concepts of poker is to win money). If you are prepared to spend a little time before you play, you will enjoy your game so much more. This is what to do:

1) Check your Mood/Attitude

More money is lost through bad attitude and responses to the vertiginous rises and falls in fortune than ever through poor poker play. You must be relaxed, have a decent amount of time to play, feel positive and optimistic, and have an innate desire to improve your game. All successful poker players, home game champs and wearers of world championship bracelets alike, know that there is always more to learn about the game – and they keep their minds open to that at all times.

If you are feeling negative, depressed, paranoid, hungover, or in a stinking bad mood with the world, don't play. Please don't play. Poker almost never improves someone's mood, but it often worsens it. This first tip alone can, if followed, save you thousands of chips. I know, because I've disregarded it, and seen the written, documented evidence to prove how much worse we all play when we are not in the correct frame of mind.

2) Money Management and Bankroll

Never increase stakes until you have won a big enough sum to form a new bankroll. Never be taken in by arguments like: 'if I play in a better-standard game, for a higher stake, my natural good play will be rewarded'. That is rubbish. If you are losing in a low-stake game, you'll lose more in a high-stake game – for certain.

Ensure that you have a big bankroll so that, if you do have a losing session or two, or three or four, or eight on the trot (and you will have all of those, however good you are), you still have money in your account to start up the fight again. I recommend that your bankroll should be twenty times the size of your regular buy-in. So, if you play in the $1/2 cash game, and buy-in for $200, you need to have at least $4,000 in your bankroll. Shocked? Most weak poker players would be. But, the less you have in your bankroll, the more you'll be thinking about money, winnings and losses, and less about the game and how you should be playing it. Poker players respect money, but they cannot worship it; as a commodity it moves to and from you in such great quantities and at such great speed that, if you value it greatly, its fluctuating movement would horrify you.

Once you've transformed that $4,000 bankroll into $8,000, you can consider moving up to the $2/4 game. However, if you find that you are losing in that new game, there is no shame, none at all, moving back down to where you were winning most of the time.

I play mid-stake cash games online: $2/4, sometimes $5/10, rarely any higher. I win consistently at those games, enjoy myself and like the fact that I am winning money. To play at higher levels would, for me, turn the game into a stressful experience and life is quite stressful enough. I don't mind in the least that some of my friends play for far higher stakes both in live games and online. Sometimes, they tell me I'm easily good enough to join them, but I'm happy where I am. There is a lot to be said for being comfortable at the level where you are winning and staying there, making profits, and enjoying yourself. If poker ever becomes a chore for you, a worry, a concern, then I urge you to reduce your stake or stop playing for a while and re-evaluate your decisions. Poker is a game – and should be relished.

3) Table Selection

Particularly when you are starting out, wanting to build a bankroll, gain confidence and practise often, your choice of table can decide whether you will win or lose and by how much. It's as simple as that. If, when you log on to your favoured site, you click on the first table that catches your eye and begin playing, you are squandering a massive advantage, pretty much unique to online play. What's more, it is a massive advantage that very, very few players take advantage of; so, for you to miss it too, is close on criminal.

The information displayed on the lobby page can reveal the type of game into which you are venturing. If you select well, you can almost ensure that it will be a game that suits you and your style of winning play. If you pick poorly, you will be virtually surrendering before the first card is dealt.

Let's look at the information and what it tells us:
Looking at the diagram of the lobby on page xxx, the two most important columns are:

Average Pot Size and Percentage of Players Seeing Flop

The reason for this is that, taking both columns into consideration, you can form a picture of the style of game being played here. If it fits your style (which may mean that the underlying style is the opposite to yours) then there is money to be won. If the style is threatening to your style, then you are likely to lose money. Poker isn't about taking on individuals . . . it is about spotting opportunities and capitalizing on them. Table selection is a basic, but vital, component of this calculation. These are the four combinations to look out for:

Large pot size, combined with low number of players seeing the flop
– this means that the game is tight/aggressive. There are limited callers before the pot and often a raiser or re-raiser with one or two callers.

Large pot size, combined with high number of players seeing the flop
– this means that the game is loose/aggressive. Typically, there are multiple callers, or raises and re-raises subsequently called by several players.

Small pot size, combined with low number of players seeing the flop
– this indicates a tight/passive game. There may be only limited pre-flop callers and rarely a raise with one caller.

Small pot size, combined with high number of players seeing the flop
– this suggests a loose/passive game with no pre-flop raises but numerous callers, who subsequently check, providing free cards on the board or, when one player bets or raises, everyone else folds.

As noted previously, 'tight' and 'loose' refer to the attitude of players towards hand selection: tight being selective. The terms 'passive' and 'aggressive' refer to betting styles, with passive suggesting checks and calls, and aggressive indicating bets, raises and re-raises.

Since, in basic terms, it is usually advantageous to you to enter a table playing a style opposite to your favoured one, you should seek out those games.

If, like me, and as recommended in this book, you prefer a tight/aggressive style, then to join a table which, up to this point, has proven loose and passive, will suit you very well. When you raise, you may get callers on marginal or sub-standard hands; when you are on a draw, players may check to you rather than betting or raising. This suits you perfectly.

Alternatively, if you like to play lots of hands and hope to hit good flops and draw-fulfilling turns and rivers, then to play at a tight/aggressive table will suit you better. Players will enter fewer hands and, when they do, you will know that they have premium or good cards; in that sense, tight/aggressive players are more predictable. Players will fold to bluff and semi-bluff raises because they prefer to make the first aggressive move themselves rather than react to actions of others.

Hopefully, just in these two examples (covering the two main, basic styles), you can see the advantages of picking your table carefully.

Look out also for stack sizes. These are sometimes displayed when you click once on the table in the lobby; sometimes you have to join the table to see them.

Imagine that, at a six-player table, there is one seat free and the maximum buy-in is $200. If the other five players have all got stacks of $500, $600 or $1,000, then those profits have been earned at that table. It may be that you have a group of experienced players who are picking off newcomers one by one as they enter the game. That table doesn't look good to me although, quite possibly, each of them has got lucky against a very weak player at some point and they are all now tired and ready to drop their chips into your lap. Personally, however, I would avoid that table for now.

Another significant element you might look out for is Time Zones.

Most sites display information about the home location of each player. This may be indicated beneath, or alongside, their name, or you may have to click on each player's name to find this out. You may even have to ask them where they are in chat. Players could invent their location, but usually it is not something about which they lie. The significance is in trying to play against someone who may be tired or drunk and therefore not fully focused on their game.

If it is 11am in London, then it is 3am in Los Angeles or San Diego. I would want to play against those players: they are probably tired and really want to go to bed. They may be chasing losses, or getting really drunk. If it is early in the USA, it is late in Asia, and so on. Finding opponents who are not at their best is a great way to boost your chances of success.

Over the years, I have taken detailed notes about my opponents, their location, their styles, their successes and failures. I credit my profits, in part at least, to choosing my opponents from different time zones and exploiting their odd hours. It won't always work; there might be an American pro who likes playing against British opponents and who plays all night and sleeps all day but, generally, it seems to work beautifully.

Which Seat?

If you have a choice of seats when you enter a table, pick carefully. In simple terms, you would like big stacks to your right, small stacks to your left. This is because, generally, chips move clockwise around the poker table along with everything else, and also because you would like the most powerful players (and a big stack means power) to act before you do, so you can judge from their decisions what to do yourself.

With more information available to you – if, for example, you have played against some or all of these players before – you would like the aggressive, raising, re-raising players on your right, where they have to act before you, and the passive, calling, folding players on your left, so that when you do call, you are unlikely to be raised; when you raise, you are unlikely to be re-raised. Where you sit at a poker table can be crucial. If you find that you aren't happy with your seat, switch seats, or leave the table. Online, there is always another table, always another game. Never feel bound to one table.

Buying-In

Everyone who gambles should have one basic concept at the forefront of their minds before they commence a session – or even start playing a gambling game in the first place: gamble only with money you can afford.

Once you have checked that you can afford to risk a couple of hundred, a couple of thousand, or tens of thousands of dollars, then you want to form a bankroll and try to keep it separate from your everyday spending.

When you decide to buy-in, make sure that you are playing in a game in which the buy-in represents no more – at most – than 10 per cent of your starting bankroll. Better still, make it 5 per cent of your initial bankroll. This is so that you can weather the slings and arrows of outrageous poker fortune without becoming overly worried about the state of your poker finances.

At the moment when you buy-in at your table, I recommend that you do so for the maximum available at the table. If you cannot afford the maximum amount, then you are playing in the wrong game. Click off from that table and try again at a lower-stake table. There are several reasons for wanting to buy-in for the maximum amount:

1) You want to appear confident and that you are a regular in the game, there to play, and positive about competing and winning.
2) To buy-in with only a fraction of the maximum will be to commit yourself to playing short-stack poker from the start. Although this may provide an opportunity to make all-in raises, the fact that you are short-stacked will reduce the fold equity of your big bets. That is to say: if you don't bet enough, the chance that you may persuade an opponent to fold to a big bluff is greatly reduced. This cuts down one of your prime methods of pressurizing your opponents.
3) Players who buy-in for strange amounts, and minimum requirements, indicate that they have been losing elsewhere and are now moving on, probably in desperation, to a new table. This is good information for you to read from other players, but not good for other players to read from you.

Statistics and Histories

All top sites now offer a button you can click to display your own statistics for the current session. Some sites provide this individually for each table in which you are playing; others combine all your tables in play to form one total set of statistics.

The value of these figures is that you can see what percentage of hands you are calling on pre-flop (generally, it shouldn't be too high); how far into the hand you are playing before folding (you should be aiming to fold pre-flop or on the flop, not at the end of the deal); and what percentage of hands played result in your taking down the pot. To refer to these statistics when you are doing very well, or very poorly, can sometimes lead to your spotting a direct correlation between your current style of play and the success/failure you are having in the game.

All top sites now offer you the option of viewing the last hand you played, as well as all previous hands for which you have been present at the table. These displays often show hands which, in a live game, would have been shown to the table but, because players check their 'muck all losing hands' box, are often mucked without being revealed. Many online players don't know this, and it provides a vital resource from which you can study what cards opponents were playing, how they played them, and what the result of the hand turned out to be.

Furthermore, if you lose a big hand, you can print out a copy of the hand history, e-mail to a friend whose poker advice you value, and see what he or she thinks you did wrong (or right) on the deal in question.

Once you have experienced a variety of different online sites, you will discover that some display this information more clearly than others. For me, the hand histories are vital research into the style and quality of my opponents and I want to be able to read off those facts as quickly and as easily as possible.

Taking Notes

I have always taken notes about my poker opponents, even when I was playing live games. I'd disappear into a rest room and write down some play which I considered to be revealing about the methods of an opponent so that I could study my notes at a later stage and be ready for those same opponents the next time I came up against them at the table.

Online, the process is far more simple. All top sites offer you the option of making notes on any opponent whom you encounter. On some sites, you might right-click on the player in question; on others, you may click a button saying 'take notes'. Whatever method is required, I strongly advise jotting down some simple notes. You may care to describe them in the basic terms I recommend: tight/aggressive; tight/passive; loose/aggressive; loose/passive.

Or, you may prefer to note down hand types played:

'played A7 in 1st position; called/raised out of position on K8s'

Whatever you choose to do, don't just write down insults:

'complete moron, has no idea, VERY lucky'

I wrote that about an online player a few years back and, boy, did it make me feel good. Unfortunately, the next time I encountered this same player, my notes scarcely enlightened me about his style of play. So, resist the notes becoming a set of caustic diary entries and personal reactions, and focus on the style of play that this player is demonstrating.

Poker Buddies

Most sites offer you the opportunity to check players whom you want to have as your poker buddies. I guess it's the online poker communities' attempt to get people to make friends. Allied to this facility is the option to search for your poker buddies when you are in the lobby. This is all charming, but a far better use for the poker buddy tag is for weak, predictable players against whom you want to play. Therefore, all my poker buddies are my chosen opponents and I get the software to search for their whereabouts whenever I log on. When I find them in a game which I fancy, I join that game and try to sit over them (to their left), so that I can pick up on their loose, undisciplined ways.

Tracker Software

At the time of writing, there is a small, but impressive, selection of poker software – some free, some available by subscription – which can track every last hand of your online play and present reports to you on demand, from which you can analyse your style, variation and success at any form of the game you choose to play. This is an excellent training tool and, if you are serious about playing online poker, is well worth trialling and, probably, paying for.

There is also software which tracks the success of all Sit & Go and/or tournament play across numerous different sites so that, when you know against whom you will be playing, you can feed their screen name and poker site into the system and get a report on their form, both over the long term and their current status. Some software even analyses their style of play and reports that to you. All the good versions of this type of software also offer lists of which tournaments on which sites are inhabited by weaker, losing players, and which ones feature a cast of successful, big money-winning players. These 'tournament selectors' can pay for their monthly subscription in about 30 minutes flat. Use them to find a weak event, buy-in, clean up and take your profits.

You will also find, amazingly, that it is not only the small-stake events which appeal to the weak players. There was a very fine $500 buy-in 6-player Sit & Go event available online just a few days ago from when I am writing this. Thanks to my tournament-selector software, it featured five huge losers and, just in time, me. I think I played fewer than ten hands to win this one. Everyone else knocked each other out in the first twenty minutes and I called a couple of all-in bets from the hyper-aggressive chip leader in the heads-up, won them both, and that was it. That was a simple way to earn $1,500 profit in under an hour at great odds. However, be aware that, even against very weak players, you can be outdrawn, become over-confident, or find that a poor player suddenly plays a hand perfectly. However, knowing that your opposition is weak to start with boosts confidence, encourages tight/aggressive play and greatly improves the odds of your placing in the money.

Making Records

I strongly recommend the small amount of extra time it will take you to make records of each session that you play. At the time, you may consider it a chore, especially if you have lost, but trust me that the information that you can extract from these records after only a couple of weeks can save you many thousands of chips.

At the end of each session of play, note down:

1) How you felt at the start of the session.
2) Your table-selection criteria.
3) What games you played: cash games; Sit & Go's; MTT (Multi-table tournaments). Note buy-ins and entry fees, profit/loss results, prizes won and position finished.
4) Have a running total for each form of the game that you play.
5) Any comments, such as changes in temperament, going on tilt, playing too many/too few hands, whether you think your cards were good or poor, how you felt at the end of the session.

When you look back at these diary entries, which should contain notes both on how you fared and how you felt, you may discover facets of your temperament, or your game, which you had not previously appreciated.

When I reviewed my online records for the first time, some six months after I first played on the Internet, I was amazed to find such a convincing correlation between feeling tired, unwell, or depressed, and enduring losing sessions.

I also discovered that I was making much more money per hour playing Sit & Go events than I was playing cash games. Since I find Sit & Go events highly enjoyable and cash games often quite stressful, this led to my changing how much of each form of the game I played. I now concentrate on Sit & Go action and play fewer low-stake cash games and only a few mid-stake cash games when the right opponents for me are all lined up. These revelations have increased my online profits substantially and, probably just as importantly, helped me to enjoy my online poker far more than I ever did before.

How Many Tables?

If you are winning consistently, play as many as you feel you can manage. I think that one high-stake game and one low-stake game is quite good. You can ignore the low-stake game if you get involved in a big hand in the high-stake one, when you can focus your attention on the high-stake game and analyse your opponents.

If you are breaking even, making a little money, or losing big, I urge you to restrict yourself to one table only. Focus on every decision, note every aspect of your opponents' games, and concentrate really hard. Until you can feel your way around a poker table, you must devote all your attention to it.

Bad Beats Online

This is one of the most important sections of this book because bad beats affect every poker player the world over and, online, you are going to see more bad beats – and suffer them personally – than you ever imagined possible. You will encounter endless speculation from other players that the site is rigged, that the cards are not random, that they are the most unlucky players ever to have walked the earth. This is not remarkable. Players who know a little about the game – but not enough – usually understand basic drawing odds and when you should be in or out of a hand, but they don't appreciate that most of what they call 'bad beats' are just the normal expectation, and the rest are simply a magnification of what has happened at poker tables since the beginning of poker time itself!

What is a bad beat?

It refers to a situation in which you are statistically hugely ahead on a hand but your opponent(s) draws successfully and much against the odds to beat you.

Let's take a look at an example:

You hold: A♠ K♠ and you raise pre-flop.

Your opponent holds: A♦ Q♥ and raises you.

You re-raise all-in, and your opponent calls.

The board comes:

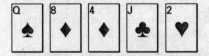

so your opponent takes down the pot. How unlucky is that!

Actually, it's not very unlucky at all, and it certainly isn't a bad beat. Let's analyse the situation:

You wanted your opponent to call your all-in re-raise and he did. At that point, you hold a 73–22 per cent lead, with roughly a 4½ per cent chance of a split pot. That is great going for you and, three times out of four – or thereabouts – you will win all the money. On this occasion, you were outdrawn, but keep playing situations like that and you will get rich. To lose a 73 per cent chance of winning is a shame, but you will see it occurring regularly, when you are involved and when other players are involved. After playing tens of thousands of hands, statistically, it is almost inevitable that you will lose six, eight, maybe ten of these types of hands in a row. It really shouldn't surprise you at all. Indeed, if you have always been the player holding AK in that situation, you will be so rich, you won't even care. So, that hand is a shame, but it's no bad beat. Don't pretend that you are the unluckiest player who ever lived. Pull yourself together and get on with the next deal.

Let's try again:

You hold: A♠ Q♣, and you raise pre-flop.

Your opponent holds: J♦ 8♠, and he calls you. The flop comes:

You bet the pot and get called. The turn comes:

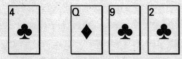

You make a big bet; your opponent calls you. The river comes:

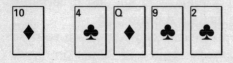

You check; your opponent makes a big bet; you call and lose.

Is that a bad beat? Yes. That is *really* annoying!

What was your opponent doing when he called your pre-flop raise on J8?

What was he doing when he called your post-flop bet?

What was he doing calling a big bet on the turn when only a ten could save him and, surely, he was worried by the three clubs on the board?

The answer to all these questions is that he was playing extremely poorly – and *that is just what you want him to do*. If your opponents don't make mistakes, you lose a vital extra way of winning – indeed, the way most good players make their money – exploiting the poor judgment and knowledge of their opponents. This type of bad beat happens to me all the time online – an unbelievably frequent occurrence. This doesn't make you supremely unlucky, nor does it suggest that the site is rigged, nor is it reason for you to move up to a higher stake or change tables. The opponent did what you hoped he would do – call for a gut-shot draw against the odds – and he happened to hit one of the three cards in the deck that gave him his hand (10♣ would have given you the flush). So, before the river, he had about a 5 per cent chance of beating you.

For years, I would fret and moan and complain about these bad beats. However, as I played more online poker, I began to realize that, despite all these horrible things happening to me, I was still well and truly in profit – sometimes substantially. That is because, for every time that an opponent hits his miracle card to beat you, he'll miss that card another ten, fifteen, twenty times. He may hit the wrong card (from your point of view) three or four times on the trot but, if he keeps playing like that, he will lose to you – and lose big.

So, these days, there is no longer a mountain of broken, cracked plastic mouses on the floor beneath my computer, the desk no longer gets thumped, nor the phone thrown out the window when it rings just after one of these bad beats. It still hurts me deep inside, makes me angry . . . but I take a deep breath, sigh loudly, sometimes growl, but, by the time I'm involved in my next hand, I'm calm again. If I'm not, I sit out from the table, go downstairs and take a one-minute walk to get some fresh air.

Learning to cope with bad beats does become easier once you realize that, when you are betting on a hand when you are way ahead of your opponent – and they are calling you – that is exactly what you want to be happening. The only way that you can suffer a truly horrible, morale-threatening reversal of fortune is if you are way ahead. Those loose, fishing, lame players never suffer bad beats because they are never ahead on a hand, always chasing. To put it another way: if you play tightly and well, you will get beaten only by an opponent getting lucky – and that luck always runs out.

Finally, let's analyse why so many more bad beats seem to occur online than in live games.

Firstly, you are playing many more hands per hour, probably four times as many – so, automatically, there will be four times more bad beats than in a live game. And that is if you are playing at only one table. Most online players play two or more tables simultaneously.

Secondly, players call far more online than in a live game. It's easier to do, less embarrassing when you have to fold subsequently, and most players online are, by nature, impatient, loose and undisciplined.

Thirdly, you will encounter more 'impossible' situations online, especially in low-stake games, than you imagine possible. When those ridiculous calls pay off, it does seem unbelievable because, unless you have been playing with complete idiots previously, you will never have seen such results. Extraordinary bad beats can occur only if the play is extraordinary.

After all that, some really important words to the wise on the subject of bad beats:

1) If a bad beat really upsets you (they do, and they will), then take a break for a few moments, until you are calm again. Doing this will save you money. This is because, in my experience, both personally and from watching others, *more money is lost by the reaction to the bad beat than from the bad beat itself*.

   On numerous occasions, I have seen players lose $100 on a bad beat, go on tilt, and gift their opponents (often the bad-beat victor) a further $400. So, if you are upset, stop playing, even for a minute or two.

2) Do not swear revenge on the hapless player who has beaten you. Don't take it personally. You don't care how you win and from whom you take chips. Indeed, if the worst player at your table wins your chips on a bad beat, that is much better news than the best player beating you since the bad player is likely to give back your chips to you later if he continues to play the same way.

3) Keep remembering that the better you play and the worse your opponents play, the more likely it is that you will see bad beats.

4) If you are not suffering bad beats, you are not betting with the best of it, and/or you are playing against players who can read your betting patterns too accurately so that they are not calling when they are behind you. If you are not on the bad end of a few bad beats, change table.

Of course, no one wants to suffer bad beats but, if you never suffer them, you are either uniquely lucky, or a major losing player who is never ahead on a hand and getting called.

Starting to Play

If you are a relative beginner as a poker player, stick to one table only and start with a low stake. The standard of poker may well be far lower than you are used to but, if you are as good as you think you are, it shouldn't take you long to record consistent profits (that doesn't mean winning every session – no one does that – it just means ending ahead as the sessions go by, increasing your profits slowly).

If you are not doing well at a low-stake table, do not make the mistake of moving up stakes to avoid the terrible beats. There is nothing wrong with playing low-stake poker and, whilst you are learning the game, it makes sense to lose small stakes rather than big ones. Only once you are beating the game which you are in for a period of time should you consider moving up in terms of stake.

Online Cash Game Strategy

Since most people online enjoy playing No-limit Hold 'Em, that's what we'll look at in these forthcoming sections on strategies for each form of the game available online.

My strong recommendation is to play a tight/aggressive style of poker online. If you are a more experienced player then you will obviously have your own preferred basic style from which you divert only when you feel that 'mixing it up' will help to disguise your normal, strong, successful actions.

When you join a table, take time to observe the action and form some preliminary opinions about your opponents. Don't rush in and play the first possible hand and end up losing it because you didn't know anything about the style of game played. (This happens a lot to online players.)

One of the elements of the online game which should be noted is the keenness for calling which is demonstrated online even by players of a decent standard. The significance is that, when you raise, you are ideally seeking only one, maybe two, callers. Online, once one or two players have called, there is a tendency for everyone else to call too. Individually, this may not be very effective play, but as a combined force, all those loose callers can destroy your premium hand. For that reason, I like to keep my starting hands strong and my betting even stronger.

Starting Hands

I would keep starting hands very tight indeed and then play them extra-strongly.

In early and mid-positions: premium hands and high/mid-pairs:

AA, KK, QQ, JJ, 1010, 99, 88, 77 and
AK, AQ

With all these starting hands, my basic strategy would be to raise. In a tighter-format live game, perhaps a raise three times or three-and-a-half times the big blind would be sufficient. Online, I like to raise a little more to discourage the start of a chain of loose calls. Four times the big blind, sometimes five times the big blind, tends to dissuade too many loose calls and leaves you only with the ultra-loose (the kind of player who calls a raise on any two cards) or the ultra-silly.

If an opponent has already raised, then with all of these hands, you should certainly consider re-raising. You must take into account from what position your opponent has chosen to raise and match that with the information you have about that player already.

For example, if you have noted that a particular player is tight/aggressive, seems patient and sensible, and has demonstrated that he plays only good hands then, if he has raised under the gun and you hold AQ, that is not a good time to opt for a re-raise (in fact, I'd probably fold). However, if the raiser is someone who raises regularly, plays every hand he can, and has shown poor judgment throughout, then you should definitely be re-raising with any of the hands above.

As always, table image is very important, and you want to lay down your marker early on. You will not allow players to draw cheaply, you will test their bets and raises with raises and re-raises of your own and, if you raise pre-flop and they choose to call you, they will, almost inevitably, face a follow-up bet from you and further pressure throughout the deal. Once you have established that image, you will usually find that the irresponsible players stop taking you on so readily and, when they do, you can then read them for having a decent hand. Establishing your own strong, aggressive image is not only good technique for playing winning poker, but it will also force the table to adjust to you; getting a table to play as you want them to is a fantastic experience and nearly always a very profitable one.

In late positions, you can add in the rest of the pairs and some sub-premium hands:

66, 55, 44, 33, 22 and
AJs, KQs

I would raise in late position with these hands, not because they are wonderful, but because you would rather take the pot down immediately than see a flop, especially if you have multiple callers. The other advantage of raising with these hands is that you will cause other players to lay down marginal hands, some of which may well be better than yours.

Of course, if you are an experienced player, taking part in a high-stake online game, against opponents you see regularly, then sticking to any kind of basic strategy for long will be a losing proposition. You need to let your imagination loose and mix up your play far more deceptively than playing what 'the book' suggests. However, the vast majority of online poker involves players who are not very good; who might have watched television and think that they know the game; who cannot be bothered to study a poker book; to take advantage of the online tips available everywhere; to join in conversations with their friends. Against these opponents, a simple, but sensible, strategy will work and it will make you money.

Protecting your Blinds

Much of the strategy concerning protection of your blinds is long-term. That is to say, if you know that you will be sitting in the same seats against the same opponents in a home game for the next eight hours, it may well pay to protect your blinds. For example, if the player two to your right keeps raising on the button, there will be some point reasonably early on when you will have to call, or better still, raise him and take him on. You may have to do this a few times so that he gets out of the habit of routinely raising on the button. You may have to do it with marginal hands and a great deal of bravery and aggression but, in the long run, it may make your life much easier.

However, please note that protecting your small blind is a waste of time and money; it is the worst position at the table and, if you don't see a premium hand there, just chuck your cards.

Online, there is a simpler method of combating a button player who raises time after time: leave the table. Don't risk your stack trying to create an image which may be lost on that opponent or which causes the opponent to re-raise you, costing you yet more money. Such a defence may prove irrelevant anyway if that opponent leaves the game at any moment. I've made a stand in the big-blind position before now, found that it's cost me a quarter of my stack and then that opponent leaves the table and another guy moves in. For how long are you going to keep doing it?

So, in short, don't waste chips playing hands out of position – you can attack your small blind if there are no others callers, naturally – instead, cash in on one of the greatest advantages of online play: leave the game and find another – instantly.

Action on The Flop

When I play online cash games, I tend to make the arrival of the flop the last moment when I decide whether I am staying in the hand or not. There will, of course, be occasions when I am called on the flop and I judge that my opponent hits his perfect card on the turn or river but, what I am trying to say is this: the flop is the time to emphasize your intention on the deal – you are either staying in and making your opponents pay to stay with you, or you are getting out quietly and not wasting any more money on the deal.

This means making strong follow-up bets, raising out anyone attempting to draw to a winning hand, and forming a decent judgment about what cards which any opponent who does stay with you may be holding.

Here are some key thoughts for low- and mid-stake cash-game poker online:

1) If you are starting out playing poker, you cannot play too tight. If you have the discipline to watch the game unfold and play only the premium hands then you will learn a lot about the game and about your opponents. The cost of learning how to play has always been how much you lose to your friends/opponents in the early days of your poker career. If you play tight, you will lose less. Also, there is the cost of the house rake (what the online card room takes from the pot every hand). The fewer pots you enter, the less of the rake you will have contributed to the house.

2) Since most television poker is tournament play and most of the hands that are shown are only a tiny selection of the tens of thousands of hands played, you will see that every hand involves a brilliant slow-play, an amazing all-in bluff, or the catching of a miracle card at just the right moment. This is not what poker is – or, frankly, should be – about. Your aim should be to keep pots small (unless you are certain that you are winning – and the nuts is rarely the absolute nuts, so often the nuts are being over-taken at the end). Poker is not about how many pots you win, not about winning lots of pots, not about the style with which you win them. Poker is about ending up with more money than you started with and trying to make the most of the money-winning situations and lessen the impact of those long, cold sessions where nothing goes your way. So, avoid all-in bets and just build your stack slowly.

3) Avoid calling. Be the most aggressive player at your table, but only when you have started the hand with really good cards. In other words, don't play many hands but, when you do, play them like a tiger.

You will see thousands of players online who might be termed 'fish'. They call and call and call some more. They'll call raises, they'll call re-raises; often they have nothing – and sometimes they have less than nothing. You won't believe how loose players are online. However, avoid letting those players set the pace. Don't fall into the trap of slow-playing them, hoping to keep them around until the end, and then hitting them with a big bet. It's all too likely that one of them will have hit something big and your big hand ends up costing you money. Keep betting, keep raising, keep making them pay to stay in the hand.

4) You are on the button. You hold: A♥ A♠. There are two callers to you. You raise three times the big blind (hoping, perhaps, to keep at least one of them in the deal). They both fold. You win two calls and the blinds. You feel sick, wasting your great hand like that.

You are in first position. You hold: Q♣ Q♦. You decide to raise four times the big blind. Everyone folds. You can't believe that you are getting so little action. All you have won is the blinds.

This goes on for a while so, eventually, when you are on the button, after two callers, you look down to see: K♦ K♣. This time, you decide that you are going to get paid properly. You just call. The small blind calls and the big blind checks. The flop comes:

Everyone checks to you, so you decide to bet. When you do, the big blind raises you. What will you do now? You decide to call.

The turn comes:

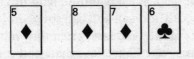

The big blind checks again. You bet again and the big blind raises you again. . . . now what?

You call. The river comes:

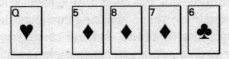

The big blind goes all-in and, since it is only a relatively small bet, you decide to call. The big blind shows you:

You lose a big pot.

Let's just think back to that feeling of disappointment when you raised with your premium hand and everyone folded. It *is* a shame not to make money with big cards, but it is a far bigger shame to lose a big pot with the same big cards because you misplayed the hand. To slow-play premium hands against more than one opponent is virtually always wrong unless you are playing in a really strong game (and even then, it can be deeply stressful).

I show you these examples because I see this kind of action online every single day. I want you to avoid losing big pots as I have done in the past trying to build pots through slow-play. It so often fails. Now, when I see this happen online, I am thankful that I have learnt my lesson.

If you are playing in low- and mid-stake cash games online (and you are the players for whom I am writing), remember this:

You will make your money in these games by value betting – betting when you have the best hand and being paid off by someone else with the second-best hand or a player who is chasing a draw which is against the odds. That is how you will win. And you *will* win – and you will win *big*.

You will *not* make money in the long run by slow-playing, running massive bluffs, playing crazy-style, calling everything, and hoping to hit miracle cards.

To win money consistently online in low- and mid-stake cash games, you require discipline, patience and excellent observational skills because it will be directly from what you observe that you will win your biggest pots. Once you think you have a 'read' on a player – a good idea how he plays and what he is showing when he takes certain actions – that will be the time to strike with a change from your usual solid, sensible, disciplined, basic strategy.

5) Analyse the flop carefully. Because the flop is usually the time when I decide whether I am in this hand until the end (barring nasty developments) or whether I am getting out now, before the deal has cost me much, the texture of the flop – and my opponents' reaction to it – is paramount.

Let me give you some examples:

a) You raise with A♥ K♠ and receive one caller. The flop comes:

This is a terrible flop for you and it could be excellent or very promising for your opponent. If my opponent bets into me, I may well just lay down my hand and move on. Even if it is correct for me to call now, I am not going to be happy with whatever cards hit the table after this point and that means I will face further tough decisions. Don't volunteer to make your life difficult.

b) You raise with A♥ K♠ and receive one caller. The flop comes:

This is a terrible flop for you . . . but it is almost certainly a terrible flop for your opponent also. I would certainly make a follow-up bet into that flop and I might well re-raise the player if he bets ahead of me. At least I will find out quite a bit about my opponent's cards if he chooses to call my aggressive action.

c) You raise with A♥ K♠ and receive one caller. The flop comes:

Your opponent checks. What should you do?
   There are several different possible reasons for your opponent's action and some of them are really bad for you. However, in all probability, there is one key

reason why your opponent has checked. It's the reason why people check ninety-five per cent of the time: he has missed the flop.

Why would we think that, necessarily?

Look at the texture of the flop. It is flushing and straightening – it is a very threatening flop indeed. If your opponent thought for one minute that he was ahead of you on this hand, he would have bet.

Imagine that he held AQ or AJ – he would probably have bet right out to try to take you off the hand or, at least, make you pay to draw. Players rarely check their hands when they have the best of it and the flop poses multiple threats like that. Maybe experts can slow-play in situations like this, but the rest of us mortals (that's 99.9 per cent of the poker-playing population) really can't.

So, you are going to make a nice follow-up bet of between half and the whole of the pot. I expect your opponent to pass but, if he calls, it probably means he has a ten. If he re-raises, I still think he's on a draw, but now you have a tough decision to make, and the passive choice will probably win the day.

d) You raise with K♦ K♠. You receive one caller. The flop comes:

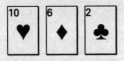

If there is one time when you might consider a slow-play, I guess this is it. You have one opponent only, you have no draw threats, and only an ace on the turn or river (or maybe, a second ten) will bother you very much.

However, generally, I would not slow-play here. Everyone can see that this is a non-threatening flop, so everyone appreciates that this might be a good time to slow-play. If I was first to act, I might try to check-raise and accept that I might be giving a free card.

If my opponent checked to me, I'd certainly bet – just as if I was making a follow-up bet with AK. Finally, if my opponent bets into me, I have a choice of plays: to call (and, in effect, slow-play the hand), or to raise immediately. Your knowledge of your opponent's betting style and general attitude will guide you how best to play the hand.

However, your default mode of play in these games should be always to bet when you believe you have the best hand.

e) You hold: 9♠ 9♥ and you raise. There is one caller after you. The flop comes:

What action do you take?

I strongly recommend betting here. If your opponent does not hold an ace, the chances are you will not be paid anything further anyway. If he does hold an ace – with a half-decent kicker – he may well think that your bet is a follow-up bet and opt to raise you.

I know very successful players in low- and mid-stake online cash games who go all-in when they flop trips pretty regularly. I confess that I was perplexed but then I saw the reason: players who have called raises with AJ and AQ never lay down their hand when they flop top pair. They can't bring themselves to do it. Of course, in a high-stake game, the pre-flop action might well have been different and the post-flop play would be more subtle but, I have to tell you, piling in the money when you flop trips seems to work very well indeed.

My own preference is to make what looks like a follow-up bet and hope for aggressive action from my opponent. If he calls, I'm betting hard again on the turn and, unless something worries me, on the river also.

The key then to successful tight/aggressive play in these low- and mid-stake online cash games is to raise with the good hands, make follow-up bets on the flop – whether you miss, hit partially, or hit beautifully. That way, you are in a strong position to steal pots and run bluffs as your image becomes established. You are, in effect, mixing up your play, whilst optimizing your money-winning strategy.

This style also lends weight to another important play which works particularly well online as part of our basic strategy.

f) A player in mid-position raises and, after one other call, you decide to call on the button with J♠ 10♠. The flop comes:

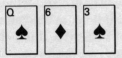

The raiser bets half the pot and the other opponent folds. What action do you take.

Hopefully, your instinct is telling you not to call (remember: we don't like calling) but to raise. This semi-bluff raise works very well here for two key reasons.

Firstly, it is generally the correct play as it offers two real benefits: it may cause the raiser to pass; it may buy you a free card when the raiser calls but checks on the turn – giving you two chances for the price of one to make your flush.

Secondly, because of the general style which you are playing, your opponent will fear that you are not semi-bluffing, but making a value bet based on your holding something like AQ or KQ, and that may make him think twice about continuing in the hand, even if he has a mid-pair in the hole. In other words, your general style of play creates a third chance to win the pot right now: to make your opponent fold the winning hand now, because he has seen you raise with the best hand on many previous occasions.

So, a tight/aggressive image bolsters your bluff and semi-bluff credentials, builds respect from other players at the table (assuming that they are watching which, online, is relatively unlikely) and that equates to one thing and one thing only: more chips heading your way.

Action on The Turn and River

Continuing to value bet is the best way both to build a bigger winning pot for you or to discern that your opponent(s) may actually have you beaten. Since most calling on the flop is from players who are on some kind of a draw (and not just straights and flushes, but those hoping to hit trips or two pair), so it makes sense to continue to pressurize them to pay when there is still one card left to come. Remember that the odds of opponents hitting their dream cards almost halve when there is only one card to come rather than two, so you should structure your bets to be big enough to make the draw costly, but not so big that you commit yourself to the pot whatever happens on the river.

The river is the place where the observation of your opponents can really pay dividends. You want to ascertain whether they are more likely to fall for calling a value bet or whether, if you check first, they are likely to bluff into you. In my experience, many online players never let go of a pot and believe that if you don't bet at the end, it must mean that you don't have much. Consequently, they bluff into you and usually it is a big bluff. If you know where you stand (and, by the river, you should have a pretty good idea), this can be a brilliant way of picking up more chips than value betting.

One of my favourite characteristics to note about opponents is their desire to bluff all-in at the end when trying to take me off a hand. I have made many thousands of dollars from knowing that this is their style and from their not having noted that I sometimes check at the end and then call the big bluffs. Your observations and the practice that you undertake in noticing these foibles will make you money time and time again.

Finally, it is worth noting that in low-stake online games, you will face a huge number of players who simply have no idea about the game whatsoever. These players can be very dangerous because, although you will certainly beat them in the long run, they may well damage you and your style of play in the short term.

For example, it may seem to you to be advantageous to have a couple of ultra-loose players around you, who call down everything, but their effect can be devastating. Firstly, when you raise and they call, this will bring in other players who recognize the greatly-increased value of calling and becoming involved in the pot. Secondly, you may be unable to bluff certain opponents because their curiosity is just so great that they call everything down even with no hand at all. Don't you believe that players routinely call you at the end with queen-high and bottom pair-low kicker? Just play some 5c/10c NL Hold 'Em online and you'll see it almost every hand – it defies belief.

All of this seems quite amusing, even entertaining but, when you find yourself well down against a table of players whom you rate well below your own standard, you may suffer a sense-of-humour failure. This may result in your making over-raises, going all-in, loosening your starting-hand requirements and calling down more hands yourself. Notice how that is the exact opposite of our recommended strategy. That is to what you must remain alert: don't let poor players drag you down to their level, nor let them alter your style in an attempt to finesse them. If you are playing against strong players, you may choose to alter your style, mix up your game, and try some unusual plays, but against weak players, any effect of occluding your play will be lost on them . . . because they aren't watching what you are doing anyway!

Against weak opponents, remain disciplined, tight-aggressive; cut down on bluffs and follow-up bets; but play your made hands a little more strongly than usual. Forget slow-playing and trying to induce bluffs at the end, just bet out your hands and get paid.

Some experts recommend playing slightly more hands than usual at a weak table because you should be able to outplay them on the flop, turn and river. However, because you have less information about your opponents (because their strategy is so random and illogical), outplaying these opponents on the board is often tough unless you make your hand.

Several further points should be mentioned in any discussion on weak tables:

1) If you find yourself losing at a weak table, don't take it personally and don't start to develop a hatred for any particular player. Remember that poker without bluffing is really just a game about making the best hand; if you find that you simply aren't hitting any decent cards, leave the table and look for fresher pastures.

2) Don't berate your opponents in the chat box; don't give them free lessons on how they should have played a hand; avoid venting your frustration or telling them how you have just finished sixth out of five-hundred players in some tournament. They don't care and you are just working yourself up. In fact, what are you doing chatting at all? Those chat boxes are the spawn of the devil. Turn them off!

3) Don't leave a low-stake game frustrated and angry and move to a higher-stake table. This is a very common mistake. You can't bear all the bad play so you figure that a higher-stake table will offer more sensible play and you will therefore do better. This is not true.

Firstly, higher stakes don't automatically equate to better play or more sensible players. Secondly, you are probably emotionally worked up and not at your best to continue playing for a while. Thirdly, if you can't beat the game at low stakes, you'll lose even more trying to beat the game at higher stakes – and that is just as stupid as the players you've got up to avoid.

Stop-Losses and Win-Protection Targets

Poker is gambling. Gamblers lie. It's endemic. I don't really care what you say to your wives, girlfriends, boy-friends, lovers or mates, but don't lie to yourself. If you do that, it will all finish badly. Keep a tally of your wins and losses and, if you are losing too much, take action. Call Gamblers Anonymous; confide in a friend; reduce the size of your stakes; study more before playing; play at only one table; take a break from poker for a couple of weeks. Whatever you do, do something!

Some players decide that when they have lost two buy-ins, they will stop for the day. That seems like a wise move to me. However promising a table looks, there are days when nothing is going to go your way. You have to learn to recognize those times and act on them. If you have followed the advice earlier in this chapter to have at least twenty times your buy-in in your bankroll, you needn't feel too bad if you lose two buy-ins. It happens to all of us. Spend a few minutes going over your own notes, rereading parts of this book, or watching the play at a table where you feel you might learn something.

When you are winning, it is easy to believe that you will continue to win. And, indeed, there is no reason why you shouldn't. However, if you are still building a bankroll, you might decide to apply a win-protection element. For example, you buy in for $100 and, after an hour, you find that you have $275 in front of you. You might at this stage apply your win protection: that is to say, you will play with 50 per cent of your profit but, once your stack dips below that point, you will leave the table. So, you have about $90 of profit to play with and, if you continue winning, you can apply that same protection clause to the next figure. This doesn't mean that you can't go all-in if you feel that you have a hand won, or make a substantial raise if required, merely that if your bankroll fritters down to half of your profit, that will be a good time to leave.

If you are truly honest with yourself, how you feel, what your place is in the game in which you are currently playing, then you may decide that there is no need to place restrictions on yourself. If the game seems profitable for you, you have a good read on your opponents and you feel patient enough to wait for the big score, then continue, but keep evaluating your own performance as well as that of your opponents.

Quick Summary of Online
Cash-Game Basic Strategy

- Take your time when you enter a new game to observe your opponents and make preliminary observations about their styles of play. These observations can make you money and save you a fortune.
- Play a tight/aggressive style. Pick premium hands and raise/re-raise with them. Avoid calling. Back up raises with follow-up bets and sustain pressure on players who merely call. Avoid giving free cards.
- Don't seek to protect your blinds; if your opponents to your right are consistent late-position and/or button raisers, consider moving table. Remember that for every small-blind hand you muck, you are saving half a big blind. After a few hours, these savings add up to a lot of chips.
- Study the flop carefully and ask yourself not only whether it hit your hand but also how it might have enhanced your opponents' hands. Observe texture and form of the board and exploit any show of weakness from opponents who check into draw-potential flops.
- Avoid slow-playing pre-flop and, unless against one known opponent, value bet consistently post-flop rather than seeking to check raise or slow-play.
- Study actions of opponents to judge whether, at the end, a value bet or a bluff-inducing check will lead to a bigger pot for you.
- Be honest about your bankroll and adjust your table stakes accordingly. Do not believe that bad players can be beaten quickly or chase losses to bad players by continuing to play at an unreadable, illogical table. Accept your losses and find another game (without raising the stakes).

- Remain aware of your own mental attitude, level of concentration and take notes for further analysis.
- Set stop-losses and win-protection targets and, if you do set them, stick to them.

Online Sit & Go Tournaments

Sit & Go tournaments are a fantastic way to practise your poker, knowing that your liability is only as great as the entrance fee. There are hundreds available every minute of the day, with entry fees ranging from $1 to many thousands of dollars. Apart from being highly entertaining and often very exciting, the single-table format replicates a final table in a big tournament. You have to remain aware at all times of your opponents' stack sizes as well as your own, and not allow yourself to be blinded away. Aggression is the key to success and the great news is that your standard tight/aggressive persona is exactly the right starting place not only to enjoy Sit & Gos but also to master them.

Once you have registered for a particular Sit & Go event – having looked at your options in the Sit & Go Lobby area – the moment the table is full, you will be taken automatically by your poker site to the table and shortly afterwards the action begins.

Whether it is a nine- or ten-player table, a short-handed five- or six-player table, or even a heads-up (two players) match, each player will start with 1,000, sometimes 1,500 chips. The blinds usually start at 5/10 or 10/20 and will rise every few minutes, or after a particular number of hands.

My advice would be to avoid 'Turbo' or 'Hi-Speed' Sit & Gos, since these rely to an even greater extent than usual on luck. The more skilful you are as a player, the more time you would like to assess opponents and build your bankroll slowly but surely. Turbo events are for adrenalin junkies who would rather trust as much as possible to luck and as little as they can to skill. These high-speed Sit & Gos are often completed in just a few minutes. Recently, online, I witnessed a nine-player $500 high-speed Sit & Go – the winner walked off with $2,500 in eleven minutes!

Playing in a normal-speed Sit & Go is still a fast-action event. Sit & Gos usually last about an hour, but they can end very quickly or go on a little longer. Eventually, the blinds get so high that anyone left has to go all-in on virtually every hand and trust to luck.

Most sites offer similar pay-outs for Sit & Gos, but check yours to ensure you know where you stand on the pay-outs for each one. Usually, the pay-outs would be as follows:

Heads-Up matches: winner takes all

5 or 6-player tables: winner 70 per cent; runner-up 30 per cent

9 or 10-player tables: winner 50 per cent; runner-up 30 per cent; third place: 20 per cent

You can see that there is no reward for finishing third in a five- or six-player event, but you would double your money for finishing in the bronze-medal position in a nine- or ten-player Sit & Go.

Sit & Go Strategy

The strategy suggested here has proven to be highly successful for those players of a good standard who have followed it. As a basic strategy it allows you the freedom to mix up your game a little depending upon your preferred style, but it also contains plenty of key advice for consistent success. Although there is a considerable luck factor in Sit & Go events (since you are playing a limited number of hands), if you master this strategy you will be able to make consistent profits online.

I know of many semi-pro players who make a good living playing online Sit and Go tournaments; they wouldn't go back to playing cash games for anything.

It seems amazing to me that although this strategy is fairly well known and many (if not all) experts seem to agree that it is the best basic strategy, there are still millions of poker players out there who don't agree, haven't heard of it, or simply ignore the advice.

I like to break any tournament down into sections, usually four, hence my name for them: quartiles. You must judge for yourself where the borders of each quartile lie and, as you become more experienced, you will be able to feel the moments when you are moving from one part of the event to another and how your strategy needs to change.

The background of this strategy is simple and based on several factors which, to a greater or lesser extent, are always present in Sit & Go events.

1) A basic understanding that to double your chip stack at the beginning of an event is far less important than to double it late into an event. Although an early lead gives you a chance to impose your leadership on a table, the risk of losing all your chips is too great.

2) There will always be super-aggressive players battling it out for supremacy early on. During this time you have an opportunity to observe the styles of your opponents and to see some of the cards being played by them. Usually, whatever stake the Sit & Go may be, you will discover exceptionally loose, poor play. It is very unusual online not to see at least one player, sometimes two or three, knock themselves out of the event even before the first level of blinds is complete.

3) There will probably be a player who does not 'turn up' for the event as he has been distracted by something

else. As time goes by the blinds will whittle away his stack completely.

There will certainly be players who are not paying attention, or who are showing off to friends at home, or who have rarely played Sit & Go events previously.

You want time to identify these players and to observe the basic styles of other players. For example, you will often see players calling raises with any ace – however awful the kicker. If you note that they continue to call down hands with such cards, you will know how easily you will be able to take their money when you play aces with premium kickers.

You should also take time to note which of your opponents routinely use the action buttons in their software to fold automatically; check/fold; fold to any bet, etc. If you find that you have several of these players around you, you should use this information to your advantage by raising consistently, even if it is to only twice the big blind: you will often find that everybody folds.

The prevalence of use of auto-action buttons in Sit & Gos is down to the fact that most online players undertake several Sit & Go events at once and, as they dart to and fro between them, it helps to save time by selecting their action in advance.

I strongly advise playing only one Sit & Go at a time, unless you are confident enough to wait to make your decisions when it is your turn – and not to use the auto-action buttons.

4) Since you will get paid if you finish in the top third of the field (more or less), early on, your ambition is to be in with a strong chance of reaching the prize money. That means that, early on, you must preserve your stack and not squander it on speculative draws.

If you play well, and receive your fair share of luck, you should be in a position to challenge for the top prize on the vast majority of occasions.

Let's take a look at the four quartiles of a Sit & Go event:

First Quartile

Use the early stage of the event to review notes on players present and form basic opinions as to the styles of play being demonstrated by each opponent.

Keep your starting-hand requirements very high in early and mid-positions, and raise/re-raise with them to protect your hand:

AA, KK, QQ, JJ, 1010 and
AK, AQs

I suggest a substantial raise to prevent one loose caller bringing in a whole set of players and devaluing your premium hand, probably fatally. Five to six times the big blind is a perfectly reasonable raise to make in a Sit & Go. You will be surprised that sometimes when you take this action, you still receive four or five callers. This is normal for a Sit & Go. However, more often, you get one caller and he usually hangs around for ages, calling you down.

Do not worry if you play no hands whatsoever during the first-blind level. Your table image will be very tight and that will benefit you later on if you have to bluff to remain in the event.

You can also play, in late position:

mid- and low pairs (calling at a nine- or ten-player table, raising at a five- or six-player table)

ace-small suited

high suited connectors, such as: K♣ Q♣, or 10♦ 9♦

The idea of playing these hands is:

with pairs: to hit trips on the flop

with ace-small suited: to hit the nut flush draw and to be able to take it cheaply

with high suited connectors: to hit a straight flush draw, or two pair

If to draw costs you too much, fold the hand; if you hit top pair with ace-small and someone bets into you, fold the hand. Take no risks other than good pot-odds-based draws – and even then, do not allow those draws to be costly, since to preserve your stack and gain information is your aim in this first quartile.

Many players feel that the small size of the blinds early on is the ideal time to go fishing for miracle flops. And, indeed, it's not a terrible idea. The problem is that they forget to fold their cards when they don't hit the perfect flop, and that is why so many players crash out of Sit & Gos early on. If you call on A♣ 4♣ and hope to catch the nut flush draw, what are you doing calling a pot-sized bet when the flop comes:

Unless the bettor is bluffing, your kicker is almost certainly losing, and the two low cards on the board make it even more likely that if you and your opponent both have aces, kickers will play. More importantly, the reason you called was not the ace in your hand, it was the chance of the nut flush draw: don't forget that. Really, the flop missed you completely and you should fold to a serious bet.

If you do hit a great flop, then play it aggressively. Slow-playing works even less well in the Sit & Go format than in a cash game or big tournament.

Avoid bluffing or taking risks of any kind.

By the end of the first quartile, you should have a basic opinion of the style of game in progress, the basic outline of how each opponent seems to play and find yourself with the average number of chips – or just below – but with several players eliminated already. Do not worry for a moment that one or two players may have doubled through in the first few minutes; the chances are that they will have those chips back in play again very soon.

Second Quartile

As players are eliminated, remain aware of what the average chip stack should look like. For example, if you are competing at a nine-player table, and three of the players are eliminated, what should your chip stack look like for it to be average?

If each player started with 1,000 chips, there are 9,000 chips in play. If there are only six players remaining, the average stack should be 1,500. If you slide well below the average, prepare to become more aggressive in late positions, raising to try to steal blinds.

By this point, there will already be some short-stacked players and you should be keen to attack these players, pressurizing them to put their entire Sit & Go event on the line. Be aware of raises into short-stacks, however, since they will probably be pretty desperate by now. Having played too many hands early on, they may feel that they must continue to press, gambling for a double-through, or give up. When you opt to raise short-stacks, ensure that either you are prepared to call an all-in re-raise, or you have contributed sufficiently little to the pot to fold to an all-in move and still have sufficient chips to continue the battle. So, if you are prepared to call an all-in, you can continue to raise four to six times the big blind; if you want to pressurize but not commit, you may find that a simple raise of double the big blind is sufficient to scare off the short-stacks. Often, a small raise looks more threatening than a big one, as short-stacks may suspect that you are trying to suck them into a hand that they cannot win.

You should also be aware of which players seem vulnerable; sometimes these can be the chip leaders, who have got lucky early on, doubling up after an outrageous all-in bet. There may also be some players who won't fold to any bet – and those must be marked as unlikely to be bluffed, and approached in a different way.

If, at any time, you fall to within five blind rounds of extinction, you must change gears immediately. During that round, you must take a stand on any hand which offers at least a 35 per cent chance of success. This usually means ace-high hands, hands with two face cards, or any low or medium pair. In this situation, you would quite like a caller and try to double through and get back into the game. However, because of your previously tight image, it is probable that you will be able to run an all-in raise several times before anyone plucks up the courage to call you with anything but a good or premium hand. Your tight start has helped you at your time of need.

Assuming that your chip stack seems healthy, you need to remain aware of the blind levels and how they are likely to affect your opponents. Your stack can be fine one moment and, a few hands later, without any action from you, your stack suddenly seems a bit weedy. Imagine, for example, that your chip stack was 600 chips. If the blinds are 10/20, that's just fine – you have plenty of time to build your stack. However, if the blinds are 100/200, then you have only two rounds before you are blinded away: you must act now (in fact, you should have acted earlier).

Remember that the later you opt to change to an ultra-aggressive stance to regain your position in an event, the less the power of your stack. If you have 600 chips remaining and all your opponents have 3,000, if you go all-in, anyone might take a gamble to knock you out. If you have 600 chips and everyone else has about 1,200, that's quite different: an all-in raise by you will still have plenty of fold equity (the extra chance of persuading opponents to fold).

By the time you reach the end of the second quartile, it is quite likely that you are almost in the money. Short-stacks will have recovered or been eliminated, and the overall chip-stack position will usually have equalized somewhat.

Third Quartile

You may be in the money already; you may have almost everyone still seated. In the former scenario, the remaining players will have big stacks and you will have time to select some decent hands to try to increase your stack. If almost all of the original players are still in their cyber-seats, then the chip stacks are likely to be quite even, although the size of the blinds will ensure that everyone will be under pressure to increase their stack or go out. From this point onwards, you must be prepared to wager all your chips at any given moment, probably as soon as you pick up a good, very good, or premium hand. You will still find that plenty of players will call you with sub-standard hands, so your chances of doubling through are probably better than 50 per cent. With the blinds high and the pressure mounting, do not be afraid to use your position to its best possible advantage. Whilst everyone at the table still thinks they can make the money, the more selectively aggressive you are, the more likely it is that you will wear down opponents' stacks and build yourself one that can survive the odd 50/50 gamble.

Assuming that, as you usually will, you find yourself left with just a couple of other players, remain aware of where the pay-outs begin. No one wants to finish on the bubble and it is a major psychological barrier for many players, especially if they have paid more for their entry fee than they might normally stake for an evening's poker.

Use that bubble barrier to good effect. You should not be intimidated by the thought of going out on the bubble. If you are fearless, combined with picking your position and opponent, you will be able to bully many chips out of all the remaining players, since they will fear being eliminated and missing out on the money. If you see other players who become quite aggressive at this moment, you can rate them as knowing something of a winning strategy for poker: exploit opponents' weaknesses. More likely, you will see everyone tighten up and play extremely carefully hoping that two opponents get into an all-in battle and one gets eliminated. Rather like calling as opposed to raising, this is a reactive, passive strategy and one which, ultimately, will prove a big loser to you over time.

In these tense moments, do not be afraid to re-raise if you sense any kind of weakness. Average players understand that raising provides an extra chance to win a pot, even though opponents may suspect them of stealing. And, when the pressure is on, stealing is usually what they are doing. A re-raise, however, seems to be such a strong move that it is rarely called, other than with a premium hand (which is very unlikely) or if the initial raiser is now pot-committed (he has to call for the last of his chips and/or the pot odds are so attractive that, even if he is behind, he feels he must complete the deal).

Comparing the size of the initial raise with the opponent's stack and seeing whether he could reasonably fold to a re-raise is something that should be considered routinely. Only when the conditions are right, your position is good and you feel that such a play might work, should you then re-raise.

One little tip which I have found quite successful is that if you do not have to go all-in yourself, just re-raise the exact amount that would force your opponent all-in. This seems to work because a player going all-in at this point in an event looks like a gamble, whereas to bet the exact amount to force your opponent all-in looks like a more measured decision, designed to pick the last meat off the bones. For that reason, the frequency of folding from a player who has previously raised is higher when his opponent's re-raise matches exactly the raiser's remaining chip stack than when the re-raiser just pushes all his chips into the middle.

Finally, here is a little bit of extra detailed strategy.

Imagine that you are in the last four players at a nine- or ten-player Sit & Go. There are three prizes and you are currently in second position. You could sit tight and hope that a player is eliminated. If you do, you are likely to be in last place as you battle for the top prize. Instead, you want to be attacking the others in order to gain chips by stealing blinds so that you are in a commanding position when it comes to deciding who takes which prize home with them. Whom should you attack most aggressively?

Most players think that you should always attack the shortest stack, but there are substantial advantages from attacking another player instead. Let's see the position in the event:

Player A   4,000
You   3,500
Player C   1,700
Player D   1,000

The problem with attacking Player D is that he knows that if he doesn't double through soon, he will be out of the tournament. For this reason, he is less likely to fold to a pressurizing raise. Instead, he will look at his two face cards, or ace-high hand, and take a stand. If you lose this 50/50, 60/40 type gamble, you will have been wounded.

The player for whom the pressure of a big raise would be greatest is actually Player C. In the back of his mind, he is thinking that he is currently in a money-winning position and if he can just sit tight, he can take home the bacon. He will be far less likely to take a gamble with you, feeling that if he can hold on a little longer, someone may knock out Player D, the real short-stack. So, bluffing, pressurizing raises should be directed towards the second short-stack in these situations, because they are more likely to fold than the shortest stack at the table.

During these latter stages, ensure that you take the first positive action on any hand: raise, re-raise, bet out. Unless you are trapping with the nuts, you don't really want to be calling and hoping.

Remember not to become so short-stacked that an all-in bet from you (or even a crafty smaller raise) will no longer exert some pressure on your opponents. Once you become too low, all you can rely on is luck and that is not really the way to win at poker.

Fourth Quartile and Heads-Up Play

Assuming that your aggressive pre-bubble hasn't found you eliminated (and, on occasion, it will), you should find yourself in a strong position to contest the various pay-outs.

You will find that, if the blinds are sufficiently high, you may face all-in raises on every round. You must not be afraid, either to call these raises from opponents or, better still, to make them yourself. If you are up against the standard aggressive online player, they know that the time to be selective about starting hands is long over, and they must play any hand over average very strongly. Typically, when you do raise all-in at this time, you get only one caller; the other player is delighted that his two opponents are bashing each other around. However, that does mean that, when you are down to three players with the blinds high, you will be considering going all-in on:

any premium, very good, or good hand (naturally, you may wish to play AA or KK more slowly in an attempt to lure a player into a pot)

any pair

any ace

any king

QJ, Q10

some high suited connectors.

In simple terms, you may raise, or go all-in, on any hand which offers some value should it get called.

Personally, I think you can usually afford to pass one or two hands at this stage and, if you are being dealt 32 off or 73 suited, you might just be patient for a moment longer.

Once you reach the heads-up stage, unless the blinds are relatively low (in which case you will have time to pass a few raises and fold a few small blinds), you will have to remain ultra-aggressive. Every pot you win now is doubly valuable because, not only does it increase your own stack, but it also directly reduces your single opponent's holding.

When you win, as I hope you will, celebrate by all means, but also note down any final observations about your heads-up opponent. They might prove vital if you meet him in the future.

If you discover that you have an aptitude for these single-table tournaments, you may find yourself choosing to play them online as your preferred game. I know several semi-pros who make a fine living playing Sit & Go events, and I have found them to be my most profitable online poker for the last few years. There are just so many poor players out there and Sit & Gos seem to bring out the most idiotic elements in them.

Tournament Poker Trackers

Several of the best poker trackers and search engines now examine the Sit & Go events across a multitude of different sites. They are able to show you which events feature strong, successful tournament players and which are populated by weak, losing players. If you hold an account at several sites, as many online players do, you can then select the ones you feel will be most profitable for you.

These poker trackers are advertised on sites and forums and most offer a small free trial. Others offer a free membership period if you join one of their affiliated sites with a small deposit. Even if you have to pay a monthly subscription to use one, if you are serious about playing Sit & Go events, it is well worth the investment.

Quick Summary of Online Sit & Go Tournament Strategy

- Use poker tracker software or your own knowledge to select appropriate Sit & Go events across any of the sites of which you are a member. Do not play in a high-stake event simply because there are no low- or medium-stake events available right now – in a minute, there will be.
- Avoid 'Turbo' or 'Hi-Speed' events, which rely almost entirely on luck and reduce the influence of good play from better players.
- During First Quartile: preserve stack by taking few risks; observe opponents and style of game at your table;

keep raises high (× 4 to × 6 the big blind) to prevent multiple callers of premium hands. Avoid bluffs and speculative calls.

- During Second Quartile: loosen slightly in late position to attempt blind steals; retain substantial raises when you do play pots; keep an eye out for the average chip stack. Change gears immediately should you fall within five rounds of being blinded away.

- As you enter the Third Quartile, remain fearless as the bubble approaches: it is better to be eliminated positively now, than to limp over the line and finish just in the money but with no chance of winning.

    Attack second-to-shortest stack, or any player short, but who still stands a chance of finishing in the money. Short-stacks tend to call for gambles; mid-stacked players often fold more readily to preserve their position.

    Reduce the size of your raise to × 2 or × 3 the big blind so that you have the facility to fold to an all-in re-raise. Measure raises and re-raises against the remaining stack(s) of opponent(s) to judge whether they may feel pot-committed or, if they fold, whether they will still feel they have sufficient chips to continue.

    Remain aggressive around the bubble and don't let up once you are in the money.

- During the Fourth (and final) Quartile, you will be battling for which prize you take home. Remain aggressive and be prepared to bet/raise all-in on any above-average hand. Try to take the lead as often as possible, leaving opponents to take the make-or-break decisions.

At the end of the Sit & Go, win or lose, make notes about opponents, especially if you faced one heads-up, and then enrol for your next challenge.

Online Multi-Table Tournaments

The strategy for online MTTs is very similar to that for live-game play, although there are some small differences and additional points. Here are the most important elements to remember when trying to improve your showing in online events:

1) Play Only One Table

Remain focused on the tournament and do not be tempted into playing cash games and Sit & Gos while you are competing. Online, you are frequently moved from one table to another, and it is vital that you concentrate on learning as much about your new opponents as you possibly can. Only by observing can you decide how aggressively they are playing, how loose they might be with their chips, and how willing they might be to stake their entire tournament on a big bluff. This knowledge will convert directly to chips.

2) Take Advantage of The Breaks

All online MTTs will offer competitors a break every hour or so. It is important to stand up, stretch, take a walk, and grab some fresh air while you can. If you are successful and last deep into the event, you will have been sitting for many hours. Those who are freshest, clearest-thinking, sober and awake will have the best chance of cashing in on the really big prizes available at the Final Table.

3) Increase Raise Size Early On

Because the standard style of play online is looser than in live games, when you have a genuinely strong hand (or when you are trying to represent one) make your pre-flop raises a little larger than usual. I recommend four to four-and-a-half times the big blind, adding further if there are more than two callers ahead of you. At the very least, you want to prevent two players calling and then other players being drawn in behind them because the pot is offering such great odds.

4) Attack Cautious Players around The Bubble

Be prepared to bully and increase the level of risk around the two 'bubbles' in an online MTT. The first, genuine bubble is the point at which prize money starts to be awarded. Be aware that many online players will be delighted to make it into the money, even if they are on their last legs by then. Use your knowledge of these players to pressurize them as the bubble approaches, making more aggressive raises and all-in plays on decent draws – such as flush and open-ended straight draws. Make them put their entire tournament at risk just to call you.

From time to time, you will be called and you may require some luck. However, if you follow this strategy each time you play, you will find that the aggressive stance is usually more effective than tightening up.

The second bubble is when the Final Table beckons. Once again, you will find other players tightening up, unwilling to risk their chance to make the Final Table (and tell their friends about it). Your attitude should be that you want to play at the Final Table only if you have plenty of chips in front of you. So, once again, bully and pressurize your opponents and, for the most part, they will give in to you.

5) Understand The Pay-outs

At some point during the event, familiarize yourself with the scale of pay-outs for the event in which you are playing. Some MTTs pay much more to the Final-Table players than to anyone else; others have a sliding scale where the differences between pay-outs gradually increase towards the winner's big prize.

Set yourself a target as to where you want to finish in the event and play towards that. If a top-fifty finish pays you four times your entry fee and, realistically, that is as far as you can expect to get, then protect your bankroll as your own personal bubble approaches. However, my strong advice is almost always to play for the maximum chips available. The occasions when you might concede a premium hand in order to watch two other players battle it out are very few and far between. More importantly, if you do hold a premium hand online, the winning tactic in the long run is to play it aggressively.

6) Check That Pay-outs Are Made

Most online poker rooms have efficient accounting mechanisms but, even so, there have been instances of pay-outs not appearing in a player's accounts. When you win a prize, check that you have been credited with that amount and, if there is an error, contact the poker room immediately.

HOME GAMES

One of the most enjoyable ways to improve your game is to form a poker school of your own, with friends and acquaintances. The great thing about a poker night in a private house is that you are not at the mercy of a casino or card room for drinks, food, timings or people; there'll always be a game at the time you want, because you are organizing it! Better still, there are no table charges or house rakes.

The key to a successful home game is to ensure that you have a group who are genuinely up for meeting every week/fortnight/month and can take it in turns to host the evening. If only a couple of people have apartments or houses big enough for this task, then the others must take turns in providing food and drinks, and hosting the evening (ensuring that everyone has what they want, when they want it).

There are two downsides to Home Games; the first is that when you host an evening, it is almost inevitable that you will not have your entire brain focused on your poker. This is because you will be busy answering the door, taking phone calls, supplying food and drinks (or, at least, directions to the food and drink) and generally being a good host.

The second is the question of friendship and money –
a combination that can often cause great strife. The key
here is that whilst you are selecting your likely group of
players, and, indeed, whilst you are all meeting, you need
to keep an eye on your mates to see that they are not
losing too much money: whether it be in your game, or
generally, over all the poker games they currently play.
Once you have accepted that they can afford to lose as
well as win in your game, then you must adjust your
mindset so that you are as aggressive and ruthless against
your friends as you would be against any other opponent.
At the end of the game, you can all be friends again, with
the ties and looking-out-for-one-another attitude that
comes with the territory: that is the time to commiserate
with them if they've taken a big hit or two. During the
game itself, you simply cannot afford to take pity on
opponents; imagine a rugby or American football team
taking pity on the opposing team: it would never, ever
happen, would it? You play hard and to win. Once the
whistle has blown, that's a different matter. If you can't
bring yourself to squash and humiliate your friends, and
then squash 'em again when they are down – and take the
same treatment yourself – then don't play poker with
friends.

So, having established all that, you have put together a
group of about twice as many people as you want. That is
to say, if you want to play an eight-player game, you'd
better have sixteen potential players to ensure that you
have a quorum each time that you want to play.

Finally, someone has to take on the onerous task of
being game manager or secretary. To try to sustain a game
without one person being in charge of telephone calls, e-
mails, acceptances, etc., will almost inevitably lead to
trouble at some point. However, I don't think you will
find it too hard to identify people in your game to act as

managers, since there are so many people who love being in charge of anything.

My recommendation would be to use e-mail. It's cheap and reduces the need to suffer endless answer-machines and broken promises of return calls. To e-mail your school with the time and date of the next game allows you to run a first-come, first-served system to encourage prompt replies without the need to follow up messages. If they don't reply, they're probably not keen enough for your poker game. In this way, you can quickly fill each game you arrange, with a waiting list (in the order they responded) so that you never need suffer a short-handed game again.

Cash or Account?

In those good old days as a hustling poker player, you'd be on the road and visiting a different town week by week or even day by day. In any of these places, you were the outsider and if you played poker and won, the locals were inclined to take against you, either individually or as a group. Bankrolls were seized, usually at gunpoint, and you guarded your cash with your life. Thankfully, these days, no one pays much attention to the Home Games, but if you live in a part of the world where going home with a wad of notes (be it $100 or $10,000) is likely to provoke attention or place you in danger, then clearly to arrange an account system is a good idea.

- You can have an arrangement where losers deposit cheques into one designated account, which are not cashed for three months in case they can win it back.
- You can run a tab system, where everyone's pluses and minuses are entered into a ledger, initialled by the player, and that account is settled twice a year: losers paying and winners cashing out. If the poker game you

are playing in is reasonably well-balanced, this should result in small payments moving between players as the luck element evens itself up somewhat over the given period.

- You can play for lower stakes with all losses being paid into a holding pot. Twice a year, that pot can then be used for:

dinner out for the entire poker school;

first prize in your own tourney where the winnings might pay for an entry to a big poker tournament, or major satellite for a WSOP event or WPT event;

a big donation to charity.

Cash Game or Tournament

The main advantage of a **cash game** is that everyone can stay in for as long as they want or their bankroll allows. Players can arrive and leave early or late; drop in and out of the game; take a break for a drink, meal or smoke; and the whole session is likely to be more relaxed and, certainly, require less organization.

However, disciplined players may pass a lot of hands and play only a few strongly so that you find that the game tightens up and stays that way. Largely, what happens to a regular cash game will depend upon the characters within the game and how their styles of play fit, or do not fit, with one another.

Increasingly, **home tournaments** have become popular, since they offer a fixed entry fee (plus, perhaps, rebuys and add-ons), so no one has to worry about losing too much money. They also offer a big profit to the winner, and a decent return for second place (and, depending upon the number of entrants, third and fourth places too) and the timing of the session can be reasonably exact. For example, if you want to play for three hours, it should be possible to structure the event to last almost exactly that length of time.

Another benefit is that you can run mini-satellites for events in casinos and poker rooms. For example, if ten players each put in $25 to a home tournament, the winner – if he takes all – would have earned $250, which might pay for an entry into a regional poker event, or maybe a satellite to something really big, like a WSOP or WPT event. The big downside of a home-game tournament is that, once you are eliminated, it's the end of the poker for you.

Some home games now combine a **tournament with a cash game**, which forms as players are knocked out of the tourney and other players arrive a little later in the evening. This can often be the best combination, since the money-winners from the tournament often join the cash game late, with bulging bankrolls, and frequently flash some cash about to keep everyone happy.

To see how to structure and run a tournament, a selection of home-games tips, and some winning strategies, take a look at our Home Game Poker Guide at the end of this section.

Forms of Cash Game

Dealer's Choice
This is still the most popular variation in home games – certainly in the USA. Either the dealer picks the form of poker just for his deal, or for a whole round, until the deal returns to the player on his right.

As well as alternating between popular forms of the game such as Hold 'Em and Omaha, Dealer's Choice usually features fairly mad variations featuring wild cards, draws and swaps, hi-lo variations and pot-building multiple-betting rounds.

In their favour, these games usually aren't dull. Unfortunately, the wilder the variation, the less skill is required or, indeed, rewarded. This is purely entertainment poker, often accompanied by a good deal of drinking, eating and making merry. But, it is not the type of game to get into if you are seeking to improve your own game and gain experience.

This is not to say that there aren't some poker schools of the very highest calibre who play Dealer's Choice. But the choices will usually be between established forms of the game, the stakes high, and the skill level even higher.

As mentioned elsewhere, for players trying to improve their game, swapping from one poker variation to another is not the best way of establishing a disciplined rhythm. However, to become a truly well-rounded poker player, it's important to gain experience in as many different forms and variations as you can, so, for more experienced players, a Dealer's Choice game may hit all the spots.

Single Variation Games

When you settle down to play just one variation of poker for a whole evening, you are committing yourself to a level of mindset and concentration which, if achieved, will almost certainly add to your knowledge and experience of the game, and this is certainly my personal preference. Many players start off playing casual, fun-based home games and then tire of the high luck factor. This is why, at the time of writing, more and more players seem to be opting for more serious styles of play – including sticking to one form of the game for the whole session.

By far the most common form of home game is to play a Limit Hold 'Em cash game. Whatever form of Limit poker you decide to play, you should also define your re-buying rules.

The most common structure would be to allow a re-buy the moment a player drops below 50 per cent of his original buy-in. So, if everyone starts with $100 each, when they fall below $50, they can top up their bankrolls to a maximum of $100 in front of them. This ensures that no one can lose too much on any single hand, but also prevents players from being forced to play short-stack poker until they go bust. Some poker schools prefer that latter method, allowing you all-in opportunities. However, there are complex strategies for playing short-stack Limit poker and, unless you are familiar with them, it is better to play with a full stack if you possibly can.

With the amount of poker being shown on television, almost all of which is No-Limit Texas Hold 'Em, more and more private games are switching to that form of the game. The problem is often that whilst the coverage on television is of fast and furious, hyper-aggressive tournament play, a No-Limit cash game is still one which requires great discipline. I think that this means that a disciplined, self-aware poker player, even of modest ability, can do pretty well in a No-Limit game, because the vast majority of players are too impatient and too loose to be able to win consistently.

One of the psychological problems of winning consistently in a home game, made up of friends and colleagues, is that, without doubt, a slow, patient approach will lead to success. However, in many home games, you will be teased mercilessly by the other players for being tight and slow and even frightened. If you can resist the catcalls and jibes and just focus on your game, you can prevail but, if you are affected by this teasing, and, consequently, you loosen your game, you may end up losing in a game in which you should really succeed. When strangers taunt me, I find it quite easy to resist; when my friends provoke me, I usually rise to the bait because I sense a need to keep everyone happy and entertained and enjoying their poker, even though it's not my sole responsibility to be ensuring this.

Many poker schools have been reluctant to swap to No-Limit, because they are afraid that the money side of the evening will get out of hand. It is certainly true that a No-Limit game can up the overall turnover of cash in a game, but there are ways of controlling this. The simplest is to allow add-ons and take-downs.

In this form, every player buys in for an agreed amount – let's keep it at $100 for the sake of simplicity. Anyone who dips below $100 can, if they wish, top up their chips so that they have $100 in front of them. Anyone who wins and has more than $100 in front of them at the table can take this excess down and pocket it, provided that they leave a minimum of $100 on the table.

This ensures that you can't lose more than $100 on any given hand, allows you to play short-stacked if you want to, and permits a successful player to take some of his winnings off the table if he wishes, so that he can control any change in fortunes and lock away some profits.

Generally, you will find that, after playing the above methods for a few sessions, you all get an idea as to how much you want to put at risk for a session of No-Limit poker and you can then adjust your house rules accordingly. Most cash games I play in are friendly but highly competitive. We agree that the original buy-in is fixed and that you can have two further buy-ins of the same amount. After that, you have lost enough for the evening and you have to bow out. This protects anyone on tilt and keeps the game pretty friendly. As much as you might want someone in your game who just blows money every session, enriching the whole school – and it is necessary to have someone like this from time to time to keep all the players happy – I think that it is only ethical to know that this player can afford his losses and to offer him some form of protection against too many losses. Doubtless there will be poker players reading this and thinking that I am deluded but, for me, that is one of the big differences between a home game and poker club or casino. In the latter establishments, it is up to the players themselves to deal with their wins and losses and you must not worry about it. I believe that in a home-game poker school, ideally, everybody, but certainly somebody, should be able to have a word with the big losers to check that all is well for them. However, that done, once their money is on the table, then it is fair game for you to target it with all the resources at your disposal.

How to Run a Home-Game Tournament

To play a No-Limit tournament is always fun. The action is usually exciting from the very first hand and, whilst there is always more luck in a time-limited tournament than in a long, rolling cash game, the better players should rise to the surface over time.

Tournaments seem to work better for larger groups also – a ten-player cash game can be quite a dull affair, particularly if you are trying to win and you are playing tight. Finally, the fact that players know how much the evening will cost them is a reassurance to many. Amongst my poker-playing friends, tournaments are now the mainstays of their home games and, even those who have played cash games for years now play a mixture of tourneys and cash games.

If you have never run a tournament before, here's the perfect guide for you to become the ultimate poker host.

Equipment

Table

Preferably, round or square, large enough to hold the number of players you are inviting. It is better to have too big a table than too small, since standing up to deal is quite a common sight in poker rooms. In addition, there is nothing worse than finding yourself with no elbow room, zero privacy and not even a place for a cold drink. If you must play on a small table, make sure that there are side tables, window ledges or shelves on to which people can place drinks.

Personally, I'd avoid like the plague those cheap, plastic table tops with nasty baize, cup holders and chip trays. They look horrible, feel cheap and sleazy (but not in a good way) and will make you feel like you are slumming it.

Table Cover

Ideally, some green, dark-blue or deep-red baize or velvet, all available from the high street. However, a blanket or a standard tablecloth will also serve your purposes. If you are playing on top of a shiny table, you may want to attach to the surface of the table, at each side with a small piece of sticky-tape, some old newspapers. This will cut down movement of the cloth on which you are playing and means that when you pull in your pot, you don't pull over everyone else's stacks, drinks and ashtrays.

Poker Chips

Poker chips are available everywhere now and there are some great deals on the Internet. I recommend at least four different colours and a robust carry-case with strong latches (to prevent accidental openings in the street during transport). There are two main styles: cheaper plastic chips, which are light and feel nasty, and the heavier clay-style chips which are used in most casinos and card rooms. The fact that the price of these chips has fallen so much in the last few years means that even the most modest home game should be able to afford a decent set.

Make sure that you bargain into your online deal (or purchase separately) a **Dealer Button** to complete your professional layout.

The minimum for tournament play would be 300 chips, ideally, 500. Many sites allow you to order your chips in bundles of 25 or 50 and you should take care to order your colours carefully.

I like to use Las-Vegas-casino colours for my chips:

Red   = $5
Green   = $25
Black   = $100
White/Blue = $500

If you are regularly going to run tournaments, you will probably start with $1,000 or $1,500 worth of chips for each player.

If you plan to order 500 chips, I would recommend ordering the following selection:

  50   white or blue chips
150   red chips
150   green chips
150   black chips

This will give you sufficient chips for almost any eventuality and avoid the common mistake of having far too many high-value chips and not enough lower-value denominations.

To begin with, you might want to print out a little key to the value of the chips, so that everyone can see. The smartest way to do this is to place one of each of those chips in a neat row in a computer scanner. Having scanned the image, type in the value of each chip beneath it and then print out on a colour printer. This looks smart and professional and will ensure that players don't waste time asking everyone what the chip colours mean.

Format of The Game

The organizer of the game must decide on the style of the game. In this example, the tournament featured will be No-Limit Texas Hold 'Em. The buy-in will be $100, for which each player will receive $1,500 in chips. We will also have re-buys and add-ons.

Re-buys

If you play without the opportunity to re-buy, you will make the game much tighter as players are terrified of being knocked out within a few minutes of the game beginning. It is probably the way to improve your game, since it makes it tighter, but as a home game is supposed to be entertaining also, re-buys are often popular. They also boost the prize pot and that is always welcome. Indeed, sometimes you get so many re-buys, so frequently, that you end up with a huge prize pot. If you have resisted re-buying (or adding-on) and you then go on to win the event, you'll find that you have made a huge return on your money. Indeed, if your style follows that suggested within the pages of this book, you'll find that you rarely re-buy, and that you are playing with a great chance of winning a substantial prize.

How you introduce re-buys into your game is another consideration. The more you permit, the looser and more aggressive the early rounds of play will be, since players will try to build an enormous stack, knowing that, even if they go bust, they can re-buy into the tournament. If you want to lower the skill factor but increase the prize money, then make the re-buys cheaper than the buy-in. For example, you might say that if you go bust, you can re-buy for the full $1,500 of chips for $50 (rather than the $100 for which you bought in). This will make everyone hyper-aggressive and the prize pot will grow hugely (probably two to three times what the initial buy-ins contributed). However, don't expect much subtlety in the style of play if that is your format.

Most re-buy periods last for the first hour of an event. If you make it longer than this, there will be more chips in play and the skill factor will reduce even further as the blinds continue to rise; players will be forced into making big decisions quickly for all their chips.

In my view, the best format is to make re-buys available at a small premium (to reward those who do not re-buy) and also to ensure that if you do lose all your chips, your re-buy doesn't put you back ahead of the patient, disciplined players.

To this end, I would propose that you can re-buy at any time your chip stack falls below 50 per cent of the starting stack. The cost of buying half your starting stack should be a little more than the original buy-in: so, make it $60 for 750 chips. This way, players who take a substantial hit early on can get back into the tournament at a small premium, boosting the prize pot, but not adding too much to the rate of inflation at your table.

Add-ons
An add-on is an opportunity to purchase further chips to add to your stack before the tournament becomes a freeze-out (when you've lost your chips you are out).

At the end of the re-buy period – say, the first hour of play – if you wish to offer an add-on, this will also swell the prize pot because almost everyone will take it. Again, the price should be at a small premium to the original buy-in. I would offer half the original stack (750 chips) for $60, but you might offer a figure equal to the original buy-in (1,500 chips) for $120 or even $150.

The more chips you allow players to add-on, the more important it will be for them to do so – or risk falling substantially behind the others – so, once again, the figure will depend on how keen you are to increase the prize pot and how much everyone wants to stake for an evening's tournament. This is something your entire poker school needs to discuss so that you are all happy with the arrangements for your game. Naturally, you can also trial different elements so that players can judge whether or not they like the latest innovation.

Once the add-ons have been purchased, anyone losing all their chips is eliminated.

Prizes

How you choose to distribute prize money is, again, a decision which should be taken by your entire school (or, at least, the founding, regular-attending members) but, generally, I would suggest the following:

5 players or fewer: winner takes 100% of prize pot
6–8 players: winner takes 70%; runner-up 30%
9–10 players: winner takes 50%; runner-up 30%; third 20%

These are fairly standard pay-outs and reward the player who actually wins rather than those who just hang around by playing ultra-tight.

The organizer should announce the prize scale at the outset of play and then fill in the detail after the add-ons and re-buys are completed so that everyone knows for what they are playing.

Organizer

I think that every game should have an organizer who, for this game at least, is in charge. You may make this the person hosting the game, the most experienced player in the school, or swap roles each time you meet.

Do you really need to go to all this trouble just for a casual game of poker at home? My answer would be yes. Whenever money is involved, small or great, amongst friends or strangers, there is always the potential for disagreements or arguments. I like to foresee these situations and head them off before they occur and, for that reason, having one person in charge of each game is a sound idea.

The organizer should state at the beginning of the game what are the house rules so that everyone knows in advance of play.

So far, my recommended announcements would be:

- length of play – let's say 3–4 hours
- buy-in $100 for 1,500 chips
- re-buys for first hour when stacks fall below 750 chips
- re-buy costs $60 for 750 chips
- at the end of the hour, an add-on will be offered: $60 for 750 chips

Blinds

A tournament creates so much action because the level of blinds is raised regularly. You can structure those blinds according to how long you want your event to last and, although you can never predict exactly the duration, you can do pretty well by following the table. This shows what the blinds should be and how often they should rise. The organizer needs to keep an eye on the clock and apply these blind raises strictly to time so that no one feels that they are running into a rise in the blinds deliberately.

Timings
The shorter the tournament, the more luck comes to the fore; certainly, aggression is often rewarded. The longer your event, the more the skill factor rises. You must decide what sort of game suits your school and whether your friends would enjoy two or three quick tournaments or one long, more skilful one. I'd certainly opt for the latter.

Quick Events
If you have a short-handed game, say, 4–6 players, it may work better to play several short tournaments so that a player knocked out knows that there will be another game starting relatively soon.

For a quick event, raise the blinds after every round – once everyone has been dealer at each level. If a player gets knocked out, raise the blinds immediately. This usually results in a tournament lasting between 45 minutes and an hour.

Longer Events
For longer events, everything from two hours upwards, you can follow the table overleaf to show you what the blinds should be and how often they should change. If the pace seems too fast or too slow, the organizer can delay the blind raise, or add in a blind raise each time a player is eliminated.

In the table overleaf, the length of each round is set at 20 minutes. This will produce a tournament which is likely to last up to four hours.

To reduce the likely running time to three hours, simply

adjust the round length to 15 minutes before each blind raise.

For a two-hour event, reduce the round length to ten minutes and raise the blinds every time a player is eliminated.

Table: Home-Game Tournament

7–10 players; 1,500 chip buy-in; with re-buys and add-on

Estimated Time: 4 hours

Level	Round length	Blind Sizes
1	20 minutes	10/20
2	20 minutes	25/50
3	20 minutes	50/100
4	20 minutes	75/150
5	20 minutes	100/200
6	20 minutes	150/300
7	20 minutes	200/400
8	20 minutes	300/600
9	20 minutes	400/800
10	20 minutes	500/1,000
11	20 minutes	750/1,500
12	20 minutes	1,000/2,000

Re-buys available during levels 1–3
Add-On offered at conclusion of level 3
Total prize money declared during level 4

Basic Rules and Requirements for Poker Games

I would propose that all rulings are done in a friendly style so no one feels that anyone else is throwing their weight around. There are really only a few rules which need to be applied to ensure a smooth running of the game.

1) Cut for Table Positions and Dealer

Since your table position, in relation to others, is crucial and can make a huge difference to your chances of success or an early exit, you must randomize the seating positions in every game.

At the start of the game, get everyone to pick a card from the face-down outspread deck, and place it in front of themselves, face up. The player showing the highest card is the dealer and picks his seat. The next highest card sits on his right, the next highest card on that player's right, and so on, until the lowest card is in the small-blind position and the next-to-lowest is in the big-blind position.

If two or more players pick cards of the same number, then an order of rank for the suits kicks in, similar to that in the game of bridge.

Spades   (is the highest ranking suit)
Hearts
Diamonds
Clubs   (is the lowest ranking suit)

This ranking does not apply at any other time in the game of poker.

2) Keep your Cards above The Table

This is a sensible rule because not only does it reduce the chance that anyone might cheat (I have known cards swapped under the table even in a friendly home game) but it also makes it much easier for the dealer to see who is still in the hand when indicating to players whose turn it is to act.

I usually like to make a joke of it by pointing to a light

fitting in the ceiling and telling players that they must keep their cards and chips where the cameras can see them. Some of the more naive newcomers in the game actually believe that there are cameras up there and they behave impeccably.

3) State your Actions Audibly

To prevent string bets (where a player puts down some chips and then tries to add some more to them) and skulduggery, all players in your game should state 'Fold' or 'Pass', 'Call' or 'Raise'. When 'Raise' has been stated, players must then either announce the size of the raise or place their bet clearly. If you fail to announce your action then, if you are betting, it is taken to be a call.

4) Don't Retain your Cards while The Deck Is Being Shuffled

Many players become so enamoured of their winning hands that they hang on to their cards even when the hand is over. They are mentally staring at them (usually because they have just won a hand, or because they have just taken a bad beat). Either way, this disturbs the shuffle and holds up the game. Propose a fine for any player who, after two warnings, fails to give back their cards: maybe, he should pay the price of a small blind and give it to every other player at the table. That usually works wonders for people's concentration!

5) Side Pots

For some, the concept of a side pot is incredibly simple; for others, it seems an impenetrable science. Forming side pots is necessary when players become short-stacked and go all-in, but there is still further betting amongst other players at the table.

Let's look at an example:

Three players remain at the table.
Player A has 3,500 chips
Player B has 2,000 chips
Player C has 500 chips

On this hand, player A – on the button – raises to 200
Player B calls this raise
Player C re-raises, going all-in for his last 500 chips
Player A re-raises again, making his bet a total of 1,000 chips
Player B calls

There needs to be a side pot because Player C has contributed only 500 chips to this pot. He cannot win more from other players than he has contributed himself.

So, 500 chips from each player, plus any blind bets, get placed in the main pot in the middle of the table. This pot is now fixed and can be won by any of the three players in the hand.

The remaining chips (in this case, 500 each from Players A and B) go into a side pot. This pot can be won only by Players A and B, and it can be boosted by those players if there is further betting on the flop, turn and river.

At the end, the side pot is decided first, either because player A or B folds, or at the showdown.

Once the side pot has been awarded, Player C shows his cards to claim the main pot, or folds his hand and concedes.

If the blind bets exceed the amount that the all-in player has left, then only the blind bets up to the value of the all-in player's chips can be added to the pot, and the remaining amount from the blinds goes into the side pot or, in the event that no one calls the all-in bet, is returned to the big-blind player and, if applicable, to the small-blind also.

The key to remember here is: a short-stacked all-in player cannot win more than his stake from any other player or the blinds. That money, and only that money, is placed in the main pot. All other stakes enter the side pot or are refunded.

6) Split Pots

If a pot is split and the total cannot be halved precisely, I recommend that any small extra amount is given to the shorter-stacked player. For example, if there are 475 chips in the pot and it is split between two players, since the smallest denomination of chip in play is 5, the player with the bigger overall stack receives 235, the shorter-stack, 240.

7) Keep The Game Moving

Finally, and probably most importantly, whoever is in charge of the game must ensure that it keeps moving. It is all too easy to waste a huge proportion of playing time chatting and arguing whilst the cards are being shuffled. The organizer needs to keep an eye on the shuffler and dealer to make sure that they keep up the pace.

In my view, if a player is faced with a tough decision, I think that he should be given time to make that decision. However, once too much time is taken, the organizer should announce, 'One minute remaining', and count aloud at 45 seconds, 30 seconds, 10 seconds and then a countdown. If the slow player has failed to act when the count reaches zero, he is deemed to have folded.

One innovation which features in many home games in which I play is the 'Two-Deck Solution'. Although it is not traditional, having two differently-coloured decks of cards in play does make sense. While one deck is being dealt, the player to his right is shuffling the other deck ready to pass over for the following deal. In this way, no time is wasted on the shuffling (which should, in any case, be thorough) and the extra time gained can be used to play more hands and take time when close decisions present themselves. I am slowly becoming converted to using two decks for home games because it leaves maximum time for the reason why we are all gathered together: to play cards!

You don't need to announce all these ideas at the outset of every game, but you might show your school this section, or print out copies, so that everyone knows the basic rules of your home game. Once again, this may seem like a bit of work but, with money and egos involved, it is a great idea to have everything agreed before play commences.

LIMIT HOLD 'EM

It's widely played in casinos and card rooms, and is still popular in home games throughout the world. The stakes are limited and so are the liabilities: you'll have to win or lose a string of big hands to end up with a serious profit or a bankroll wipe-out. This makes it sociable, seemingly more gentle, sometimes even predictable. Whilst those traits may make the game sound slow or boring to you, to others these are attributes which make it their game of choice.

In this section we'll talk about casino and card-room limit poker – and you will soon see what differs from your home game. If you're going to Las Vegas, or venturing into a card club or casino for the first time, this is the information that you'll need to enable you to fit right in.

Stakes

First off, you'll need to decide on your stake. Largely, this will depend on your own bankroll as it's not necessarily true that the standard improves with the size of the stakes. Certainly, if you are making your first appearance in a card room or casino, play your first game at a low-stake table to give yourself time to get used to the etiquette, speed, and style of the game. Even if you are a decent player, opponents at higher-stake tables are likely to latch on quickly to the fact that you are a new face in town and will use that information to intimidate you and to make better decisions against you. Players at the lowest-stake tables are usually more interested in their own cards than in the behaviour of the other players.

Make your first port of call, in a new card room, the manager's desk. There you can talk to card-room staff about which games get started when, and which table or tables you would like to join. Sometimes you will be directed straight into a seat; more often, you'll have to wait a few minutes for a seat to become free. Use this time to observe the action at other tables so that you quickly become familiar with the etiquette of the games played in this particular card room.

The stakes at each table may be displayed simply as: $3/6 Limit Hold 'Em – meaning that for the first two rounds of betting, pre-flop and on the flop, the bets and raises must be exactly $3; for the second two rounds, on the turn and on the river, the bets and raises must be exactly $6. When displayed like this, you must ask, or better still, observe the size of the blinds.

Alternatively, you may see the stakes advertised as: Limit Hold Em $1-$3-$6-$6; this shows that the small blind is $1 (the big blind will be double the small blind), the first two rounds of betting, $3 and the final two rounds, $6.

Bear in mind that, if you are playing tight (as you should be), even if you fold every hand, you will committed to posting the blinds. At $1 and $2, that's $3 per round. At four to five rounds per hour at a full table (more in a short-handed game), that's costing you $12-$15 per hour just to sit there and grit your teeth. Now, think about the bigger blinds that will operate in the $10/$20 and $30/$60 games. This must be a consideration when you choose your stake.

House Rules

The house or table rules should be displayed close to the stake sign. Study these carefully at another table before you sit down in your own game, so that you are aware of any peculiarities.

Usually, house rules will state most of the following: one player only per hand; check and raise permitted; maximum three (maybe five) raises per round (sometimes heads-up pots are excluded from this regulation); no string bets; food at table; dress code; behavioural regulations; card room manager's decision is final.

Picking your Table: Tips for Picking The Right Game for you

If you are playing in a busy, popular card room, you may well have the choice of several low-limit tables. Pick your table (and, if possible, your seat) very carefully. Good game selection is a long-term big-money winner, and you should start the practice immediately. Let's take a look at the outward signs to which you should attend:

Tables to avoid:
- Silent, concentrated, humourless tables, where the players are taking the game very seriously.
- Tables where everyone seems to be a regular: if they all know one another, they may deliberately, or subconsciously, gang up on you when you cut into their game. Look to see if, when a new player joins their game, they glance at each other knowingly, or whether they seem relaxed and recognize the new player.

- Tables where casino employees tell you there are good players, or local 'pros'. The most dangerous low-limit players are the locals who have all the time in the world, have got used to being ultra-patient, and who make their money slowly but surely by grinding out profits from impatient 'tourists'.

Tables to which you should make a beeline:
- Noisy, friendly, talkative tables. You want people to be having such a good time that they don't mind losing a bit of money to you.
- Tables with plenty of alcohol being consumed. Outright drunks slow down the game, but relaxed, drinking players are usually loose and ready to gamble, which is what you want them to do.
- Tables with anxious, nervous players: players who fiddle, diddle and dawdle; players who play too many hands because they are bored and want to do something with their hands (both their poker hands and the hands attached to their wrists); nail-biting, ring-twiddling players; people looking at their watches because they have only a limited time in which to play and will therefore play too many, sub-standard hands which are odds-on to lose.
- Tables with players playing out of their chip racks – a real amateur, inexperienced move.
- Rich, glamorous, well-dressed people, who are probably thinking that this poker lark is just the kind of excitement they are looking for and which makes them feel like James Bond. These people will play way too many hands.
- Ladies, or men, who are wearing a lot of expensive jewellery: this won't have been paid for from poker winnings, trust me. (NB: this is not true if you encounter Phil Hellmuth Jnr wearing all ten of his WSOP gold bracelets.)

Buying In

How you buy into a game will depend upon the card room or casino in which you are playing. Some will expect you to visit the cashier to exchange your cash for chips (or checks); others will allow you to sit down and hail a card-room employee to change your cash into chips for you.

Finally, in a few card rooms, chips may be purchased at the table from the dealer. However you physically get your hands on your chips, they will probably come in plastic racks for easy transportation. When you sit down, take the chips out of the racks, or, at least, sufficient chips for you to play without having to dip into them, and stick your empty racks under your chair.

To play with the chips from the racks is a very amateur move which usually slows down the game as you struggle to take out the bet you want to make. I've seen racks knocked over, chips flying all over the table and on to the carpets (casino carpets are usually highly-patterned so that they don't show stains – this has the effect of not showing the chips either, so you may well lose money in the pattern of the carpets). So, take the chips out and stack them professionally.

For how much should you buy-in? In my opinion, you should always buy-in for the maximum you can afford. If you have $300 with which to play, don't buy-in for $100, lose it and re-buy for another $100. You'll look cheap and, far more importantly, you'll feel cheap. Buy-in for the full $300 at the beginning. Keep $100 back in a rack, perhaps, and play with $200, but have the money on the table.

Apart from giving the impression that you are a serious and determined player, at the table for the long term, you will also feel under less pressure than if you are constantly playing short-stacked. Let's say you lose a pot relatively early on which costs you $30. Instead of that being almost a third (30 per cent) of your bankroll gone, it is actually only a tenth (10 per cent). Just that simple mental analysis can make a big difference to you psychologically. Losing 10 per cent of your bankroll is an everyday (several times every day) occurence; losing 30 per cent shouldn't be.

Demeanour

When you arrive at a table, by all means say hello and acknowledge greetings. After that, batten down the chat hatches and get yourself sorted out and ready to play. You will always be given time to do this, and you are usually not required to play the first round of blinds which come to you, giving you time to prepare and observe the action at the table. Look serious and focused and don't get drawn into conversations with other players yet. If, subsequently, you discover that this is a friendly table and that you can concentrate on your game without a problem, then there is no harm in joining in. However, at the outset, assume that any interaction with other players will simply serve to help them gauge the type of player you are. Poker is, intrinsically, a game of information, and you want to provide as little as possible to your opponents.

The Rake

Depending on where you play, the casino or card room will take a rake from each pot. This may be anything from 1 per cent to 5 per cent, up to an advertised maximum. This is taken only from the pot, and so affects you only if you win the pot. If you are playing in a busy, popular card room or casino, the rake will be reasonable; rooms where the rake system is too aggressive soon empty out. The good news is that since there are more card rooms than ever these days, there is more competition to provide low rakes, good service, pleasant surroundings, free drinks, freebies and surprise give-aways (such as bad-beat jack-pots and royal-flush bonuses). Ask at the manager's desk which of these are available and how to qualify for them.

Tipping

Tipping is still prohibited in some countries (such as the UK) but in most card rooms and casinos, dealers expect a tip and, by and large, deserve to be tipped. Most dealers are paid only a basic wage and rely on tips to supplement their income. If they are friendly, efficient and enthusias-tic, then each time you win a pot, a tip is probably in order. The size of the tip will depend upon the stake you play, the size of the pot, your generosity and, probably most im-portantly, the general policy of the regular players in the game. After all, the dealer cannot directly influence the outcome of any hand for you, so the tip cannot be said to be 'incentivizing'. Generally, if a hand is decided pre-flop, there would be neither rake taken nor tip expected. After that, small-pot winners in a low-limit game might tip 50c (you might throw a $1 chip to the dealer and say, or gesture, 'chop' – meaning, take half). For bigger pots, a dollar would be appropriate. Remember that the dealer will receive between twenty and fifty tips per hour, so it all adds up for them. Most importantly, fit in with the actions of the table and don't draw attention to yourself by tipping too big or too small. Since you will have observed several hands, both whilst waiting to sit at a table and after you have taken your seat, you should have a good idea of the etiquette at any given card room.

Choice of Seats

Often you'll have to go where you're put but, if you find that the player on your right is one of those who is constantly raising and re-raising so that you are seeing little or no action, declare to the dealer that you would like to swap seats when another becomes available. Most of what happens in card rooms is done on a first-come, first-served basis, so the sooner you tell the dealer, the higher up the list you will be for any movement of seats.

Changing Tables

Don't like the table you find yourself at? Either straight away or after a few people have come and gone? Don't just sit there. Get up and put your name down for a seat at another table. No other table? Then leave. There is another day. To sit at a table where you are not winning and not enjoying yourself and you feel you may be outclassed or, at least, in a poor position, is foolish in the extreme. It is up to you to influence your playing conditions as much as possible. It is part of the game and, if you want to win, it must be taken seriously.

General Tips for Card Rooms and Casino Games

Have an open-ended time schedule or, at least, plenty of time to play. If you are thinking about time, you are not thinking about your game. Don't go to a casino or card room with friends or relatives with whom you are sharing transport. One of you will want to stop playing before the other and, inevitably, that will affect you negatively: you may play for too long in a poor game for you, just to use up time; you may leave a highly-profitable game just because your mate needs to get home in time to stop his wife throwing out his dinner, leaving him, and spending a night of passion with her orthodontist!

Don't Drink
My advice would be not to drink at all, but I don't drink anyway, so that's easy for me to say. At the very least don't, whatever you do, get drunk and blow seven hours of careful, profitable play in the last hour of drunken shenanigans.

Don't Explain, Don't Complain
One of the best poker tips of all time should be etched in your brain – or, failing that, on your forehead – forever. However lucky or unlucky you may be, whatever brilliance or stupidity you unleash upon your opponents, just stay quiet.

Stay out of Arguments
Don't get involved in bad-beat recriminations (there's lots more on this later on) or arguments, especially when you are not involved in the hand. Stay quiet, keep your own counsel and look like you've seen it all before and it really doesn't bother you.

Take your Winnings
If you win the pot, get your hands on those chips before you give the dealer your cards. This stops any disputes head-on, saves time, and looks professional.

By the way, don't, as some of my friends do, fall so in love with your hand, you forget to give the cards back to the dealer. It happens occasionally and it drives both the dealer and everyone else at your table barmy.

Strategy for Low-Limit Hold 'Em Cash Games

Limit Hold 'Em Playing Styles

Because the size of every bet and raise is limited, the opportunity to vary your play with big changes of betting style is eliminated. This makes Limit Hold 'Em a much more statistical game than No-Limit (and, for ease, we'll include Pot-Limit with No-Limit from now on).

When deciding on your starting hands – those hole cards with which you will enter the betting in any given position – you must be aware that the overall size of the pot is limited and therefore the 'upside' of any action is limited. Whereas at No-Limit, you might speculate on playing low suited connectors, knowing that if you hit the right flop, you might win an absolutely massive pot, even against a single opponent, at Limit Hold 'Em, there is, really, a natural limit to any pot (excluding those weird and wonderful pots where two players repeatedly raise one another to the limit on each round of the betting). For that reason, to succeed at Limit Hold 'Em, especially when played for relatively low limits, you must be far more selective about starting hands and make speculative calls – if ever – only when there are many players in the pot and you stand to win a decent pot in relation to your risk. In simple terms, this means when your pot odds are fairly easy to calculate and – what I like to call – your potential pot odds (when one or more players come along with you when you've made your hand) can be only a pretty small addition to the standard pot odds. So, Limit is based more on odds and statistics than No-Limit and, at low limits, particularly in a full game, bluffing is almost redundant: there's usually someone who'll call you down to the end.

What does all this mean for our strategy? Hopefully, you've worked it out for yourself: a tight, disciplined approach to starting hands, odds-based reasoning for draws and an almost complete absence of bluffing except when short-handed or heads-up, or when you genuinely feel that there is evidence that such a play has merit.

Basic Strategy

How you play will determine how well you will do as a player. My strategies for all forms of Texas Hold 'Em tend to be on the conservative, disciplined side and this may not suit you. However, when starting out, either as a general poker player, or as a participant in a new variation of the game, tight is definitely right as a way to begin.

The point about Limit Hold 'Em is that there will be far more showdowns than in No-Limit and that simply means one thing: the vast majority of the time, you'll have to have the best hand to win.

In order to play a variety of hands therefore, position is going to be crucial to avoid your losing endless calls which are subsequently raised. In simple terms, the earlier the position pre-flop, the stronger you must be to play; as you near the button, an increasing number of hands can be added to your calling/raising repertoire.

Since many players like low-limit Hold 'Em because it costs them relatively little to see a flop, pre-flop raises should generally be respected as showing very strong hands. In fact, at Limit, there are occasions when to raise, even with a premium hand, is not necessarily the best policy. However, most players, including you, do best by playing their cards honestly: raising with great hands, calling with good hands and mucking the rest. If you stay patient (that word is going to rear its ugly head with the regularity of an unloved television commercial) and disciplined pre-flop, you will succeed at Limit Hold 'Em in the long run. Which brings me naturally to the point at which I remind you that no session of poker is of much consequence: out of a lifetime of poker, it really doesn't matter if you win or lose; whether you suffer bad beats galore or hit a couple of long-shot draws to wipe out the table. The most important element is that you are playing as well as you can, making the right decisions at the right time, and always – but always – striving to continue to improve your knowledge and skills.

Starting Hands and Pre-Flop Action

All ideas about starting hands and, indeed, all strategy, are going to vary depending on your own preferred style and that of your opponents. In simple terms, if the player two places to your left regularly raises, you will have to be more selective about which cards you can call originally. You may find that when you raise, this same character always folds. Knowing the likely action of your opponents is a huge advantage.

Which hands qualify as suitable starting hands will largely depend upon your position. Assuming a full (-ish) table of nine players:

Early Position: the first three players to act to the left of the big blind. These are the most dangerous positions since you have no information from the other players yet, and they still have to act, giving them the opportunity to raise or re-raise before the action returns to you or a flop is seen. For this reason, you must be at your most disciplined and selective in this position.

Middle Position: the fourth and fifth players to act after the big blind. You have seen a third of the table act, and you will be in a decent position to act post-flop, since the blinds must act before you from now on.

You may add further cards into your starting-hand category.

Late Position: one from the button and on the button. These are the most flexible positions, having allowed you to see the action from all the early- and middle-position players before you have to decide on what action to take. Only in these positions should you consider playing speculative and drawing starting hands. At least here, the chances of a pre-flop raise are now small and you will get to see a flop cheaply. Obviously, for more aggressive players, this position offers the best opportunity for a raise, ensuring a late-position decision post-flop if you receive any callers.

The Blinds: Even less attractive than at No-Limit, the blinds offer the worst position throughout the deal. At Limit Hold 'Em it is almost always wrong to make speculative calls in the small blind. What you save in a session by not calling in the small blind will be equivalent to a couple of decent-sized pots.

Early-Position Starting Hands
As you would expect, the negative elements of this position demand that you take a disciplined approach to which hands you should play.

AA
KK
QQ
AK – suited or unsuited
AQ – suited or unsuited

That's it. You can play other hands as you choose but, in the long run, you will lose with them. This is quite different from No-Limit, where subsequent betting can take another player(s) off the hand, whether or not you have hit the flop.

In low-limit games worldwide, you will see other players playing other hands in early position. Be aware that, however successful they might be in the short term, they will lose money with these other hands in the long run. You *want* them to play those sub-standard hands, because the mistakes of others equate to profit for you.

To call or to raise? I like raising with all of these hands but we'll take a closer look at that decision at the end of this section.

Middle-Position Starting Hands

This is still a very dangerous position in a low-limit Hold 'Em game and the hands you choose to play here are still quite small in number. All those early-position starting hands can be played, plus:

JJ
1010
99
88
AJ – suited or unsuited
A10 – suited or unsuited
A9 – suited
KQ – suited or unsuited
KJ – suited
K10 – suited
QJ – suited

Late-Position Starting Hands

This is your moment to add in a few more hands. How many you can add will largely depend upon how many callers there have been so far. If there is one caller, then you shouldn't be keen to play 98 suited; if there have been six callers, then you might well decide that you are getting the right odds to make a speculative call. These are the basic additions to your starting hands:

A9, KJ, QJ, Q10 – unsuited
All pairs, 7 or lower
All ace-low suited hands (making good draws for the nut flush)
K9 – suited (second nut flush draws)
Q10 – suited
Q9
J10 – suited or unsuited
J9 – suited
109 – suited
98 – suited

Depending upon the number of callers, you may choose to add lower suited connectors or semi-connectors to this list. However, please note that when you hit your flush with these cards (only 3 per cent of the time anyway) you may have the second-highest flush and subsequently may lose a large pot.

Generally, at low-limit Hold 'Em it simply doesn't pay to play low cards, suited/connected or not.

Raising or Calling

Basically, raising is desirable because it makes you seem aggressive, it cuts down the number of likely callers, and therefore protects your good starting hand. It is not, generally, good policy to start building a pot at Limit Hold 'Em on speculative hands pre-flop, so you may find yourself calling more often than you would like. That's fine, provided that, when you do hit a good flop, you now come out betting, to cut down on the number of drawing hands out against you.

However, be aware also that the more calls there are, the better odds late-position players enjoy to join the pot.

In Limit Hold 'Em at low stakes, raising may give the right impression but it rarely keeps weaker players out of the hand. Particularly if they've called already, to call your raise often seems automatic to them, so you don't gain much information about opponents' hands.

However, if you are thinking about raising, then I would; if you are thinking about calling, then *don't*. Muck all those marginal calling hands and you will save a fortune. Call only when you know that you want to call.

One idea that has helped many of my students is this: think of what will be best for your hand and then decide what to do.

What will be best for, say, KK?

I'd like just the one opponent, maybe two. That way, my wonderful hand is protected and I'll be able to better judge what to do on the flop. If I get six callers, it's odds-on that after the flop, I'll be behind.

What about J♣ 10♣?

With this type of hand, I want as many people in the pot as possible. If I hit trips, a full house, or a straight flush draw, I want to make as much money as possible; it's not likely to happen so, to make it a worthwhile bet, I want plenty of dosh in the pot.

So, that makes raising with the premium hands an easy decision: to prevent a large multi-way pot developing; to call with a speculative hand to encourage others into the pot is the right way to go to ensure a big pay-out if you hit your (unlikely) perfect flop.

There are also informational advantages to raising pre-flop. If a player re-raises, he is telling you clearly that he has a premium hand. Players raise with all kinds of rubbish, but they are reluctant to re-raise, as a general rule, and even more so when you have shown yourself to be a 'rock' up until that point.

Raising pre-flop may buy you a free card on the flop if the callers choose, as they often do, to check to the raiser to see what action you'll take. This will be useful when you are on a positive draw but don't want to pay any more to see the turn.

When to Call A Pre-flop Raise

If you are thinking about it, you need to know two things: in what position is the raiser sitting – and where he is in relation to you (which of you will be acting first on each subsequent round of betting?); what his style of play has been up to this point.

The earlier the raise, the stronger the hand.

A drunk or an ultra-aggressive youngster might raise on anything in any position. A quiet, disciplined, focused player will be raising only for a very good reason: usually, because he has a premium hand.

Next, see if any other players have called the raise. If they have, are they decent players? If so, they may hold very good hands themselves. Are they calling stations? If this is the case, you're getting much-improved odds to call with your hand.

If all else fails, ask yourself whether you think you're winning the hand right now. If you imagine that the raiser has AK (his most likely early-position raising hand) then, clearly, hands such as AQ and AJ look big underdogs, whereas any pair is a slight favourite, even by the time the river has been dealt.

Late-position raises may be made on all kinds of hands and now you must re-evaluate your hand in the light of that information: AQ and AJ now look rather better.

Finally, watch out for the action taken by the blinds when there is a raise. Unless they are poor players, the blind bettors will almost certainly pass anything but the very best hands, knowing that they are in the worst position for the rest of the hand.

Re-Raising Pre-Flop

This action will test the raiser's nerve and the value of his hand and should gain you more information about his holding which, in time, may save you money. Bear in mind, however, that the chip value of a re-raise will not push him out of the hand because the raise size is simply not big enough to have that effect, but it may sow seeds of doubt in his mind and that is never a bad thing. High pairs and AK are the most likely re-raise holdings. This isn't No-Limit where, in theory, you might re-raise on anything; this is Limit and the hand may well still go to showdown and you tend to need the best hand to win at that point!

Action on The Flop

Be aware that you are likely to be playing against opponents looser than you, so betting won't necessarily push people off the hand. However, betting from others will often push you off the hand, because this is the moment to get away from a hand: whilst the bets are still small and you have not in any way become wedded to your hand.

If you raise pre-flop and miss the flop, certainly bet, but bear in mind that a bluffing bet by you might win you the hand against one or two opponents but, if you have half a dozen callers, one of them will have hit something easily good enough to call you down to the end.

With drawing hands, once you have seen the flop, assessed your opponents and seen the action to you, then you can make a reasonable pot-odds-based decision as to whether to continue in the hand.

With only two or three players in the pot, you must bet immediately to protect made hands such as high pocket pairs and top pairs on the flop.

With multiple opponents, even big pairs are liable to be beaten if the flop is all one suit: a player might have flopped a flush; two or more players might be on a flush and/or straight draw. You're not much of a favourite and you might just be bled dry.

Low pairs should be mucked immediately when there are even two overcards on board and a bet to you. You're less than 10 per cent on to make trips now and you may well be beaten even if you do hit. Ignore low straight draws and flush draws because you will almost certainly be beaten even if you hit.

Re-raising on the flop is a pot-building manoeuvre and not in any way an attempt to get players off the hand. If they're in it on the draw, the re-raise simply won't price them out of the hand. All you are doing is getting more money into the pot when the odds favour you to win it. This is the action you'll take with top pair hidden in the hole, top pair-top kicker on the flop, as well as stronger but vulnerable hands such as trips.

Beware these holdings when there is a bet on the flop, then a raise, then a re-raise. Top pair-top kicker is probably losing now; even hidden top pair in the hole is vulnerable. These bet, raise, re-raise-to-you situations are usually best played conservatively because, even if you are ahead now, the odds may well favour your being overtaken after the last two cards are dealt.

A bluffing re-raise on the flop may be in order in a heads-up, or sometimes in a three-handed situation, where the flop is low and the raiser has acted first with a quick bet. Now, you may take him off AK, regardless of your own hand – and the raise may scare off the third player also.

Beware both calling and raising into a straight draw when there are two suited cards on the board. Players will certainly call bets to try to make their flush and they are slight favourites over you to hit their hand.

Finally, and in synch with the advice for pre-flop raises, you may buy yourself a free card by raising now. On a draw, you may get to see both turn and river for the price of one bet, and a small bet at that, as everyone dutifully checks to the raiser; if you make your hand and bet on the turn, you have gained further action with the best hand – always a desirable scenario.

Action on The Turn

The bets are doubled, but the pot is bigger, so their value is unlikely to affect greatly the decisions made by your opponents.

If you're in the hand on the turn and you think you have the best of it, you must bet it out. You cannot risk everyone checking and the river arriving for free. With multiple players remaining, it is odds-on that someone will overtake you.

Players who raise pre-flop, then bet on the flop, and then check, often hold AK. They've tried their power play to get their opponents off the hand and it hasn't worked. Keep that in mind when deciding how to act now, and see what the arrival of an ace or king on the river might do to your hand.

In multi-player pots, high cards on the turn and river are bad news. This is because many players enter a pot with any two picture cards (plus aces, naturally) so three high cards on the board may mean that there is a high straight out against you.

In keeping with the advice throughout, if you are planning on playing this hand to the end, calling on the river, then bet or raise now. You may take out players or you may win the pot at this point. This is just standard aggressive play which, when tempered with common sense, will lead to improved table image, the stealing of marginal pots and the building of bigger pots when you hold the best of it at showdown.

One tip I read years ago has certainly won me a few dollars over the years and I recommend it to you. I call it the 'Nut Flush Semi-Bluff'.

You hold A♥ and you're still in the hand after two hearts appeared on the flop. If a third heart hits on the turn, bet out looking like a man who has just made his flush. You may bluff your way through – no one else can make the nut flush, because you have the ace – or you may get called. In this latter scenario, you still have close on 20 per cent chance of hitting the nuts on the river, plus any further chances of trips or 2-pair which might make the winning hand.

Action on The River

If you're on the draw, you have to see whether the river made it for you. If you thought you had the best hand pre-river, then you must analyse if the river card may have completed an opponent's draw. Having made your judgment – or your read – you can concentrate on how to save money or make money at the end.

Certainly, if you are going to call at the end, you might as well bet out. This is standard poker practice: if you have the best hand, you may provoke a call and get paid more; if you don't have the best hand, you may on rare occasions take your opponent off the hand – you need this to happen only once out of many, many occasions to make the play worthwhile. Finally, it all adds to your serious, aggressive image.

Value Betting

Throughout the hand, if you are ahead and you bet, when you get called, you are gaining value for your best hand. To bet out with the best hand at any time therefore is considered a value bet.

At the end, apart from the slim possibility of persuading a player with a better hand than yours to fold, the main reason to make a bet on the river is to gain one more large bet from an opponent who holds enough to call (but not enough to beat you). To this end, when considering betting on the river, you do not want to risk an extra large bet if your opponent has you beaten and calls; worse still, risk two large bets if he raises and you decide to call. The fact is that you must put your opponent on a hand and check that nothing that has appeared on the river has helped him sufficiently to overtake you. If you are concerned that it might have done, then check the hand and, if necessary, call his bet at the end.

In the lowest-limit games available, it is rare to find anyone bluffing at the end unless they are heads-up, or playing against a couple of clearly nervous opponents. Not only is the size of the bet usually too small a proportion of the total pot (and therefore makes the calling of the bluff bet too promising a proposition), but there are simply too many players out there who'll call you down to the end with only the smallest of hands. The moment you move to slightly-higher levels, or if you are at a low-limit table with a bunch of very good players (not strictly a low-limit table in that case), then you'll find that bluffing occurs more frequently because opponents are good enough (ironically) to fall for the bluff and pitch their cards.

Another great tip on low-limit Hold 'Em which has served me well over the years is this: beware the player in early position who checks and calls bets throughout the hand and then, on the river, sticks in a bet ahead of you. This player usually has the nuts and he just wants to make sure that a bet is out there ready to be called by a few loose players. He daren't check, hoping to check-raise, because he's worried everyone may check down the hand. Fold in these situations unless you have a monster because you're almost always beaten.

Bluffing Opportunities

Despite the high percentage of times when a bluff at Limit poker will fail because the size of the bet itself is not prohibitive to prevent a call, you should realize that you need your bluff to work only a tiny percentage of the time – let's say, on average, 5–10 per cent of the time – for you to show a profit from bluffing play. Be aware, however, that against very weak players, you should probably cut your bluffs to the minimum since poor players always call, sometimes with whatever they have.

Your judgment about when and how often to bluff will be influenced largely by the table conditions that you encounter at any given time (being aware that as table personnel change, so do the conditions).

In pots with a small number of players, bluffs work better (there is less chance of someone having hit a monster that they're unlikely to lay down).

Against better players, or players who think they are better – usually playing mid-range Limit Hold 'Em – bluffs have a much better chance of success than against fish in the lowest-limit games.

When there have been two rounds of checks to you, some players actually hope that there will be a bet and then they can throw their cards away and get on quickly with the next hand. Watch for overt body language signposting this: you won't believe your eyes the first time you see

every single one of your opponents itching to fold to your
bet!

I have always favoured betting aggressively when the
board pairs (at low limits, especially low pairs) and when
the flop is all one suit. You often have to make a second
bluff bet/raise to take the money, but the return on
investment is good.

Beware bluffing when you see either an ace on the board,
or two connecting/semi-connecting picture cards. The
reasons for this are straightforward: many low-limit players
play any ace they find; the chances of someone having a pair
of aces when there have been multiple callers is very high
indeed; as discussed earlier, many poor players get involved
with any two picture cards; if there are two picture cards on
the board, the chances of two-pair or a high straight draw
are just too great to make the possibility of everyone passing
their hands even worth considering a bluff.

Back to The River

Returning now to the river action, just remember, in
whatever position you find yourself, your natural inclina-
tion should be to call bets at the end if you think you have
even a small chance of winning the pot: the pot odds will
be just too good to resist. For example, if a pot contains
$60 and you have to call only $6 to find out whether you
might have won the hand, you are investing only 10% of
the pot; so as long as your hands win 11% of the time, it
will be the right decision.

This is another reason why bluffing in Limit Hold 'Em,
especially at the end when the pots are relatively large, is
so unlikely to work.

So, to sum up:

Be aware of pot size and pots odds for calling, both
when considering whether to risk a bluff at the end or

whether to call a bet at the end. Players should be inclined to call bets at the end because of pot odds.

Bluff less against: pots with multiple callers, very weak players, calling stations, flops containing aces or connected/semi-connected picture cards.

Bluff more when: you are heads-up or there are few callers; against players who are good enough (think they are good enough) to fold real hands when they think that they are beaten; when the board pairs or is single-suited; when there are repeated rounds of checking to you (and players are sitting forward in their chairs ready to muck their cards with relief once there is a bet – watch for it – you will see this).

Hand Examples for Limit Hold 'Em Cash Games

The following examples will illustrate some basic Limit Hold 'Em strategy as well as acting as a test for you to check that you are ready for casino Limit Hold 'Em. Rarely in poker is any single answer the only option available to you, but the solutions suggested here will help you to become a reliable, patient, tight – and winning – low-limit player. And, if low-limit poker is your game, that's what you want to be.

Assume a nine-player table of, say, $3/$6 Limit Hold 'Em

Pre-Flop

1) You hold: A♠ J♥
   What is your standard, basic action in the following positions?
   a) 2nd seat
   b) 5th seat
   c) on the button

2) You hold: K♥ J♣
   What is your standard, basic action in the following positions?
   a) 2nd seat
   b) 5th seat
   c) on the button

3) You hold: 10♦ 9♦
   What is your standard, basic action in the following positions?
   a) 2nd seat
   b) 5th seat
   c) on the button

4) You hold: A♥ K♠
   What is your standard, basic action if there has been a raise from the 3rd seat, no other callers, and you are in the 6th seat?

5) You hold: A♥ Q♣
   What is your standard, basic action if there has been a raise from the 3rd seat, a call from the 4th seat and a re-raise from the 5th seat?

On The Flop

6) In 3rd seat, you raise with A♦ K♣ and receive one call from the 7th seat.

   The flop comes: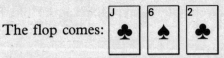

   What action would you normally take?

7) In 3rd seat, you raise with A♠ K♣ and receive four callers.

   The flop comes: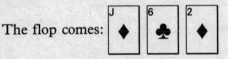

What action would you normally take?

8) In 3rd seat, you raise with A♥ K♣ and receive two callers.

The flop comes:

What action would you normally take?

9) In 6th seat, you call pre-flop with 9♠ 9♣

The flop comes:

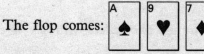

What action would you normally take?
a) with two players in the hand
b) with five players in the hand

On The Turn

10) The 4th-seat player raises pre-flop, you decide to call on the button with J♣ 10♣

The flop comes:

The raiser bets the flop, which you call.

The turn comes:

The raiser checks.
What is going on?

11) You call with A♣ 7♥ on the button. You and three other players see the flop.

The flop comes:

The player ahead of you bets and you call, leaving the pot heads-up.

The turn comes:

Your opponent bets. What action might you take?

On The River

12) On the button, you raise two callers with A♠ J♣ and both call.

The flop comes:

They check to you and you bet; both call.

The turn comes: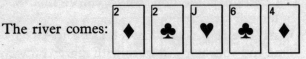

They check to you and you bet; only one opponent calls.

The river comes: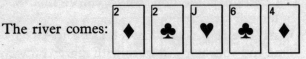

Your opponent bets. What should you do?

ANSWERS

1) a) Pass. Unless you are at a generally tight table where there are few callers, nice though this hand is, it will lose you money in this position in the long run.

   b) Call. This is a decent hand in mid-position.

   c) Call; perhaps raise.

   This illustrates perfectly how a hand can be unplayable in early position, yet be good enough to consider a raise in late position. It is *vital* to your success at Limit poker to respect position at all times.

2) a) Pass. Your hand is nowhere near worth a call; it is odds-against to be the best right now and you must fold to a raise, wasting your initial call. This is a big losing proposition in the long run.

   b) Pass. This is the classic marginal decision. If you can learn to pass all the marginal hands, you may get a little bored, but you will lose less, and therefore end up winning more. Which do you want to be? Rich and a little bored, or poor and slightly less bored?

   c) Call. You are in position and you may pick up a great flop. With no raises yet and only the blinds remaining, the odds on your seeing the flop just for the price of the call are very good.

3) a) Pass. The flop would have hit you from time to time and your gut will burn with regret. However, your brain accentuates this emotion (so that you remember it) and diminishes the dozens of times you would have missed and wasted money. This type of hand can win big for you in early position at No-Limit poker, but not when you have betting limits, reducing your upside on every hand.

   b) Pass. It's marginal again, and the key is to pass the marginal hands.

   c) Call, if there are at least three callers already; pass
      if there are fewer than three – it is very unlikely
      that you will hit a monster so, when you do, you
      want plenty of players in the pot to pay you off.

or Raise; it is generally not right to start building pots at
Limit without premium cards but, if you have no callers,
or only one, you might take down the hand now – and a
raise mixes up your action a little.

Notice, here, that with one caller before you, you'd fold
this hand or raise with it, but not call. This is, once again,
all about position.

4) Re-raise. Don't call, letting other players join this pot
cheaply, raise it up in an attempt to go head-to-head
with your opponent.

5) Pass. It's a nice hand, in a nice position, but it has
become a marginal decision. You are almost certainly
beaten by one of the three players ahead of you and
your position alone is not sufficient to warrant a call or
raise. If you did call, what would you like to see on the
flop? If an ace falls, you'd fear AK in an opponent's
hand; even if your flop was ideal, say, Q73, you might
still lose a big pot to KK.

6) Bet. Represent an overpair and put the spotlight on
your single opponent. He didn't re-raise pre-flop, so
he's likely missed the flop just as badly as you – and
you may be ahead anyway. To check is just too weak.

7) Check – and fold to a bet except perhaps if the action
is checked to the last player, who may simply be
making an (almost mandatory) bluff bet. Then,
maybe, even consider re-raising. However, basically,
your action is to check and then fold since, with four
callers, someone will have hit something or made
some kind of a draw. To bet again now is likely to
cost you in the long run.

These examples illustrate the difference in action between a head-to-head pot and a multi-way pot: the facility to bluff exists in the first scenario, but not in the second.

8) Bet. There are three good reasons for doing this: firstly, you rate to have the best hand now and betting out your winning hands in a simple fashion is the winning policy at Limit Hold 'Em; secondly, there are possible draws out there for your two callers – at least make them pay to hit their hands; finally, you want to play this hand just like the previous follow-up-bet bluffs – when you have to show down your Big Slick to win the pot, your opponents will remember that you bet your top pairs straight out, and that will make them much more reluctant to make a stand against you when you subsequently make a bluffing follow-up bet.

9) a) Bet. To slow-play trips is always dangerous, because the hand looks strong but is very vulnerable to drawing hands. With only one opponent, you might consider check-raising or slow-playing, but I advise against it. In a low-limit Hold 'Em game, to bet out your hands honestly is almost always the best policy.

   b) Bet. Definitely. To slow-play against multiple opponents is asking for trouble. And the trouble is, not only are you likely to be overtaken if you don't eliminate some of the other players, but also when you are overtaken, you'll find it hard to lay down your flopped trips, so it will cost you multiple bets to realize that you are beaten.

Slow-playing is not recommended. If you wish to give it a go – to mix up your style perhaps – do it against a single opponent, never against multiple opponents. By the way, a check-raise is a kind of slow-play, because it relies upon your opponent betting (otherwise, obviously, you miss your chance to bet on that round).

10) The raiser may well have AK, AQ or even a mid-pair. He has tried to take you off the pot with his follow-up

bet on the flop and, now that it will cost him double to bet here, he has checked. Unless you are in a slow-play mood, you should bet here. You are representing top pair now and that's what you have; if your opponent has one of the imagined hands, he'll almost certainly lay it down. You don't want him to see the river for free since any top picture card or a heart will frighten you.

11) Raise. This is a nice semi-bluff. Your middle pair could just be winning, but the third club on the board gives you the chance to take your opponent off the hand now. If he calls, you probably have aces, sevens to win and any club for the nuts and, if nothing happens, you have the aggressive option to run the bluff again, by betting or raising again on the river.

12) Clearly you must decide between calling and passing. The second two on the river is irrelevant; your opponent knows that you know that he isn't representing trip twos. So, what was he doing? He called your raise out of position and happily checked and called until this last round. Is he worried that if he checks this round, you'll check too? Experience should tell you that this is likely.

So, what does he have? Trip sixes, perhaps? You will probably be right to pass this final bet: if you don't believe me, you may have to call in this situation quite a few times to convince yourself. This is the play of a guy who has you beaten the entire hand, and knows it.

You've read the basics, answered the questions, and you're ready to roll. Before you do, let's run through a few of the key elements to which you must adhere if you are going to succeed. Most poker players fail in one of the following categories and that is what you are there to take advantage of. So, check again that you don't fall into any of these traps.

Key Factors for Success – and Mistakes to Avoid – in Low-Limit Hold 'Em

Table Behaviour

From the moment you arrive at a table down to the last hand you play, your opponents should be watching you carefully (and you should be doing the same to them). If they sense weakness, uncertainty, a lack of confidence in your place at the table, even quite poor players will pick up on this and put pressure on you.

Take time to observe the behaviour of other players in your card club or casino and then blend in quietly with them. There's plenty of time to develop a poker personality once you're a consistently-big winner. Remain alert at the table, remain calm, whatever strange thing happens – the dealer will sort it out.

Above all, keep emotion out of your system. It's easy to become disheartened by a poor run of cards, especially when you are playing a tight, disciplined system as we do, but you must ensure that you do not slip into the habit of sighing or slouching when your cards are consistently poor. More importantly, your behaviour upon receiving a great starting hand must not differ from the norm. (Incidentally, when switching from online poker to live games, this is a common occurrence: no one sees that frown or hears that groan when you're alone in front of a screen.) Even poor players, who play and lose a lot, are apt to spot basic tells such as these. This part of your game is as important as how you play your cards. Ensure that you remain disciplined at the poker table at all times and your body language will, for these games at least, be sufficiently disguised.

Play to your Bankroll

Gambling money isn't real. It doesn't exist as banknotes or coins, not as a bank balance or as an investment. It cannot: it may be there one moment and gone the next. Gambling money must be completely separate from your everyday common-or-garden money. If you mix the two together, it's very dangerous.

When you choose your stake, ensure that you can afford to weather the inevitable troughs and peaks of a poker player. I think that, when you sit down at a poker table, your bankroll should contain 200 times the amount of the big blind. That means, to play $3/$6 Limit Hold 'Em, you should have $1,200 available to you. That doesn't mean that you take twelve hundred bucks to the casino with you – far from it – it just means that you have that size of bankroll always available in your mind (or, better still, in a poker bank account). Then, never take more than a quarter of your bankroll with you to any session (perhaps, day) of poker. In this way, if you are unlucky enough to lose a run of hands and you find yourself down $300, that is still small compared to the overall size of your bankroll. You have plenty of time to win that back.

The moment that the amounts you are winning or losing is playing with your head, then you are in trouble. If your mind is thinking about money, what it can buy in the real world, it cannot make the correct decisions for you at the table. Subconsciously – or, sometimes very consciously – your brain will have converted your gambling money to real money and its true value, and you won't be making a poker-based decision.

Many players move up to higher stakes because they think that it is somehow a status symbol (both of their wealth and also of their poker ability). There is a grain of truth in this – as casinos and card rooms please you in direct proportion to your spending – but basically, unless you are moving up-stake because you think you can beat the game as successfully as you were beating your lower-stake game, then any move is just ego, just machismo.

I'm happy to confess that I'm a mid-stakes player. I like stakes so that they hurt you if you lose badly and please you plenty when you win. I like my mid-stake games because I can beat them consistently, and I measure success at poker the way you measure success of your favourite sportsman or team – how high they are in their league, how much money have they won. In poker, your chip stack is your means of keeping score – and I like mine big!

This is an important note to players who want to play poker for higher stakes: there are millions of fish swimming around the low-and mid-stake games, happy to swim about inanely for a while before being gobbled up. If you're winning nicely at your level, test the water very carefully at the next level up. If your success rate falls, dive right back in where you were king, and to hell with your perceived status. It may be where you belong.

Playing 'Intuitively'

Poker is a game of decisions based on incomplete information, but it is a logical game. Particularly at low-stake levels, it's not about superstition, or feeling that a card might come, or thinking that it was your turn to win a pot. It's about making sensible decisions – all the time. On each occasion you make a poor decision, you are offering your opponents a chance to take your money. So, decisions must be based on the poker facts – and nothing else.

The odds of any particular play being correct are pretty much set (although your opponent is an important variable). You must know the basics of pot odds, and how to calculate 'outs' correctly. If you don't know these basic things, then don't sit down to play.

By the way, the simplest method of calculating 'outs' is the two-and-four method which should be widely known.

If you are on a draw – say, for an open-ended straight – after the flop, you have eight cards which will make you what you believe will be the winning hand. The rule of two-and-four says that with both turn and river cards to come, multiply the number of outs by four – to provide a reasonably-accurate percentage chance of hitting your card.

In the case of the straight draw, that's 8 outs × 4 = 32

In fact, 32 per cent isn't far off the accurate calculation.

With only one card to come, you multiply your outs by two. In the case of the same straight draw, with only the river to come, that's 8 outs × 2 = 16%, which, again, is pretty close to the exact answer.

So, now you know how to work out simple odds on the flop and beyond, you can calculate whether it is worth a bet or not. Especially at Limit Hold 'Em, to think in any other way is just going to hand your opponents your money without effort.

However, this doesn't mean that intuition need be completely absent from your game. There are times and places for such feelings. These are when reading the human reactions around the table. Here, a precise, computer-like ability to play the hands perfectly is of no help. You must use your instincts to guide you. Yes, those instincts must be honed and practised but, ultimately, some people are better than others at reading their opponents and it is in this department that intuition, feeling, gut instinct and conviction play their part. Indeed, to trust one's first instinct in these situations often turns out best.

Playing Too Many Hands

There is one simple thing you can do now, right now, to save yourself losses and increase winnings: play fewer hands.

Particularly at Limit Hold 'Em, the quality of your starting hands will reflect in your results at the end of a few sessions. If you get bored, if you feel that you have only four hours in which to play and you want some action, if you think that calling in small-blind position is cheap – then you will lose money. Maybe not instantly, but definitely in the long term.

Playing tight and disciplined isn't a whole lot of fun. However, for me, ending up with more chips than I started with – other players' chips – *is* fun: that's why I play poker. If you want to win at poker, that's the sacrifice you're going to have to make.

Once you are an improving player, you can consider tournaments and short-handed online games, where the action is, perforce, much greater and much faster-moving. But, in low-limit Hold 'Em games, patience and discipline will win money. In the long run, assuming you know your game, those profits are as close to a certainty as you'll ever get at poker.

The next time that you have a close decision: whether to limp in, whether to call a raise, just fold your cards. Usually, when you make a close decision to proceed it is the wrong decision, and the big problem with that wrong decision is that it has cost you now, and it may well cost you again – and again – if you are persuaded into bets later in the hand.

Throwing away the best hand pre-flop is not a terrible decision; it may not even be a poor one.

Imagine you hold: A♠ J♠ and there is a raise from the 4th seat and passes to you on the button. This is a close decision – don't let the fact that your cards are suited influence you too much (see below) – and close decisions should be folded. You muck your cards and, moments later, the raiser is showing down: K♣ Q♥ and asking whether anyone will ever call him. You shouldn't feel bad. You were only a little bit ahead, and there are five cards to come. To lay down these hands is fine. To lose a big pot because the raiser held AK, AQ or AA is much more foolish.

This is an easy concept to accept on the page but when you've been passing solidly for an hour and you see AJ suited it does look like a big hand. Just take a deep breath and make the right decision.

Incidentally, there is one other possibility, if you are not sure what to do. You could raise. At least, if you raise, you gain two things: the chance to win the pot right now; and the opportunity to gain information.

In the example above, the original raiser ought to fold. He probably won't, but he ought to. When he doesn't, you are still marginally ahead. If he misses the flop and you bet again, it'll be over.

What this all comes down to is that calling is a lame action. You want to avoid it. Passing is far more decisive. Present an aggressive, positive image, selecting your hands carefully and playing them strongly with raises and re-raises.

Overrating Suited Cards

You don't need to tell me how beautiful K7 suited looks after an hour of staring at 72, 63, 93, 84 hand after hand after hand. However, you wouldn't, I hope, consider playing K7 normally and, just because it's suited (and shows up after a lengthy spell of less than nothing), you shouldn't in any way be persuaded to play it. The actual statistical advantage of holding suited cards is around 3 per cent. To flop a flush is very rare; to draw cheaply to a flush, from which you can then extract further bets from your opponents, is almost as rare. So, suited cards are a small bonus but not much more than that.

If you are looking at suited cards in the hole and you know deep down that you shouldn't play this hand, then *never* let the fact that they are suited persuade you otherwise. Keep repeating the low-limit mantra: if you're not sure whether to play the hand – don't!

Being a Television Star

Poker on television and online has encouraged and influenced the vast majority of people taking up poker in the twenty-first century. This is great news for the health of the game, the support of big businesses in terms of sponsorships, and, indeed, the entertainment value of watching the world's best players making million-dollar decisions.

For the beginner or inexperienced player, however, this is also a curse. On television there is always banter, staring down, huge excitement on every deal. One well-known commentator in the UK gets so overexcited about every hand, I seriously fear for his health (and for the well-being of viewers' ears). Of course, television is looking for excitement. It cuts and pastes, edits and manipulates, until a four-day tournament becomes a two-hour programme. Out of that two hours, there are going to be at least twenty minutes of commercials, twenty minutes of player interviews and introductions, and yet another twenty minutes of leader boards and chip counts. So, now we're down to one hour of poker action out of forty hours of action (at multiple tables – so make that hundreds of hours, thousands of hours of poker) and you can see that you're going to get only the cherry-picked action.

When Dave 'Devilfish' Ulliot raises on 73 off in first position and then takes another player off top pair-top kicker, it looks amazing. What you don't see is Devilfish trying moves like that all tournament long. Sometimes, all his opponents fold; sometimes, they raise or re-raise and he folds. The next twenty hands at that table, one player raises and everyone folds. None of this makes good television, so they don't show it – and you don't get to see it.

The vast majority of poker play is dull – really boring. Someone raises, everyone folds. There are two callers and the big blind; the flop comes and one player bets – everyone folds. Towards the end of a tournament, you'll often see tables where no one bets anything and the big blind collects the small-blind bet and the dealer deals the next hand. This is the reality of poker: it's repetitive, dull and as unglamorous as you can imagine. I know that you don't want to hear this, but it's my duty to tell you that if you want to win money at poker, this is how it really is.

I was in a big card room in Vegas recently, watching the low-stake Limit Hold 'Em tables – I couldn't believe what I was seeing. Not only was the play terrible, but the etiquette and behaviour was awful too. Players didn't seem to know whose turn it was to act; they weren't sure how big they could make their bets; they didn't under-stand when they could check and when they had to call. It was amazing. I think the dealer may have been considering taking up smoking again, and then emigrating. There were a couple of local grinders there and I'm sure they made money . . . I just wondered what it was doing to their souls. The thing that made me laugh out loud was the way the new players were looking at their cards: they were arranging them neatly in front of them, side by side, face down, just like the players on television do. The problem was that this was real poker and there were no under-the-table cameras waiting to see what they held. Nonetheless, everyone seemed to be having a good time, but it was costing them. I want you to enjoy your poker, achieve a real buzz, but also leave the table with a big stack of chips. It can be done – you just have to want to do it.

So, in short, ignore all the action on television. Many of the tricks these players play on each other are multi-layered versions of a battle they've been waging against each other for years. Some of it is just for the benefit of the cameras – poker players are show-offs too – and all of it is compressed into a rich, sticky concoction of endlessly-exciting action. Remember that poker is a slow, waiting game. If you are patient, you will win.

Incidentally, if you don't care whether you win or lose, then you can relax and have fun and let it all hang out. A friend of mine, a very decent player and a very wealthy man, plays the tournament circuit some of the year and has done really well. However, when he plays cash games – online or live games – he says that he just can't concentrate for hours on end, because the sums are just too small. He says that he starts getting loose after about half an hour, and then the pots get bigger, and suddenly he's the life and soul of the party. Only thing is: he's a self-confessed loser in those cash games. I know how successful he is in the tournaments – it's a matter of public record – he just can't bring himself to play tight and disciplined in the cash games. I thought it was big of him to admit to me that he loses year after year when he plays low- and mid-stake cash games, but it is very revealing information. The bottom line is: he doesn't care; he wins more than he loses overall and even if he didn't, he has never played needing the money.

So, if you can afford to gift your chips to your opponents, have fun, don't pay attention and play like a madman; it'll be fun and you will become poor.

For the rest of us, I recommend my tight, disciplined policy.

Reading your Opponents: Tells and Bluffs

As mentioned earlier, low-limit Hold 'Em is a fairly statistical, odds-based game, with more than its fair share of showdown action. There are only limited opportunities to bluff. However, that is not to say that you won't get plenty of action from your opponents. So, for low-limit Hold 'Em games, in card clubs, casinos and home games, here are a few of the basic tells and sources of information which you can use to fold or call or raise your opponents at the crucial time.

The tells listed below are the most obvious, best-documented observations of all. They may not be relevant to you if you play in mid-stake or high-stake games, or if your home game is of a high standard. However, I bet that you will be able to use at least one of the following in your very next game – and it will save you, or make you, money . . . hard cash.

Poker players are not traditionally sartorially elegant. For example, they aren't wearing dark glasses inside a gloomy casino as a fashion statement: they're wearing them to hide their eyes. This also goes for the high-collared shirts often seen at the green baize, even the casually-tied scarf. Again, this is not fashion (thankfully), but an attempt to hide the veins and arteries in their necks. Some players have been known to throw towels over their heads to prevent anyone reading anything from their pulse, blinking or dry mouths. Top players watch every last element of a player's game in order to gain a better idea of what they might be holding: facial movements, body language, style of making a bet, size of bet, speed of bet, reaction to other bets . . . the list goes on and on. Not only must you also look out for basic tells (information gained from a player's behaviour), but you must be on your guard to protect against revealing too many of your own.

Let's start with some really basic, but important, tells, which will crop up in low-limit games and home games:

Strong Is Weak; Weak Is Strong

The most classic tell of all occurs far more often than anyone would care to acknowledge. Almost all poker players are aware that they might be giving away information, so they attempt to balance this with a piece of classic human psychology: act opposite to your true emotions.

Players who sigh or slump when they see the flop have often hit; players who stare long and hard at either the flop or their hand have usually missed. Players who bet confidently are often weak, whereas a gently, nervously placed bet is often very strong.

Don't think that a little acting won't play to your benefit even against top opposition. Take Jennifer Harmon, one of the greatest women mega-stake cash-game players in the world: there's never a moment when she's not pulling a face, usually of a nervous or miserable variety. Sometimes, she looks so unhappy, you wonder what could have happened to her: like she's on the verge of tears. Do not be deceived. Those expressions mask a multitude of different possibilities. I've seen her on television and I've seen her live and every time she looks so utterly defeated, deflated, miserable and just sick, so sick it almost moves you to tears, when she's just about to pounce and kill some poor unsuspecting palooka: it's a thing of beauty really.

My advice for all low-limit games, low- and mid-stake buy-in tournaments and all your home games is this: when you are strong, act strong; when you are weak, act a bit weak. Everyone will assume that you're playing some complex psychological game and will misread you. The best news of all is that it requires little thought or effort on your part, is pretty relaxing, and therefore gives you maximum time and brainpower to concentrate on your own game and the reading of your opponents' tells.

Nervous Bet Placing

This is one of the strongest, most consistent tells I know. It is incredibly reliable in all low- and many mid-stake games: a bet placed with a shaking hand is a strong bet made by a player who knows that he is winning.

When most beginners and intermediate players make a bluff, they are usually very conscious of controlling their emotions and they can often ensure that their shaking is controlled. When they have the nuts, the excitement at the thought of taking down the pot, along with some extra chips from you, is just too great. They can't hide it. And it manifests itself as shaking hands.

Tells and False Tells

Any player who is showing interest in his opponents and is clearly watching their actions, attempting to get a read on what they might have, is a player to be respected. This is a type of player who may attempt a false tell to deceive you and you must be aware of that. Players who are paying no attention to their opponents will have only the most basic philosophy on tells – such as weak is strong; strong is weak. So, you need to weigh up the ability of your opponents before deciding how to interpret information which they are providing you.

Take this simple example: against an intermediate opponent, who clearly had an interest in the game and was attempting to observe what was happening, the simplest of false tells was able to bite. I hit the nut straight, well concealed on the turn, and bet into him. This is because, as above, I like acting strong when I'm strong. This guy has top two pair, maybe trips, and he calls. When the river comes, I check, and he bets. Now, I raise the maximum (it's a pot-limit game) and I look away. I know he's watching me, but he doesn't know I know. My hands move to my mouth, to my nose – seemingly subconciously. If genuinely subconsciously, these would be classic body-language indications that I am uncertain about my actions, maybe even ashamed. He catches them, thinks he's spotted a tell that I'm bluffing, and calls me down. When I show him my hand, he smiles and admits – right there, out loud:

'I thought you were bluffing then. You looked like a man who was bluffing.'

Music to my ears. But that wouldn't work against the vast majority of players: they would either be too good, or they wouldn't have been paying me any attention whatsoever, because they're just not interested in watching their opponents. It's like real bluffing: there are some players so bad you just can't bluff them – ever. You have to know your opponent and pick your spot.

This brings me to two important elements of tell reading:

Firstly, your readings are based on the action taking place at the table right at that moment. If the game is either particularly slow and tight, or fast and aggressive, it may be an aberration from the normal rhythm of the game. If this is the case, the actions and reactions of the players may be different from normal and you may receive more or less information than usual – and, possibly, in a different form. This may make normal tell-reading skills less valuable.

The key here is that when you play at a table where the action is markedly different from the status quo, your job of reading your opponents becomes harder, because everyone may be in a heightened mood of stress or extremely relaxed. To this end, try not to change the mood of the table yourself (unless it is very much to your benefit).

If you get into a loud argument with a player, making him angry, the next time he acts, you won't know whether it is his usual action, or whether your actions have provoked him into being more aggressive or passive.

If you show down a beautiful big bluff, the next time you come up against that player, you may be unsure whether he is still reacting to his earlier humiliation, or whether his action is standard.

Secondly, be careful what you say at the table, since whilst this can play on the minds of your opponents, it can also rebound on to you. This example occurred in a very mixed tournament in which I played whilst I was writing this very section; it happened to be a No-Limit table, but the point is still very much applicable to any form of the game.

At my first table, the player in second position calls and it is passed around to the big blind. The hand is checked down and, at the showdown, the second-position player shows: K♣ 4♣.

There is some friendly chat at the table about a second-position call on such a weak hand.

On the next round, I'm in the big blind and this same player calls in first position, and it is passed around to me.

When I check, I say, 'I guess a call under the gun shows king-eight then . . .'

The flop comes:

As the flop comes down, I watch my opponent out the corner of my eye and he looks interested alright. Since I hold: 10♦ 2♣, I decide to check and he checks very quickly. I suspect he may have flopped trips and is trapping.

The turn comes:

I check, and he checks very quickly, glancing at me.

The river comes:

I check and he . . . checks.

Guess I've misread that one. I can't think why he seemed so interested in this deal. We show our cards and he takes the pot with

See what happened? My opponent wasn't excited about the flop at the moment I looked at him; he was excited because he didn't understand how I'd named his hand precisely pre-flop. He asked me whether I'd seen his cards. If I had, I told him, I would have bet.

The table found the hand funny – and it was – but my big mouth had cost me the pot. If I stay quiet and he checks twice, this combined with his body language would have persuaded me to have bet at some point – and he would have folded. Instead, I'd mixed up the emotions and demeanour of my opponent for no reason and lost a reliable read on that opponent. It was my fault entirely.

So, if you have decent reads on your opponents, keep them going. Don't upset the rhythms. Of course, there are many good poker reasons why you should sometimes sweep in and upset the status quo, disturb the ordered game which may have been established, but beware the effects this action may have.

Impatience

Strangely, I think that this is a conflicting tell between live games and online poker. Online, impatience often indicates a poor hand and a desire to move on to the next one quickly. In live games, a player who is trying to get the action going usually has a better-than-average hand. It's not usually a premium hand, in which case he tends to keep quiet and try not to attract attention, but it's usually a hand worth playing (or, at least, a hand on which this player has decided that he will play). Raising is unlikely to work against this guy; he's decided to play the hand, so play he will. Often, it's better just to count him in as a future caller and adjust your decision slightly if it affects you.

Change in Behaviour

It's obvious once you've seen it for yourself, but up to that point players are often unaware that their opponents are changing their behaviour at all, let alone that they them-selves are changing theirs.

In simple terms, players who talk a lot, seem relaxed and sociable, often clam up once they've decided to play a hand, and that usually means that they have something decent.

There are some players who, quite correctly, don't look at their hole cards until it's their turn to act and then, whatever they have, they keep quiet whilst they consider the action to them, their own position, and whether or not they will enter the action, and how.

Basically, however, look for quiet players becoming boisterous, or noisy players becoming quiet and focused. These changes usually indicate, at the very least, cards worth considering more carefully than the usual peek and muck that most good poker players find themselves doing more often than they would like.

Intimidation Plays

Any play that is intended to intimidate, especially a single opponent, is likely to be weak. With a strong hand, why not just bet normally and hope to get called a few extra times? These aggressive plays include the following:

- The Directed Bet
  When a player pushes his chips towards the pot, but directs them at his opponent, this is usually a weak bet attempting to push the opponent off the pot.
- The High-Velocity Bet
  This is when a player places his bet in an exaggerated or aggressive style (up to and including chips bouncing on the baize, rolling away from the pot and careering off the table altogether). This is sometimes an almost subconscious show of strength to back up a lousy hand, and you should consider such bettors as likely to be weak.
- The Staring Bet
  This is when a player makes his bet and blatantly stares at his opponent. Yet again, this usually reveals weakness or, at the very least, uncertainty about his position in the hand.

Many top players recommend raising against any of these styles of bet and the big advantage of such a play is that if your opponent really is weak, he'll probably lay down his hand now, so the re-raise will produce a win immediately or provide crucial information. This is an excellent time to watch carefully the reaction of your opponent. If you are lucky, you may even witness a squirm (always my favourite) but if not, you'll almost certainly get a subconscious body-language tell because low-limit players aren't used to their basic tactics being attacked so aggressively. So, if he doesn't fold, he'll almost certainly reveal his true feelings about this development.

Staring at The Flop

You see this a lot and it usually means just one thing: the player missed his draw. If a card comes that worries him, he'll usually look away and consider what it means to him and his opponents (he may even look up at you); if a card comes that makes his draw, he'll be trying to look nonchalant, and staring at the flop does not achieve this.

Against intermediate players, try a false tell when you hit your draw by staring long and hard at the flop. If they're watching you, they should read you quite incorrectly and start raising you – now, you can act like a calling station and call gingerly.

Calling Speeds

As a general rule, players who vary their speed of action when it is their turn are revealing extra information about their hands. Being predominantly an online player, I have found these tells to be less reliable than some of those above, but almost everyone cites these as being important in low-limit live games, so keep your eyes open:

- Fast Calls
  These usually indicate weakness or a drawing hand. If you had strength, you'd usually mull over your best course of action for a while before acting.
- Slow Calls
  Advanced beginners or intermediate players may be calculating pot odds; others may be considering the chance of hitting trips or two pair. Either way, they are usually on a draw. A bet on the next round should sort out whether they are fishing or not.
- Out-of-Position Calls
  Pre-flop, this is usually a mistake and doesn't often indicate great strength, just a resolve to play this hand, often on quite marginal starting values. Players with premium hands usually take the time to check that they are playing in turn and not drawing attention to themselves or their big hand.

  Later in the hand, players who appear to be reaching for their chips are usually trying to obtain a free card. They hope that you'll be intimidated into checking, after which they will also decide to check so that they get their extra card. When you see this, definitely bet, or raise, and most often, you will see your opponent reveal his true colours – and fold.
- Help with Your Calls
  In most low-standard games, players who try to help their opponent with a decision whether to call or not, almost always want you to fold. If a player had a good hand, he would just keep quiet and hope that you call. In high-standard games, such action could mean anything: it'll be part of an ongoing mind-game with an opponent.

Note that many of the above basic tells are simply variations of the weak-is-strong, strong-is-weak basic psychology.

Here is one last basic tell that I really like and, I confess, although I've noticed it happening, I haven't really used it to my advantage. I think it's quite an advanced piece of poker thought, but it's still beautifully simple and, best of all, as it involves the players no longer in the hand, it's likely to be a very accurate tell, since they have nothing vested in the hand to want to fool anyone else.

Reaction on The Flop of Opponents out of The Hand

Low-Limit players who are not in the hand tend not to be watching the actions of their opponents, but wondering whether they might not have played their dodgy hole cards after all. When a juicy flop hits, such as:

You may well see a player roll his eyes, bang the table, or even utter an under-his-breath expletive. That usually means that one of the outstanding jacks is catered for.

Even a pair of fours in the hole is not that great now, but if you've just mucked Q♣ 5♣ – as you should have done – you may well react badly to this flop. Knowing that the nut card is accounted for – and two further clubs – may be enough for you to alter your own view of the developing situation.

The case jack may well appear as if by magic. Most inexperienced players laugh when the flop is tripped, because they haven't seen it happen that often; if an opponent looks sick, the case jack is in the discard pile – and that can be reassuring to you. Indeed, sometimes, if you keep your ears pricked, you can hear one opponent whisper to the other that he just passed a jack.

So, these are some of the main, basic tells for which you should be looking out, and those which you should consciously try to avoid yourself. Indeed, let's take a moment or two to work out the best basic strategy for table image in low-limit games.

Table Image and Resolutions for Success

As previously discussed, poker is not really a barnstorming, glamorous game; on television, directors have often had to try to persuade the players to sex up their behaviour so that the game seems less dull. However, if you want to win at poker, you must treat it with respect and a determination to concentrate and improve your game. To this end, these would be my suggestions, when playing in a casino, card club or serious home game.

1) Choose your game carefully. We'll talk a lot more about game selection, particularly for online play where there are so many tables from which to choose but, in a live game, play at stakes with which you are comfortable, for sensible sums, against opponents who are not known to be much stronger than you. If you can't find a game in which you feel happy and confident, hard though it will be, resolve not to play that day.

2) Blend in with the table. Discover the rules and styles of play before sitting down (it is better to ask someone at the card-room manager's desk, rather than the dealer at

your table, where your opponents will witness your enquiries).

Acknowledge opponents and dealer, but keep yourself to yourself whilst you watch the initial action unfold.

3) Buy in for the total sum you are prepared to stake, preferably the table maximum. By all means, retain some of that stake in its racks, or to one side, but stack your chips and look like you are sitting down for the long haul and that you are a serious player who's come for business (and not just to fritter your chips away for a thrill).

4) Pick a strong hand to play as your first. You'd like to win that first hand (it's good to play with your opponents' money from the start). If you have to pass every hand for the first hour, so be it. This will bolster your image as a serious, selective player and may allow you to loosen your style to steal blinds or run bluffs at a later stage.

5) Be patient and disciplined. Stick to the tight starting-hand selections and play them strongly. This tight/aggressive style will serve you well. (Tight/aggressive means be tight in your selection of starting hands, and aggressive in the way you play the hands you select.)

There may be hours of passing marginal hands but every one that you choose to muck will be money saved in the long term. If you can save money on your poor and intermediate hands, then your winnings from your strong hands will be worth much more to you and your bankroll.

If a starting hand is marginal – don't play it.

6) Do not waste down time at the table by dreaming, fretting about poor cards, or wandering off to play a few hands of Blackjack. Observe your opponents carefully and try to learn about their individual style of

play, body language, and reactions to the unexpected. Try to put them on a specific hand and compare that to what they may show at the end. Remember that, since low-limit Hold 'Em hands often result in showdowns, you will be offered information – you must resolve to be bothered to take advantage of it.

7) Don't look at your hole cards until it is your turn to act. Instead, watch your opponents as they look at their hole cards. To know that the two players to your left are disgusted with their hands and are preparing to throw them away can be a huge advantage when deciding what action to take.

Harder than this is not to look at the flop, turn, or river cards when you are still in the hand. Continue to observe your opponents. Less experienced players will give away how they are feeling about the hand as it develops and you must be looking to spot this.

At first, doing this may seem very odd to you; indeed, you may find it nigh on impossible, especially if you have played only a few hands up to this point. I guarantee you that, not only will it become second nature to you quite quickly but, the moment you make a great play based on the reactions of your opponents, you will be convinced that this is the way to go. If that doesn't happen for you straight away, bear with it, because it will happen soon, and you will love it.

8) Try to keep your betting decisions consistent.

To avoid revealing information by your betting speed, I recommend counting to ten in your head whenever you are considering what to do, from starting hand to action on the flop. This takes discipline when you had a great hand, were called, and now suspect you've been overtaken, but just do the count and then pass. Once you master a fairly-consistent betting speed, you will be able to forget about it, knowing that you are hiding a valuable source of information from observant opponents.

9) Whenever it is your turn to act, however you have been behaving previously, keep quiet and concentrate. In this way, whether you just decide to pass or whether you take more dramatic action, your opponents will be used to seeing you focus when the spotlight is on you – regardless of whether your hand is any good or not – and they will therefore be less able to draw conclusions from your change of behaviour.

All this may seem like hard work to you but, I assure you, it really isn't, especially once you get into the habit of doing it. Think of it like driving. When you first learnt to drive, you probably thought that the coordination required would be tough to master: the gear changes, checking the mirror, parking, managing on the freeways, getting through narrow entrances. Now, you take all these for granted and you drive, concentrated, but relaxed. So it is with poker.

But, you may say, it's supposed to be a game; it's supposed to be *fun*. Well, you can treat it as an idle pastime if you wish; just be prepared to lose money doing it. I can't think of any game of skill, be it physical or mental, that does not require practice, concentration, dedication and self-awareness. Any game worth playing will demand these elements from those wanting to become successful. Of course, natural talent will help but do you really think that Tiger Woods doesn't hit thousands of practice shots, or Roger Federer doesn't consult his coach on strategy, fitness and shot selection? You bet they do. And, so do the top poker players. If they don't study, they sure practise – and so must all of us if we're going to compete with them.

Finally, if you are scoring with money, why would you not want to score your maximum? I've played Blackjack all

over the world and I am consistently amazed to find that
only a tiny percentage of players follow the basic strategy.
Anyone who is keen on cards could learn this in about an
hour. It would reduce the house edge to a bare minimum
and give any player a fighting chance. But, people can't be
bothered. So, they lose their money and call themselves
unlucky.

What I'm trying to say is this: whatever your level at
poker, if you pick your game carefully, follow the advice
above, and pay attention, your likelihood of winning is
greatly increased. Indeed, I'd go as far as to say: if you
know your basic poker, if you are prepared to be patient
and follow this advice, you *will* win. Maybe not on your
first session but over, say, ten sessions, you'll record a
profit.

As you improve, so you can change styles of Hold 'Em,
swap games, increase stakes, try out different playing
styles. However, you will always have your default, sensible, winning style on which to fall back if things aren't
going well. Learn it well, and it will serve you well
throughout your entire poker career.

Short-handed Limit Hold 'Em Cash Games

The strategies that we have been discussing have been
based on a standard full, or nearly full, table of eight or
nine players. However, there will be many occasions in
casinos and card rooms as well as in home games when you
find yourself at a table with four to six players. This is
officially a short-handed game. Three players really isn't
much fun and two players is Heads-Up, which requires an
entirely different style of play and is rarely played for cash
(see Heads-Up Strategy in the Tournament section).

A short-handed game may be all that there is on offer or
your full table may become short-handed because people

leave. If it is the latter, check that it is not all the weaker players who have been busted out, leaving you with just the stronger stock against whom it may be difficult to make an impression. If you're not happy with the make-up of the game, just get up and leave. There will be another, better game for you later on. However, don't leave just because the game has become short-handed since if you adapt your strategy to the new conditions more effectively than your opponents, you will find yourself with an excellent opportunity to make money.

In simple terms, the fewer the players in a game, the lower the likely value of the winning hand. In short-handed games, high cards and single pairs frequently take down pots, whereas in a full game, those hands are likely to be second- or third-best, costing you a lot of money.

Basic Strategy for Short-handed Limit Hold 'Em Cash Games

Be more aggressive.

That's it.

Well, OK, let's delve a little deeper . . .

Because there are fewer players, the blinds will come around to you more frequently and you will need to be involved in more action to avoid being blinded away. In any case, you will want to be more involved pre-flop and on the flop, because the chances are that no one will have hit the flop really convincingly. The more players you can get off the hand, the more you reduce the pot odds for players on the draw and, ultimately, the more likely it is that you will take down the pot at the end.

How will that affect our starting-hand policy? To keep it simple, I'd recommend upgrading all the categories by one.

With the premium hands:

AA
KK
QQ
AK – suited or unsuited
AQ – suited or unsuited

You'll raise in any position, and re-raise also.

In addition, with the good hands, you'll consider raising too:

JJ
1010
99
88
AJ – suited or unsuited
A10 – suited or unsuited
A9 – suited or unsuited
KQ – suited or unsuited

Any of these hands might be raised in any position (early position isn't nearly as significant in short-handed games since there are still only two or three players to act before the blinds).

Notice that there are two glaring omissions in this section: Firstly, there is no reference to suited cards – this is basically because in the short-handed game, even if you hit two cards on the flop towards your flush, the pot odds are unlikely to be right for you to continue – there simply aren't enough bets in the pot to make it a profitable bet for you. Secondly, there is no mention of *mid* and *low* suited connectors. This is for similar reasons: draws for straights and flushes generally won't be worthwhile and whilst you might hit a low pair, those hands usually cost you money in the long run.

Conversely, when you hold top pair, two pair or trips and a threatening straight or flush card appears on the river, generally you do not need to be as afraid of this development as in a full game. The chances that players are drawing are relatively small; more likely they have a hand on which they think they may be winning and are calling you down.

Pre-flop, many experts like to raise and re-raise with any *mid* or *low* pair, and raise with any ace in late position. You have to be pretty good to play on the flop when you play as aggressively as this, but it will get your opponents thinking and worrying and that is exactly what you are seeking to achieve.

Let me give you an example:

Imagine that you are in first position and you decide to raise with 8♥ 8♠ and the player on the button re-raises you with 5♥ 5♣. You call and the flop comes:

You can see that when you check, as you likely will, and your opponent bets, you have little choice but to lay down your hand. Aggression is going to count for a lot in this short game.

Your style can loosen a little in a short-handed game, provided that you retain (indeed, increase) your aggression.

You can bet a little more, which is in keeping with your aggressive stance. Betting out middle, even bottom, pair is not outrageous.

You may well have the best hand now and take down the pot straight away.

Slow-playing when you are heads-up or in a three-handed pot is slightly safer, since your opponents are unlikely to have played cards simply because they are connected or suited. I would still urge you to bet out your hands in a fairly straightforward, aggressive way, because you will still get called down, since the game has become generally looser.

Finally, because you are likely to be playing more pots against one or two opponents, bluffs and semi-bluffs are more likely to yield a better percentage rate of success and therefore become a more attractive proposition than in a full game.

Casino and Card-Room Tips for Short-handed Games

If you are playing in a casino or card-room cash game and you find yourself playing in a short-handed game, either early on or after a full table has been in operation, one of the players might ask the dealer for a 'rake break'. This would reduce (and sometimes cancel) the rake taken by the house out of every pot. Since pots are likely to be smaller, and most casinos take a percentage up to a maximum, the rake is taking a proportionately larger chunk out of each pot.

If you don't enjoy the extra pressure that comes with short-handed play, don't forget to ask to move to a full game as early as you can, since most requests are dealt with on a first-come, first-served basis.

Do not be afraid to leave the table if the game no longer suits you. Learn to resist the likely complaints from other players that you are 'breaking up the game'. They are saying this only because they think they can beat you – otherwise, why not let you go? You are a free agent and it is absolutely not your responsibility to help out the casino or card room to fill their tables. Go get a drink, meal, stretch your legs and see what's available when you return.

If nothing suits you, tough as it may be, call it a day and come back another time.

Higher-Limit Hold 'Em Cash Games

Even if you can afford to lose thousands of dollars per session and you want to play with better players, I strongly advise you to serve your apprenticeship at low-limit tables. You may argue that you lack the patience to play for such small stakes, but what you are really saying is that you lack patience – period. Better get used to displaying some then, because that is what Limit poker is all about. And the best place to prove to yourself that you can be a grinder if you need to be is at the low-limit tables.

At the higher limits, you may not find that the standard increases greatly; it will depend upon where you play. But beware the mid-range stakes in major gambling cities, like Las Vegas and LA, London and Vienna. These zones are often populated by pros: patient, grinding, experienced professional players who make almost no mistakes. Winning at these tables will be tough and, as your stack diminishes each round by the size of the higher blinds, you will be tempted to play marginal hands. This is just what the experts want: you lose patience, they clean up and leave with your money.

It's back to game selection again and my advice would be this: if you've learnt nothing from this book that you didn't already know and regularly practise, then maybe you are ready for the higher-limit games.

If any of this stuff was new to you (hopefully, inspirational), then stick to a modest game in which you can continue to improve your results.

Finally, let your bankroll guide you to the higher games. At your current level, earn two hundred times the big blind of the higher game you want to join, and then if you lose it all, it's your opponents' money you've lost, and you return to your former game and build it up again.

In addition to having two hundred times the big blind for your new game as your bankroll, also earn two hundred times the big blind for the smaller game you are leaving so that if it all goes pear-shaped in your new game, your stake is just waiting for you when you return. Many of the world's top players have in their pasts moved to higher games, lost it all and returned to their lower-stake game. There is no shame involved. Eliminate ego and pride from your poker considerations, be a free man (or woman) and play smart.

Developing Higher Limit Hold 'Em Strategy and Table Understanding

You're going to have had to develop your own winning strategies before moving up. Your default tight/aggressive game will still serve you well, but you will need to mix it up deceptively to ensure that you get paid for your good hands.

Consult books dedicated to the subject of Mid- and High-Stake Limit Hold 'Em cash games.

Be prepared to be scrutinized much more, and much more effectively, by your opponents. You will have to increase your powers of observation and hand-reading accuracy also.

Your opponents will likely make fewer costly mistakes; so developing pots and taking them down will be that much harder.

Finally, some good news. You may find that in your card club or casino, the mid-stake, or even high-stake, games do not contain that many professionals and strong players – just rich, foolish ones. Learn from your fellow card-room players, sympathetic staff and dealers, and keep your eye out for passing wealthy palookas who venture into the room for some quick, satisfying action. That means they will be loose and you will be there to catch them. This does happen and if you are in the right place at the right time, you'll be able to cash in.

Limit Hold 'Em Tournament Play

Like cash games, Limit Hold 'Em tournaments are more of a showdown game than Pot-Limit or No-Limit where big pre-flop raises or enormous bluffs at the end can steal the hand without any cards being shown. Nonetheless, as in all tournaments, the blinds will rise steadily and the pressure to increase your chip stack will become ever greater.

My conservative, tight/aggressive style is, if anything, even better suited to Limit tournaments than No-Limit events. However, if you have developed a consistently successful alternative style, then stick with it; but the methods briefly outlined below have served me well.

A poker tournament breaks down into different sections during which your aims and playing styles should adapt to achieve what is required to keep in the event and, ideally, gain chips to improve your position.

I definitely favour a disciplined, tight approach during the first half of the event, loosening slightly to apply pressure in the third quartile, playing the best hand strongly and making early folds if the cards don't hit for you. I'm a great believer that, if you can be there with a half-decent chip stack as the money-cut-off point approaches, you are in a good position to attack the conservative and nervous players with pre-flop raises and re-raises, as well as mopping up those players who are short-stacked and have to risk their chips on sub-standard starting hands. When this strategy works, you are not only in the money, but also in a good position to challenge for the poker player's 'Mecca' – the Final Table, where the big-money prizes are distributed.

Overview

Throughout the event, you should be aware of the number of players who started, plus re-buys taken (where applicable), so that you know the total number of chips in play. Then, as players get eliminated, you can calculate (roughly is fine) what the average chip count should be and therefore understand where you lie in the tournament as a whole. Your position will go some way to determining how aggressive you should become at different stages. Most big tournaments will provide you with information about players remaining, average chip stacks, and the times at which blinds will rise and breaks will be taken. You need to remain focused and alert to all this information as well as concentrating on the players around your table and your own game.

First Quartile

Whilst some players favour a super-aggressive style from the start, I definitely favour a slow, steady beginning. It is important, particularly if you are not very experienced in the tournament arena, that you should spend time analysing the players at your table, especially the four players surrounding you: the two directly to your right and the two to your left. Once you have formed an opinion as to their basic style, you have the beginnings of a read on their actions if you come up against them in a big hand.

During this time, you should play only the premium and very good starting hands:

AA, KK, QQ, JJ
AK – suited or unsuited
AQ – suited or unsuited
1010, 99, 88, 77

My suggestion would be to raise with all of these hands –
and also to re-raise with these hands. This may seem very
aggressive (particularly with the mid-pairs) but aggression
used on good starting hands is a sound, solid style of play
which has proven very successful.

The advantage of the re-raise is that if you are called and
the flop appears, if your opponent misses the flop (and 80
per cent of the time he will do) then a further bet by you
may well take the pot there and then – even if you too have
missed the pot.

If your further bet is then called, you may yet still have
outs which would give you the winning hand because you
started with a premium hand.

The mere action of passing many hands, followed by
raising and re-raising when you do play a hand is sufficient
evidence for your opponents to read you as a tight/ag-
gressive, strong player, and this in turn will provide lee-
way for blind stealing and occasional bluffing during the
later stages of the event.

Second Quartile

You should maintain your tight image. Be aware that, if
you have changed tables or if several of your original
opponents have been eliminated and replaced by new
players, you may need to re-establish that image.

If you have less than the average chip count (or if you
have played almost no hands whatsoever), this is a good
time to loosen your starting requirements a little, but only
in late position to an unraised pot. Since the blinds will

still be reasonably small, you want to try to pick up some pots reasonably cheaply. Do not be tempted to enter the action in any other position than late (that means: one from the button and the button).

Additional starting hands:

AJ – suited or unsuited
A10 – suited or unsuited
KQ – suited
KJ – suited
Ace-low – suited

Whilst you might choose to raise with AJ and A10 in late position, the other hands are more likely to be played by calling to see a flop cheaply. Notice that, apart from AJ and A10, each of these hands is very flop-sensitive. If you don't pick up solid top-pair hands, 2-pair, trips or straight draws, then it will be best to go quietly. In the case of ace-small suited, you are seeking only a cheap nut flush draw, or perhaps 2-pair or trips on the flop. If you play these lesser hands tightly on the flop before the size of bet increases on the turn and river, you have a chance to hit some big hands without denting your chip stack too badly.

Obviously, if you become aware that the two players to your left are very tight, then you may use that information to steal blinds with weaker hands on deals where there is no action to you. Otherwise, keep to premium starting hands and play them aggressively – with raises and re-raises.

Third Quartile

As the third quartile of the event approaches, so will the point at which the cash prizes will start to be paid. All poker players have an aversion to being eliminated 'on the bubble' (one place off the money) and many will do anything to avoid that fate. You will see almost a physical tightening, as well as in their style of play, from these players and it is these individuals whom you must target for attacking play.

I believe that to have any chance of a Final-Table appearance, you must be fearless at these stages, stealing blinds and raising anyone who seems to want to see a flop cheaply. By this time, your tournament eye should be well enough focused to be able to spot the attitudes and styles of your opponents and to vary your play accordingly.

If your entire table seems to fall into a conservative, tight style of play, then you should loosen up yourself and become more aggressive, stealing blinds and bullying your opponents; if your table is aggressive and wild, then hunker down, wait for a premium hand, and sock it to 'em!

I do think that, for less experienced players, to survive to the latter stages of a tournament is fantastic experience: you get to play against the best players in the field and improve your game, whilst still receiving a prize for lasting so long. Once this has occurred a few times, you will be in a strong position to challenge for the Final Table and even one of the really big prizes for the medal positions.

Fourth Quartile

If you make it this far, you have certainly experienced one or more of the following:

- good cards at good times
- fine play by you
- excellent luck
- poor opponents

In truth, you often require all four conditions to make it to a Final Table in any half-decent tournament. To make it up the ranking lists and increase your prize money, you certainly seek good cards at a good moment. Because the blinds will be so high at these latter stages, I think that you should remain patient and play only the hands listed in the earlier sections. Experts may be able to play weaker hands and judge accurately their actions on the flop. Unless you are completely confident of doing so, your best chance is to wait and hope for serious action on the good hands which you choose to play. Remain positive and aggressive and, with a little luck, you have a chance of increasing your stack and providing a serious threat. If you get knocked out, having been beaten on the draw when you have held AA, KK or AK, you just have to accept that these things do happen and the odds were in your favour. Keep playing with those odds and you will succeed.

Practice Tips for Limit Tournaments

If you are planning to play in a serious Limit Tournament, then practise with your regular school for a few sessions. Many players swap between No-Limit and Limit and find that they are mentally unprepared for the big changes in style required. More often than not, regular Limit players lose far too many chips on marginal hands when they switch to No-Limit; and No-limit players forget that more hands get called down to the showdown at Limit and find themselves unable to bluff opponents off a hand. So, prepare for a Limit event by playing Limit poker.

The change between a Limit Hold 'Em cash game and tournament is also huge, most obviously in that the blinds never rise during a cash game and therefore there is no pressure on you to accumulate chips. If you usually play a cash game with your friends, try to persuade them to play a tournament with you instead.

Finally, playing online is a fine way to practise and Limit tournaments are available somewhere every hour of every day. There are also Limit Sit & Go events (one-table tournaments) which provide an excellent practice ground for the Final-Table scenario. Although online poker and live poker differ quite considerably, simply becoming fluent in the form of game you plan to play will benefit you enormously. Take a look at the Online-Poker sections of this book to give yourself the best chance to win money whilst you practise.

OTHER LEADING POKER VARIATIONS

This book has concentrated on Texas Hold 'Em because it is the most widely played poker game in the world. In terms of numbers, the players who enjoy Hold 'Em dwarf all the other variations put together. The combination of television coverage of Hold 'Em tournaments, that the WSOP Main Event is No-Limit Texas Hold 'Em, and the fact that the game itself is a vibrant mixture of luck, skill, aggression, patience and drama has made it, indisputably, number one.

Although Texas Hold 'Em is played by almost everyone at some point in their poker careers (and many play nothing else), there are many other excellent poker games as well as countless home-game variations featuring wild cards, change of seats, card swaps and . . . well, you name it!

Here, in a very concise form, is an introduction to some of the most popular varieties, still widely played today in card clubs and casinos. No sooner is the ink dry on these entries than another form will be invented which, one day, may take over the world.

To play any of these games for money, study at least one good book on the subject, practise online or with friends for minimum stakes and develop a feel and understanding for the game which allows you to concentrate on the table, and not just on remembering rules.

Omaha

In many respects Omaha is similar to Texas Hold 'Em. However, there are considerable differences in the value of your hole cards and, because you have four of them rather than the standard two, the hand values become much looser – meaning that you and your opponents are more likely to show down big hands than at Hold 'Em. One of the major problems for Hold 'Em players switching to Omaha is that every hand looks enormous (with four hole cards as opposed to just two, the chances of picking up high pairs and running cards are much higher). However, all that glisters is not gold – and Omaha proves it!

As well as seeing four hole cards, there is a total of five community cards, revealed as flop, turn and river as in Hold 'Em, but in Omaha, you must use only – and exactly – two hole cards and exactly three board cards to make up your hand. You have no flexibility in this regard. In the same way that your hand develops and changes as the board cards appear at Hold 'Em, so does the value of everyone's hands at Omaha – only a great deal more. This makes Omaha a real roller-coaster ride.

Limit Omaha

As with all forms of Limit Poker which we discuss here, the bets for each round are limited to particular sums which you will see posted at your table. Since there are always four rounds of betting, if you are playing $10/$20

Limit Omaha, you will be limited to bets and raises of $10 for the first two rounds: pre-flop and post-flop; and then bets and raises of $20 for the second two rounds of betting: post-turn and post-river.

How many raises and re-raises you are permitted will be down to house rules. Five raises is typically the limit in many card rooms.

Finally, assuming that there are still players in the pot by the end, players reveal their hands for the showdown. Amazingly, even good players still misread their hands occasionally at Omaha and, if you are a regular Texas Hold 'Em player, you will find that it is sometimes difficult to determine who takes the pot. Remember that every hand must consist of exactly two of the hole cards and three of the board cards. So, if the board reads:

only three of those cards can be used by the player. So, you will need to be holding two cards matching the community cards to make your straight, or two higher or lower running cards to make up a higher or lower straight.

If you held:

you could use J♥ and Q♦ to add to the board's 10♠ 9♦ and 8♠ to make the high straight, or with

you could use 5♣ and 6♦ along with the board's 7♥ 8♠ and 9♦ to form the low straight, but your J♥ could not be used, because you would only have four cards in sequence before you had to use your second hole card – and nothing there completes the straight.

For each of these variations, consult at least one specialist book to study strategy, and practise online or with friends for low stakes whilst you put your plans to the test and pick up on some of the subtle nuances of the games.

Pot-Limit Omaha and No-Limit Omaha

Both Pot-Limit and No-Limit Omaha are identical to Limit Omaha, except for the betting structure, which is modified accordingly. In Pot-Limit, you can bet up to the entire value of the pot at your turn. In No-Limit, you can bet whatever you wish, up to all your chips, at your turn.

Naturally, each form of betting demands a different response from the players in terms of strategy and it is often tough to switch from one form of the game to another. It is perhaps harder to switch from playing Hold 'Em to Omaha – since at the latter, every hand looks so full of promise.

Omaha 8 or Better (Hi/Lo)

This version of Omaha is even more crazy than the standard versions above and yet it is fast becoming one of the world's favourite games. This is mainly because it provides a massive amount of action, with players vying to win the low hand, or the high hand – or sometimes both – and with multiple opportunities for your hand to develop during the course of the deal. Better still, according to some, even the world's top players haven't worked out the best strategy for this game; in fact, they can't even agree on which cards qualify as good starting hands!

The game pays half the pot to the best high hand and half the pot to the best low hand, assuming that it is at least 8-low (as the name suggests). If there is no 8-low or poorer hand, then both halves of the pot will be won by the high hand. Sounds complicated?

Let's qualify some of the elements. For the low hand, you must have five cards no higher than 8. Flushes and straights do not count as made hands, but pairs and trips do, so you must have five cards, unpaired, from the 8 downwards. Aces count both high and low, so the best *low* hand is A 2 3 4 5 – suited or not, and the worst *low* hand is 4 5 6 7 8 (which are the five highest cards, unpaired, that can form a low hand).

Indeed, reasonably often, there is no low hand available. For example, if the board came:

How could you form a low hand with two of your cards and three from the board? Only one six can play, since pairs are not permitted, so that leaves 4♠, a 6 and Q♦. Since the low hand must be no higher than 8, there cannot be a low hand makeable on this board so now all attention turns to the high hand, which will win the entire pot.

If there are three or more low, unpaired cards showing on the board, then there is a chance of a low hand, and you must take your two lowest cards from your hole cards to complete your low hand. Since the ace and the 2 are the two lowest cards available to you, they are the best starting cards for your hand to contain if you are going to have a shot at the low half of the pot.

Now, let's introduce the last nightmarish element to this explanation. You must use two cards from your hand to make the low hand, and you must use two cards from your hand to form the high hand – these cards can be the same two, just one, or a different two for each hand you are declaring.

If you hold these cards in the hole:

And the board comes:

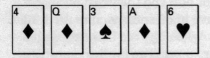

you can form the low hand by taking 2♣ and 7♦ from your hand, making:

and for your high hand, you can take A♠ and Q♥ to make:

That's a pretty-nice low and a pretty-decent high hand. You're in with a shot at both halves of the pot here. Notice that you used two completely different cards to create each of your hands.

Bear in mind that once you are used to the game, it is reasonably easy to see from the board whether there is a low hand available (there must be three unpaired cards no higher than 8 showing) and to calculate what the winning low hand will be; but it is also not difficult to work out the highest-available high hand.

Since you must use two cards from your hand, there must be three suited cards showing for a flush to be possible; a pair on the board to be able to create quads; three cards in sequence to create a straight. Trips and 2-pair are rife at Omaha.

Starting Hands

Since there are two halves of the pot to consider, it is helpful to describe the starting hands which you might consider playing. The best starting hand would be: A A 2 3 of any suits and, best of all, when one ace is suited with a low card, and the other ace is suited with the other low card. This gives you the top pair right now, maximum potential for the nut flush in the high hand, and A 2 available for the ultimate low hand.

Any starting hand containing A A 2 is a premium hand as it immediately bodes well for the best low hand and is ahead right now for the high hand also.

Even hands containing A 2 are strong and usually worth playing, becoming premium hands if they also contain a high pair, such as A 2 K K or A 2 Q Q.

Other starting hands, still strong but less so than above are:

A A 3 any
A 2 3 4
A 2 3 any
A 3 4 5
A A 4 5
A 3 K K

Four high cards (10+) are reasonable, as are:

2 3 4 5
2 3 4 any

Beware hands which contain low and middle pairs since if you don't hit trips, your pairs are bound to be beaten by most of the remaining players and when you do trip them, you may lose a bunch of chips calling down one, or more, higher tripped hands.

The flop, turn and river strategies start as simple and quickly become very complicated. Much of the expert play revolves around trying to occlude your hand so starting hands which seem perfect for a raise may be slow-played and the strong (but not premium) hands sometimes get played very strongly indeed. Search out a specialist Omaha 8 Hi/Lo book before sitting down at anything but a beginners' table. The speed of the game and the size of the pots make it a dangerous game for the inexperienced up against those with a decent under-standing of the game.

Five-Card Stud

This is the classic form of poker, with each player being dealt five hole cards and the betting running on those cards alone. With no open or community cards and no draw, this was always a battle of psychology and, for modern tastes, lacking in action. Variations with mini-mum hands and wild cards abound.

Five-Card Draw

In poker, the draw was a major innovation. Players could swap between 1–5 cards (or none at all) with new cards from the deck. The draw provided an extra round of betting: pre-draw and post-draw, as well as producing a far wider spectrum of likely makeable hands. The psychology of swapping a particular number of cards, along with the pot odds for making your hoped-for combination made it a far more complex game which soon became de rigueur throughout saloons and back rooms.

Seven-Card Stud

Some consider this to be the ultimate poker game of skill and judgment. Played in many variations of Limit and No-Limit form, there are no fewer than five rounds of betting – producing all the action the hardened gambler could want – with changing odds, psychology and judgments at every turn. At a full table, there will also be many face-up cards, allowing you – should you have the capacity to do so – to re-calculate odds more accurately. Above all, Seven-Card Stud is a memory game, not only about your opponents and the styles in which they played their cards and dealt with various situations, but also about the cards which appear and then, when a player folds, are turned over. Remembering those cards and their ability to make the probability of hitting your draw stronger or weaker is a major part of the skill required to succeed at Seven-Card Stud.

Seven-Card Stud features ante-bets rather than blinds so there is no rest from the endless drain from your stacks. However, the ante should be only a small proportion of a starting bet (usually 10–20%) so there is no question of protecting antes in the same way that you might – just might – consider doing so at Hold 'Em. Also markedly different from Hold 'Em or Omaha is that the dealer, despite moving in a clockwise direction, has no positional advantage. This is because, as you will see, the player 'under the gun' is actually the one showing the lowest card (or highest card in Razz – see below). Therefore, the betting position is effectively randomized. As for me, I hate being the dealer at Seven-Card Stud. There are lots of cards to deal, and I'm trying to concentrate on everybody's hands as well as my own, thanks. The good news is that in many casinos and card clubs a professional dealer will sort it all out for you.

Let's see how the game works: each player is dealt two cards in the hole and one card face up. For the first round of betting, the player with the lowest up-card is first to act (ties are split by order of suit; as in bridge, highest to lowest rank: spades, hearts, diamonds, clubs).

This player must make the bring-in bet, and then the action moves clockwise, as ever, with players calling, raising or folding. When that round is completed, the dealer provides every player remaining with a second up-card and another round of betting begins – this time, and for the remainder of the hand – starting with the player showing the best hand with his up-cards. A third up-card is now dealt to all remaining, followed by another round of betting, followed by a fourth up-card. More betting follows before, for all players remaining, a final card is dealt face down to each. Like the first two down-cards, this final down-card is seen only by the individual player. Again, the player with the strongest hand showing in his up-cards starts the betting and eventually players fold or come to a showdown.

Like many forms of poker, Seven-Card Stud values starting hands very strongly; if you start with the best, you'll likely end up with the best. However, unlike most forms, you can actually see one third of your opponents' starting hands (since there are two hole cards and one up-card for each player). This means that you may have a great hand but you suspect from the cards showing that it may not be the best.

Let's take a quick look at the best starting hands:

trips – that is to say, a pair of queens in the hole and a queen showing [Q Q] Q

high pairs in the hole [K K] any

high pairs, with one card in the hole and one up-card [Q any] Q

suited connectors (I like the high ones only, but lots of players go wild for these whatever their size)

[A♥ Q♥] K♥ or [Q♣ K♣] J♣

after that, weaker hands, which may not be worth playing unless raising:

any pair in the hole [7♠ 7♣] any

any pair [8♠ any] 8♦

semi-suited connectors (again, preferably high ones) like [K♥ 10♥] Q♥ or [Q♠ 9♠] 10♠

As ever, the advice is absolutely clear-cut: study and hours of dedicated practice. This is truly a game where the skilful will enjoy their edge sooner than in most variations.

Razz

Razz is Seven-Card Stud LOW, so that your aim is always to make the lowest hand possible. As with most other low games, straights and flushes don't exist, so the best low hand is A 2 3 4 5.

This variation is dealt the same way as standard Seven-Card Stud, but here, the bring-in bet is placed by the player boasting the highest card showing, and all subsequent rounds are started by the player showing the lowest hand in his up-cards.

HORSE

Many expert poker players find that, because of the multitude of online players qualifying for the World Series of Poker final event – the $10,000 buy-in No-Limit Texas Hold 'Em Tournament – the field is so enormous that to reach the final stages has become too much a matter of luck. To try to return the game to its roots of skill, versatility and stamina, a new form of poker tournament has emerged at the start of the new millennium: the HORSE tournament.

HORSE stands for:

H = Hold 'Em
O = Omaha
R = Razz
S = Seven-Card Stud
E = Seven-Card Stud Hi/Lo Eights or better

If you are playing a HORSE game in a club, casino or at home, the style of poker played rotates through the variations every time the dealer button makes a full round. In tournaments, the game changes at the end of each round, with blind levels rising after each set of variations has been completed.

In 2006, the WSOP introduced a major new event, in the form of a $50,000 buy-in HORSE tournament. Only 143 players entered – the small field being an indicator of just how tough it is to be able to master all these variations and end up on top. Most competitors were well-known poker professionals with years of experience and even they looked shattered by the end.

In the old days of poker, almost every professional was proficient in every form of the game imaginable. Nowadays, more players choose to specialize in just one game:

for tournaments, usually Hold 'Em; for cash games, often Seven-Card Stud or Omaha. To win a major HORSE event is a true sign of great poker talent across the many variations played today.

100 TIPS FOR TEXAS HOLD 'EM

Assuming that you are playing low- or mid-stake No-Limit Texas Hold 'Em in a live or online game, these tips should hit the spot whenever you are in need of some inspiration. For other forms and variations of the game, many of these tips will provide sound guidance.

1 Ask yourself: Do I Want to Play Poker, or to Win at Poker?

This is a crucial question since it may well decide whether you will thrive, or merely survive, at the green baize. It is the first question in a series which will lead to sufficient self-awareness for you to be a genuine force at the table.

If you have merely watched poker on television or online; if you fancy a life without a traditional pattern of work; if you think that the life of a professional (or semi-professional) gambler is glamorous and exciting, then I urge you to pause.

To win at poker requires discipline, patience, self-awareness, a desire to observe and learn, and guts. If you can't be bothered with any of this, and what you really want is action, then decide right now, that to play poker is your goal. You'll enjoy it, you may win a little for a short time, you may live your dream. However, if you aspire to be in contention for a WSOP or WPT bracelet; if you'd like to make consistent pocket money – or much more; if you enjoy learning and derive enjoyment from the process then, if you put your mind to it, you will play better poker, you will win more, more often, and better still, you'll continue to improve every time you play. But, it does take effort. Are you up for it?

By the way, there is nothing to be ashamed of should you choose just to enjoy your game and make no effort. I know many people who accept that they have no desire to take poker seriously, to be patient, to take notes, to read books, to practise online. They play and they have fun. They play little home games, mid-stake ring games in card clubs, high-stake casino poker; they're even playing in the WSOP events. I love these guys – and so should you – these are the very people against whom you want to play, because your skill advantage will make you a winner over time – inevitably.

Finally, if you are as keen to improve as I hope you are, do remember that this is just a game, and should be enjoyed as such. Personally, my enjoyment is derived from improving, honing my skills and aiming for the top (even if I acknowledge that there's a long way to go). However, don't let poker make you miserable: because you aren't improving as much as you'd like, because you're enduring a terrible run of cards, because it's ruining a relationship or stunting your social life.

Answered that first question yet? Player or winner?

2 Assess your Current Poker Standing – Accurately

The first question is: are you winning or losing? There really are only two categories: breaking even is more a state of mind than a reality. If you look deeper (through taking notes and making records of your play), you need to ask yourself this: is my profit generally greater from winning sessions than my losses from poor sessions? Typically, a top player will lose $500 one day and win $1,000 the next; a beginner loses $300 and then wins $50.

From this, you can extrapolate that not only must you strive to increase your winnings (a concept with which we are all familiar) but you must work equally hard to limit your losses. For every hand you correctly pass, for each second-best hand you lay down on the flop, for every opponent's value bet you don't pay off, you are saving money – and ultimately that will convert into bigger profits. Yet, despite their equality, most players think only of greedily building the pot and never of saving that small blind or not calling a little bet even when you know – for certain – that you are beaten.

Are you playing in the right game? Successful poker is about good table selection. Unless you are playing a tournament, you get to choose whether you play at a certain table or not (in a home game you're tied to one table for the duration but, if the game is so bad for you, you should duck out of that school for a while). You must use wisely that freedom to pick your game. You must eliminate peer pressure or personal ego when it comes to this decision, because it is your money you are talking about.

If you are losing in your current game right now, consider moving down to a lower-stake game for a while. Build your bankroll and then move up again, together with greater confidence and increased skill. Never believe that if you move to a higher-stake game (and therefore, usually, a higher-skill level) you won't suffer so many bad beats or idiotic calls because, to win at poker, you need your opponents to get into situations like that. If that's the game you are in now – great. Stay there, remain patient, and eventually you will clean up. Then, move up a level. Remember that the pros who made this game great did so by hustling their way around the country, finding little games, building their bankroll and finding bigger games and building it some more. Once their bankroll and skill levels had increased in tandem, they were ready to take on the world. That, I believe, is how you should structure your own road to poker greatness.

3 Be Aware of your Own Image

Since you are in the business of trying to decode the meanings of your opponents' actions, remain cognizant of the fact that their actions will always be influenced by yours – as an instant reaction, or as a long-term formation in their minds of your image – and that awareness of your own image is therefore essential to reading your opponents.

For example, if you are playing well, and you are aware that your opponents show you respect, then show them respect in return when they act aggressively towards you.

You might raise under the gun with A♣ Q♦ and the player in third position re-raises you. What does this mean? He believes that, despite your show of strength, he has you beaten. Since you could not be worse for your raise in that position, you must fold.

Contrast that with an early position raise from a loose/aggressive player who has been raising once every five deals. Now, a re-raise from an opponent represents a far wider range of hands: a premium or very good hand, any pair, high suited-connectors . . . nothing.

One re-raise is quite different from another because of the initial raiser's image.

Similarly, you might have presented a loose/aggressive image throughout and raise on the button with the same

A♣ Q♦. Now, when you receive a re-raise, you can re-raise. You know that your opponent knows that you could have raised with anything in that position, hence he may have very little, and you can put him to the test.

4 Buy In for The Maximum

If you can afford to do so, always buy in for the maximum amount. Equally important: if you can't afford to buy in for the maximum, play at a lower-stake table.

The advantages for a maximum buy-in are many:

You have sufficient funds that a series of small losses will not affect you psychologically – you cannot worry about money and play good poker.

Your stack size will prove a threat to your opponents. Subconsciously, the sight of big stacks may alter your opponents' actions: they may choose to check rather than bet, call rather than raise or re-raise – this is to your advantage.

Players joining your table will wonder whether you have won those chips and while they are wondering that, you will be winning their chips.

Players may feel that they are playing catch-up from the moment that they join the table – this will make them over-eager and cause them to push too hard.

The ultimate effect of the maximum buy-in is to re-enforce your confidence and to present a confident image to your opponents: this is the perfect combination.

5 Mix Up your River Betting

Particularly online, but also in low- and mid-standard live games, players miss opportunities to make value bets (an extra bet which could lose occasionally but, in the long run, will prove profitable – based on holding what you believe is the best hand) which optimize their chances to make a little extra from the hand.

Equally, to check at the end when out of position, despite holding what you believe is the best hand, can be profitable to you – again, especially online. Players who have been calling or raising into draws which you know they have missed can often be relied upon to try to steal the pot at the end. Since you have checked, this leads them to believe that a big bluff will take you off the hand. This is exactly what you want since, in these situations, a value bet by you is unlikely to be paid off, whereas you can call, or even raise, the big bluff. Online, it is not unusual to see players going all-in to try to bluff you off the pot. Prepare for some very indignant donkeys when you call and take the hand with the nuts!

6 Beware The Fast-Changing Online Table

You have carefully selected a table ideal for your game. You sit down, win a pot or two – it's going well. Then you notice that two players have left and their seats have been filled by new personnel. Assess these characters carefully because, if they spoil the game, you must react quickly. Imagine that your lazily fishing table is suddenly transformed by two raisers and re-raisers, preventing you from maintaining control of the game. Online there are thousands of tables from which to choose. Don't be so lazy that you can't be bothered to move when unsuitable opponents join your game. Don't feel that you have to outplay anyone who joins your game – just leave and outplay some less demanding opposition. This is your money we're talking about – surely your hard-earned cash is worth protecting with a two-minute delay and a couple of mouse clicks?

7 *Standardize your Reaction Times*

When it's your turn to act, do you fold quickly with a sigh, call smoothly and grandstand a raise? If you do, you're letting yourself in for trouble in the future. Good players will soon learn to recognize when you are between actions; your reaction time will tell them. Even online, the speed of your action (or, worse still, the use of auto-action boxes) may, at a crucial moment, telegraph what you hold – to the profit of your observant opponent.

Ideally, you seek to take all actions in the same tempo. Perhaps, count up to five slowly before acting. Then fold, without any sign of reluctance or frustration, announce your call or raise, and push in your chips. If you practise this for a while, it becomes second nature pretty quickly (you need to keep checking on yourself, because you can slip back into bad habits very easily). The advantages may seem intangible but, to your opponents, your new un-readable style will prove frustrating – and that is exactly what you want.

Some experts say that to pause momentarily before making any move is a very good way of sowing doubt in opponents' minds. Players often misread your hes-istation and find themselves drawn into hands that they should be well out of, or being driven off winning positions.

Incidentally, maintaining this tempo is relatively easy when things are going anywhere from not-too-well to really-quite-well. When they get dire and desperate or you are on a tremendous rush, then these rituals are often abandoned. Ironically, these are exactly the times when your discipline will convert most rapidly into saved chips or increased winnings.

8 You Don't Have to Do Anything

Most players get bored and then do something: usually they start to call. When you call on marginal or substandard hands, you have only yourself to blame when your stacks shrink. No one is making you enter a pot; no one is forcing you to call that raise. It is your choice. You are doing it. If you don't feel that you should do something at the poker table, then don't. Trusting that instinct, that gut feeling, is a very important part of poker.

You are, as Anthony Holden observes so wittily in his great poker book, *Big Deal*: 'Master of your own destiny'.

And your destiny may require you to fold the next thousand hands you pick up.

Being a tight/aggressive player, I spend many long hours folding hand after hand. I hate calling raises because I feel that it is a passive move, and I like to be setting the agenda for every hand in which I'm involved. That probably means that I fold too many hands pre-flop. However, the effect of this is to leave me with fewer tough flop, turn and river decisions: decisions that can cost hundreds of dollars. When my opponents comment on how tight I am, I smile to myself. I'm very happy to promote that image because a time will come when I can exploit it to my benefit. But, it never makes me feel that I should play more hands.

I got an e-mail recently to my website from a player to ask me whether she could have played a particular hand better. See what you would have done . . .

At an eight-seater $2/$4 online table, in first position, a supposedly decent player raised three times the big blind. The next player, supposedly also decent, raised to six times the big blind. My student, on the button, held: A♣ K♠. What should she do?

She told me that she folded and that, when she'd told her husband, he had laughed at her and told her that she should have pushed all her chips in.

Well, let's see. If you have noted the player UTG to be decent, and the same for the player in second position, what cards are they likely to be holding? Pairs, I should think. Maybe mid-pairs, more likely premium pairs, perhaps even AK also.

Thankfully, we know what happened, because the hand was played out when the re-raise was called. The flop came:

The first player bet and the second player called. The turn came:

Then the betting dried up and the river came:

The first player made a small bet, and the second player called. The first player showed QQ, the second, KK.

So, what should my correspondent have done?

In a tournament, if she was in any way short-stacked, she should probably all go in, but in a cash game . . .? She could have called; she could have raised – as it is, she would have won, although she had less than a 30 per cent chance of catching an ace on the board. And would she have called on the flop?

The fact is that her fold of A♠ K♠ turned out to be fine. She was behind, and she believed that both her opponents held very strong hands. That's a great time to fold!

The point is: she didn't have to do anything she didn't want to do.

Once you understand that you can trust your instincts for being ahead or behind on a hand, then you realize that you can do whatever you want at the poker table whenever you want – or do nothing at all. It's up to you.

Five Basic Errors to Eliminate . . .

9 Not Thinking about What your Opponent(s) Holds

Too many players look at only their own cards and take no notice of the fact that poker is a game of relative values. If you hold the top flush, that's great, but you must be aware of a possible full house. The reason why this tip is so important is that more money is lost with the second-best hand at poker than with any other.

The betting may reveal the likelihood of your opponents holding the cards they need to beat you – stay alert to it. It can save you a fortune.

Incidentally, equally important is not to get over-imaginative about what your opponent might hold when he makes a big bet into your very powerful hand. Keep in mind that while straight flushes and quads are very rare, big overbets on the river are common. Don't worry yourself into folding that nut flush or big full house.

10 Failing to Keep Notes and Records

To play online without keeping notes of opponents is verging on the criminal; it is certainly a waste of money.

Even the simplest of observations can save you thousands of dollars over a short period of time. To know that a player is close to un-bluffable; is a rock; will call any raise; will never raise into draws; generally fishes with nothing: any of these observations can make or break a poker hand.

The world's best live-game players are those who remember every hand they've ever played against you (and some of them when they weren't even involved personally) and use that information to judge your hand the next time they meet you. Online, the notes should make this gargantuan task much easier for you.

Keeping track of your session location, type of game, time of game, length of session and wins/losses will provide you with essential information to increase your bankroll.* For example, after a few weeks, a study of your records might reveal that you win far more consistently in one card room as opposed to another, at one stake rather than another, at one time of day as opposed to another. This information adds to your overall bank when it comes to table selection, which is of prime importance in optimizing your skills and boosting your bankroll. Remember that for most poker professionals, their income is based less on their own skill level, but on that of those they choose to play against. If the pros know that table selection is key, then so should we.

11 Playing Marginal Hands

Every time you choose to call a raise with A7 or KJ you hurt yourself doubly. Not only do you start the hand with chips committed when you are, statistically, well behind, but you also open yourself up to a whole world of pain when you face action on the flop, turn and river. We

* In some countries, for tax purposes, you are legally required to keep an accurate record of your wins and losses.

remember when these hands win pots because the win is usually accompanied by a great deal of risk. However, over time, you will lose a lot of chips this way, even if you play the hand really well when you are ahead.

Equally, when you call pre-flop with marginal hands, you are, statistically, frittering away your chips because, in the long run, playing these cards has a negative expectation and, eventually, the odds come home to roost! The next time you refuse to call $1 pre-flop holding Q7, remember to pat yourself on the back for just saving, maybe, five cents. Think how many times you face those decisions every time you play and work out how much money you can save over just one session. The problem is that we get bored and crave some action, so we start to limp in with the marginal hands. Forget it. Put up with the boredom a little while longer (and, if you must create action, pick a late-position hand and raise with it – at least, you are taking the initiative and pressuring your opponents). Better still, sit back, fold those marginal hands and reflect on your ever-growing wealth. Making money for doing the right thing! Sounds good, doesn't it?

12 Failing to Adjust to Different Forms

Players moving from cash games to tournaments tend to play too cautiously, failing to exert maximum pressure when the odds favour them. The raising of the blinds is the key problem for cash-game players when they move to a tournament. Learn to make a clear distinction between the two games so that your brain clicks into the right mode.

Moving from tournaments to cash games can prove quite exciting for the first half-hour or so. If you continue to play as aggressively in a cash game as you were in a tournament, you may steal some early pots and take players off hands but, eventually, one of them will lure you into a costly trap and, if you don't adjust quickly, the same will happen again and again. Your game is predictable – and that is a losing game.

13 Playing 'Turbo' Tournaments

Success in any poker tournament requires more than your fair share of luck: they are indeed far more reliant on luck than a steady cash game. However, the amount of luck involved tends to depreciate in relation to the length of the event. Hence, the WSOP final event, the $10,000 NL Hold 'Em, has been played over ten days with blind levels changing only after two hours. After all this poker, usually only pretty good players survive to the Final Table.

Online, most sites now offer 'Turbo' or 'Hi-Speed' versions of their Sit & Go tournaments as well as some MTTs. I urge you to resist these since, as the blind levels rise every few hands, or every few minutes, the luck factor is at its very greatest and any skill advantage you hold over the opposition will be negligible.

Really, these events are for folks who have a two-minute attention span and for the online poker rooms who charge far too much of an entry fee for such a short event. From their point of view, the more of these quickie tournaments you play, the more entry fees you'll pay and that suits them just fine.

As your game improves, you will want to play against predictable, poor players, over a long period of time. That combination increases the certainty of your winning. To play against unknown players, in an unpredictable format, over a short time span is exactly the opposite of the correct playing conditions if you want to win.

14 Get Out on The Flop

To call loosely pre-flop can be a winning tactic, provided that you have the discipline to make good lay-downs on the flop. To call for the turn starts to look like a passive, desperate tactic and will prove costly.

At No-Limit (and Pot-Limit), when the flop appears, make your decision to stay with the hand and to play it aggressively and positively (in other words, cut down on the checking and calling, and step up with a bet or a raise – at the very least, you will gain vital information about your opponents' hands) or lay down your hand now.

At Limit Hold 'Em, your decision must be based on the pot odds, and you are far more likely to call on marginal hands since you stand to win so much more in return for a call. Indeed, some players fold too eagerly on the flop at Limit Hold 'Em, neglecting to consider that two-pair and trips opportunities exist at the correct odds to continue in the hand.

Whatever the form you are playing: treat the flop as a key moment for a positive decision one way or the other.

15 Don't Look at your Hole Cards until it's your Turn to Act

The moment that you start to play at a half-decent level, this becomes a very important tip because it works on several levels.

Firstly, if you look at your hole cards when you receive them, then you have taken your eye off your opponents. Your attention should be wholly focused on their reactions to their hole cards. As you practise watching them, you will discover that you begin to get feelings, inklings, about what they hold: a sudden tension in the shoulders (a very good or premium hand); a stolen glance to see who is on the button and therefore in what position they are sitting (a good, or very good hand – but probably not a premium one); a slow release of breath, a shoulder slump, a sigh, a look of disappointment (all indicating a continuation of perceived poor cards). Some of these tells are incredibly obvious, but occur for only a split second – if you miss them, they're gone.

Secondly, you may react yourself to what you see you are holding and other good players will be watching you. Especially if you are used to playing online poker, where your own physical reactions are of no significance whatsoever, it is quite likely that you will reveal information about your hole cards when you look at them. For this reason alone, it would be better not to look at your hole cards until it is your turn to act.

Thirdly, players who are disciplined enough to wait to view their hole cards, who watch their opponents rather than the appearance of the board cards, these are players who present a strong, positive, professional image and, immediately, that lends weight to the actions which they take. Since your aim is always to be believed, that is a great image to project.

As you practise observing your opponents, try to remember how they looked or behaved in a certain situation and then compare that with the cards that you get to see at the showdown. If you don't get to see their cards, observe their behaviour at the end of the hand. Often, you will see from a player's reaction that he was bluffing, semi-bluffing, or really did hold the nuts. Add those observations to your earlier ones and you are beginning to form a data base, not only of individual opponents' tells, but also an increased, almost subconscious awareness of what is happening at the table . . . and all without seeing their hole cards.

16 Ask yourself Three Questions before Making A Big Decision

If, in a No-Limit game, your opponent suddenly makes a play which presents you with a big decision, take your time. Even online, many sites have a button you can click to provide you with extra time. Ask yourself these three questions:

1 What does my opponent hold?
2 What does he think I hold?
3 What does my opponent believe I think he holds?

Often, especially online, your opponent hasn't even considered questions two and three, which makes your reading of him that much more difficult. However, the more that you practise this art of reading your opponents' actions, the quicker you will find that you begin to develop a true poker sense and, from time to time, it will come to your rescue in a big way.

17 Choose your Seat Carefully

If you have a choice, use it wisely. Ideally, you should favour aggressive, raising players to be on your right, and passive, calling players sitting on your left.

This set-up allows you to come over the top of an aggressive raise when you hold a premium hand and, in all likelihood, contest it with just that one opponent (your re-raise tending to push others out of the pot) and, equally, permits you to limp into pots, knowing that a subsequent raise from the calling, passive players to your left is highly unlikely. This scenario also lends itself well in terms of position later in the hand, when you will be sitting over the aggressive players, and ahead of the

passive ones in all subsequent betting rounds. Blind
stealing and pressure raises now bite most effectively.

Remain aware of the value of seat choice both in live
games and online. In the latter format, you have thousands
of tables to choose from and have little excuse for finding
yourself in a poor seat at any table.

Incidentally, stay alert to changing personnel at your
table. Especially online, you can sit down with everyone
just where you want them and then, five minutes later,
find that every player has changed. Take time to reassess
your seat in the light of that knowledge.

18 No Matter How Good you Think you Are, you Have to Do it

There will be poker players reading this book who are
well above average standard, yet they still don't record
consistent wins. They may blame this on luck but,
more likely, they realise that although they know the
correct way to play winning poker, they just can't seem
to do it.

As discussed previously, to optimize your chances of
becoming a consistently successful player, you must adopt
disciplines and routines which, to many, may sound like
hard work. Actually, I think these requirements are so
simple and undemanding that anyone can achieve them
without more than a modicum of effort. However, because
we are all impatient, and in search of a bit of a thrill, an
adrenalin boost, we decide that, maybe just today, we
won't bother with the preparation and discipline: we'll
just relax and enjoy the game. Whether we win or lose that
session, the die is cast and we become more and more lazy,
and we fail to utilize our strengths to help us to win. We
start to rely on luck and the mistakes of others; we
minimize our wins and maximize our losses.

So, to succeed at low-stake, mid-stake and even in some high-stake games, all you need to do is to bring your knowledge to the table and put it into action. Do it! Focus on the game in hand, resolve to stay tight and disciplined and aggressive and, no matter what the cards throw at you, stick to it. That way, if you are good, you will win. For certain.

19 When you Think you Have The Best Hand – Bet

I witness it all the time and it happens to me as well. You decide to make one little check to feign weakness and the next thing you know, the board has brought a really threatening card and you have no idea where you stand any more. Those pots often cost extra bets, big bets.

Almost every poker player you talk to, regardless of their standard, will tell you that they hate to be bluffed off a pot. In the back of players' minds is the thought that you don't have as good a hand as you really do. For this reason alone, when you think you hold the best hand, you should bet out. This includes really good hands, such as top pair with top kicker, two pair and trips.

There are still more reasons why this is right:

- If you bet out with the best of it, when you bet out on the next hand, perhaps merely making a continuation bet having missed the flop, that bet will carry more weight and more threat.
- If your opponent calls lamely, you are building a pot which you expect to win.
- You gain information: if your opponent calls, or raises, you will limit the range of hands he could hold and possibly allow you to make an accurate read.

- If your opponent has any kind of draw, you may be pressuring him to play against you with the odds stacked in your favour.

A couple of slightly wild examples perhaps, but even stronger hands can be played simply:

This, from a televised tournament where a top pro faced an internet qualifier. The qualifier calls pre-flop with 10♦ 9♥; the pro raises on the button with A♠ J♥. The qualifier calls and the pot is two-handed when the flop comes:

The qualifier goes all-in instantly (about five times the size of the pot). The pro scratches his head and puts his opponent on a draw with maybe a pair also, so he calls. The turn and river bring him no help and the qualifier doubles through. No need for subtlety; no need for finesse.

In the next example, from a tournament of inexperienced players, a lady in red raises with 8♥ 8♣ and is called by a dapper chap holding A♠ Q♠. The flop comes:

What does she do? You guessed it: all-in, as quickly as she can push those chips forward! The chap calls – rightly or wrongly – and she takes down the lot. The turn and river don't bring a spade so it is unlikely that her opponent would have paid to see the river or tried a bluff at the end. She definitely got the most out of her quads.

I don't recommend either of these plays, but they illustrate the fact that, however wrong making a big bet with the best hand might seem, it often results in you getting paid off as well as you could be.

Exceptions to this rule abound, of course, and your poker sense will guide you in some situations. The most obvious is when you have an aggressive bet-bet-bet player sitting to your left. Now, you can safely check your big hand, in the great likelihood that your over-aggressive opponent will bet it for you. This allows you to re-raise him immediately, or to slow-play the hand – but with extra chips in the pot.

20 Never Show your Cards

If you are a wonderful player or, at least, the most wonderful player at your table, then you might show some cards for advertising reasons. When you make what might have been a continuation bet and everyone folds, you might choose to show that you had top pair. Do that two or three times in succession and, consciously or not, your opponents are likely to show your bets on the flop a good deal of respect in future. Basically, however, to reveal your cards is just giving your opponents information. It is much better to keep them guessing, because then they can never match a hand to your actions.

To show bluffs, satisfying indeed, is an even worse proposition because if affects not only the opponent whom you humiliate, but also the entire table. The actions of your opponent and others at the table will be skewed by the revelation of your bluff: you won't be able to read a call or a raise or a re-raise again.

To show your cards at any time is to connect your actions with actual cards and situations; experts will use that information against you.

Oh, and one more thing: never show your cards to kibitzers (onlookers). They may be future opponents of yours, their reactions might be revealing and, finally, it'll make you look like a complete amateur.

Snap Out of These Five Poker Delusions

21 I've Watched Poker on Television and I Know Exactly How to Play

In fact, there's not much to this game; it's mostly luck and balls – and I have both.

The problem is that poker on TV is fast, furious and shows only the best bits (and usually the strange bits too). It will inspire you in quite the wrong way.

22 I've Won A Couple of Times at $1/$2 so It's Time to Move Up Stakes

My dog could win a couple of sessions at low stakes, so your doing it doesn't mean anything. You have to be winning consistently and confidently. Incidentally, dogs are fine playing online, but in live games, although they keep poker faces just fine, if you watch their tails, you can soon see what kind of hand they've got.

23 If I Play for Higher Stakes, I'll Get Fewer of These Ridiculous Bad Beats and Silly Calls, my Raises Will Be Respected and I'll Win Some Sensible Pots

The problem here is that, however frustrating loose play can sometimes prove, you need opponents to play badly to give you an extra edge over them. Sure, you won't get so many bad beats in stronger games, you'll just get beaten fair and square by better players.

24 The More Hands I Play, The More Chance I Have of Hitting A Flop and Beating Up my Opponents

Tight play is dull and boring and those players never win anything.

It's true that loose/aggressive play is more exciting than tight/aggressive play, but it is also a very tough style to play successfully. If you find that you can judge flop, turn and river play very well, then it might be for you. However, for the rest of us mortals, playing weak cards leads to losses as surely as night follows day. That's why tight/aggressive should be our default style of play – because it does, in the long run, win you the most.

25 The Online Sites Are All Fixed

The casino's shills win all the money; this dealer is jinxed; I always lose after I cash in some of my winnings; I've left my lucky mascot in the car; that pit boss is a Sagittarius and they are seriously bad luck; I'm just an unlucky guy; I've had more bad beats than anyone I know; and so on . . . Using anything other than your own skill and a long-term view of the vagaries of luck as reasons to moan is just to make excuses for inadequate play. Unless you are playing on very dodgy premises, the casino and online games are run carefully and legally and they don't need shills; mascots and star-signs are for the illogical and irrational, and finally, no – you are *not* the unluckiest man alive (there are millions of other poker players claiming this title).

26 A Simple Guide to Tightness

Play a tight/aggressive style of poker as your default playing method: it will make you money in most games, and simplify your poker decision-making. However, it is possible to play too tight and, in doing so, squander opportunities for greater success. Whatever your underlying default style may be, you must always be ready to adjust to whatever playing conditions you find yourself in, mixing up your play when you can.

Particularly, pay attention to position and the opportunities that favourable position can produce for varying your play with an aggressive raise to steal blinds or push out opponents. Position is a key part of 'finding your spot' in which to make a positive play. You may sense weakness in opponents, be able to exploit your history against a particular opponent, or generally feel confident that you can outplay someone on the flop or at the end.

Tightness should not lead to predictability: if your actions, however correct they may be, become predictable, it will not take long for the better players to start to read you, avoiding strength and exploiting any weakness you may show. So, mixing up your game is important, but must not be an excuse to fritter away your stacks.

You can mix up your level of tightness also. They key here is that to play tight, you need to play only a little tighter than your table generally, and the benefits of that tight/aggressive style will still be present. However, by loosening your play a little, you serve to mix up your game, for your own enjoyment and to the hoped-for befuddlement of your opponents.

27 *If you Plan to Call a Bet, Bet Out First*

A well-known tip, but one that is neglected all too often. The advantages of betting first are so many, it seems amazing that anyone interested in poker could ignore them for long:

- Everyone else may fold.
- You sow a seed of doubt in your opponents' minds as to what you might be holding and you may set up a possible bluff scenario at the end.
- You may build a bigger pot to win.
- You may persuade opponents to check on the next round providing you with a free card.
- You perpetuate the image of you as an aggressive, positive player, an image you would like to cultivate and advertise.

Remember that to call is a passive move, the success of which relies on only one thing: your making the best hand. That offers only one way to win; to bet, or raise, offers many others.

28 Money Already in The Pot Is Gone

Less experienced players confuse pot odds (what the pot stands to pay in relation to the price of a call) with what they have contributed to the pot. In fact, once you have bet, that money ceases to exist as a single entity; it is merely absorbed into the pot. It is certainly not yours any more.

When you come to make decisions whether to continue in the hand or whether to fold, what you have contributed to the pot bears absolutely no relation to those questions whatsoever. All you have to consider is: how much do I have to pay now (and maybe subsequently) and how much do I stand to win? You judge every decision on the financial prospects at that point in relation to the current size of the pot (and, to some extent, the likely size of the pot at the conclusion of the hand), but never on how much of that pot was once yours.

29 You Have to Bet to Get a Read on your Opponents

You might get something from them when you call, but you'll gain a whole lot more if you bet out in front of them, or raise their bets.

A common scenario in low- and mid-stake poker is that someone makes a small raise pre-flop and a player or players call him. He bets out small on the flop and he gets called; he bets out small on the turn and gets called – and then he bets big on the river – and no one knows where they are. Usually, everyone folds.

Apart from the fact that this is horrible poker: reactive and feeble, it is also a really poor use of your chips. Try a re-raise, if not pre-flop, then at least on the flop. Firstly, you might find out what you are up against in the raiser's hand; secondly, you may push out other opponents allowing you and the raiser to contest the pot alone; finally, you might well take down the pot there and then (after all, pre-flop raisers have been known to make continuation bets having missed the flop completely).

At the very least, for the same price as calling two or three times, you have gained information and given the impression of aggression and strength.

The next time that you call optimistically twice in a row, ask yourself whether you wouldn't have done better by raising or re-raising the first time.

Take a look at this example from a pretty wild mid-standard cash game:

Player A holds: Q♥ Q♠; Player B holds: J♥ J♣. A player under the gun raises three times the big blind (let's say to $30). Player A re-raises three times the raise, making it $90 to go. Player B re-raises double the pot (making it $180). Only Player A calls him. There is about $400 in the pot. The flop comes:

Player A bets $200; player B calls. The pot stands at approximately $800. The turn comes:

Player A bets $200. Player B calls. The pot stands at about $1,200. The river comes:

Player A bets $200; Player B calls.

Player A wins a $1,600 pot.

There are many actions which both players could have taken differently – and many different ways to play the hand. However, one of the worst elements of Player B's play was that he bet a lot of money and never found out anything about his opponent's hand.

Let's replace just one call made by Player B with a raise. Imagine, when the flop comes:

When Player A (holding QQ) bets, player B raises. If Player A calls now, surely Player B can give up on the hand, folding to subsequent bets. What can Player A have if he calls (or raises) that raise? Surely, for the pre-flop betting to make sense: trip aces or a higher overpair?

So, if Player B tries to define his position in the hand by raising on the flop, he gains information and saves himself money. He calls the total of $180 pre-flop; then raises to $400 on the flop. After $580, he can bow out, reasonably certain that he is beaten. As it was, he wasted a total of $780 repeatedly calling. Not only could this player do with saving himself $200, if he plans to call opponents down with that kind of hand in future, that'll be a lame way to lose his chips.

30 Beware The Thought That you Can Beat Most People on A Hand

This scenario affects many players especially, it seems, when you have only a short time in which to play. Let's look at an example:

You have been folding in a disciplined manner for the last hour and suddenly you see: A♥ 10♣ in the hole. It's not a great hand, but you are in position and it looks great after zero action for so long. Before the spotlight falls on you, the player in second position raises and there are two callers. After a little thought, you decide to lay down your hand. This is a good play. You should be patting yourself on the back. But, instead, you are thinking: here I am again, watching when I could have been playing and I bet I'm beating at least two of those other guys.

Well, you probably are but, equally, you are almost certainly not beating all of them and, to reiterate, the second-best hand is the most costly hand in poker.

To put it another way: if you are more disciplined in your folding with marginal hands than your opponents, you will win in the long term.

31 Spot The Tourists

Vegas pros, who play the low- and mid-stake games, have a vast array of mildly abusive names for the hordes of

tourists who swamp Las Vegas on a Friday night for a
weekend of gambling and wild hedonism. What they
recognize, however – and what we should add to our list
of observational benefits – is that tourists playing for only
a short period of time are always overeager, unfocused,
and likely to play too many hands. In other words, prime
candidates to be fleeced by the patient, disciplined tight/
aggressive player, for every last cent they have on them.

Watch out for players who are:

- asking basic questions about the game;
- showing off to their friends;
- drinking and smiling and having a great time (whatever
  their stack sizes);
- announcing that they are jet-lagged and that they'll play
  only one more hand and who then stay playing, usually
  haemorrhaging chips, for another four hours flat.

In any game, you should be able to spot a tourist: players out
of their depth in terms of standard or stake players; unused
to a particular game, venue or country; players who keep
glancing at their watches wondering where their wives/
girlfriends/boyfriends/mistresses might be; even players
online who announce that they're about to go to bed and
arrive with the remains of their bankroll eager to spill it.

All these traits represent good poker opportunities for
you. Better players will prey on you and you must prey on
those weaker than you. That is the law of the poker jungle.

32 Use Time Zones to Benefit you

In Vegas you can see poker players so jet-lagged that they
can't open their eyes or sit up straight. You lose your usual
tells on them, but their mistakes usually end up being
more profitable anyway.

Online, you can use time zones to your benefit if you join a number of different online sites, based on different continents. For example, if you are playing on a North American site in the UK at 9am GMT, the American players are probably still up in the early hours – that may give you an edge. In Asia, morning play may catch the Europeans sleeping (or, at least, sleepy) while evening play will catch the Americans beginning to feel drowsy and perhaps a little drunk too.

Referring to my own records whilst writing this tip, I notice a definite correlation between increased winnings and when my choice of site includes reference to the variance of time zones. So, it does work.

Finally, it is worth mentioning that there is unquestionably a difference in playing ability between guys coming home from a long week of work and playing in a Friday night home game and the guys who are retired or self-employed, or even just men of leisure. Home games often feature four hours of disciplined sensible play, followed by an hour of madness. Resist the urge to go crazy with them, and calmly pick up the towers of chips building those monster pots.

33 Adapting to The Modern Game

If you play home game poker, then when you hit a card club or casino, you will find that the games are very different. The standard may well be superior, even at low stakes, and the attention to detail, rules, and standard games may seem almost dull in comparison to your freewheeling home game.

One way to prepare to extend your poker playing is to persuade your own poker school at home to adapt to some of the modern methods. Perhaps you can do away with the wild card variations, and instead stick just to one form of poker, at least for an hour or two, if not the whole evening.

Any of the HORSE (Hold 'Em, Omaha, Razz, 7-card Stud, Eights or lower Omaha) variations are fine, although No-Limit Texas Hold 'Em is by far the most popular game at the time of writing.

In our Home Games section – page 223 – you can see how to organize No-Limit Hold 'Em cash games and tournaments, and really jazz up your home games.

The advantage of playing more seriously is that you will all improve your poker as the skill factor returns to your game. You can learn from one another and help each other's games; you can even play tournaments with the big prize being an entry into a proper tournament or cash game in your local card club or casino.

You may have slightly fewer laughs, but I guarantee that you will remember the game in greater detail, analyse how your poker buddies play, and look forward to your next game more then ever.

34 Beware The Eyes!

The eyes, the eyes, beware the eyes. The eyes in question are your own and the times to be most wary of them are when you find a premium hand in the hole, the flop hits you perfectly, or you realise that you've just rivered your opponent in a big pot. What your eyes tend to do is to look downwards towards your chips. This is a tell that experienced players pick up very quickly. Even if you are sporting a pair of very dark glasses (so passé, by the way) your head may tilt downwards slightly. And, better yet, if you are observing rather than perpetrating such a poker sin, is that your hands move to your chips instantly also. It's a natural excited reaction, but you must be aware of it and learn to counter it.

I found myself in a strong game in Vegas a while back and, when the flop hit me and I checked, my opponent bet, and my hands moved, almost without my knowing, to my chips so that, when I raised, my opponent smiled a little and folded his hand quickly. I have never been so mortified at the green baize in my life. I was, quite frankly, ashamed of myself. But, it was the wake-up call I needed, and I redoubled my efforts to be self-aware and disciplined. I even got a chance, about two hours later, to make amends: against the same player, I found myself heads-up and, this time, the flop missed me completely. I checked, he bet, and deliberately I made my hands reach down for my chips. Again, my opponent smiled, and again he folded, but this time I won a pot where I was certainly behind. I'm sure that opponent has me down as a rank amateur, but that's alright now; my human frailty cost me chips, but I made it make me some chips too. And I think of that every time I'm going to play and I remember to beware the eyes . . . and the neck . . . and the hands.

Fight These Five Poker Delusions – They All Cost you Money

35 I've Kind Of Hit The Flop

This can be a major leak in your game, grasping for your chips and taking them from you slowly but relentlessly. When you pay to see a flop, it is almost always because you are hoping to hit a flop (for a change). When you do hit, or when no one else appears to have done so, you can take positive action. When you miss, and especially when an opponent seems to have hit, you may not feel great but your decision is easy: you fold. The delusional element is when you hit a bit of the flop, but it wasn't what you were hoping for. Now, you become tempted to remain in the hand, hoping to hit again. Perhaps at Limit poker the pot odds may be positive for you but, generally, you will playing with negative expectation . . . and away go your chips.

A simple example might be:

You hold: A♠ 8♠ on the button. There is a raise and three callers so you decide to play, hoping to spike, specifically: a decently-priced nut flush draw, trips, or two pair. You know that anything else isn't what you are looking for. The flop comes:

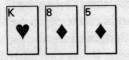

The raiser bets out and gets one caller. You have to resist the temptation to play on here. You've missed the flop (again). Fold the hand.

36 I'm The Best Player at The Table: I'm Gonna Win Consistently Here

No matter how much stronger you are than almost everyone, or even absolutely everyone, at your table, poker remains a game largely of luck and anyone can win for long periods of time – no matter how lousy they are. If you start to feel frustrated, you must resist the temptation to push too hard, to strain to show off your superiority. If you are patient, you will be presented with opportunities to exploit your skill and win extra chips; it's just that sometimes it takes much, much longer than you might expect.

This is prime tilt territory where frustration and impatience combine to persuade you to change your style to wild and aggressive. Against weak players, this can be a catastrophic decision. Beware.

37 I'm Wedded to my Hole Cards

Particularly if you play the recommended tight/aggressive style, you often have to wait a long time to see action. When you do pick up a premium hand – perhaps AA or KK – they seem invincible. Do not remain so tied to those wonderful cards that you ignore betting that tells you that you have been overtaken. This is especially true for the tight/aggressive player because, if you have been patiently playing only very good hands, when opponents play back at you they know that you have that very good hand, and they are still taking you on. That's noteworthy. Be prepared to pitch the very cards you have been, all evening, longing to see.

38 It's A Game, I Should Be Enjoying myself

Of course, folding poor cards repeatedly is very dull, while playing them is exciting, but if you want to win, poker isn't always fun. Play poker merely as a game if you wish, but the road to true poker satisfaction is to play each hand well and enjoy the long-term pleasure that you can beat any game you choose.

Learn to enjoy the ambience of your card room, to imbibe that magnetic atmosphere of gambling. Discipline yourself to observe the actions of your opponents, knowing that when you do enter a hand, you will have more information on them than they on you. I enjoy these things; these are part of the pleasure of poker.

By the way, what worthwhile game can you name that is unmitigated fun every time, all the time?

39 I'm Eager to Play

Unfortunately, this usually means: I'm eager for action. There wouldn't be any point in playing if you didn't look forward to it, but your enjoyment will be enhanced if you are winning. To increase the chances of your doing just this, don't be overeager, straining to play. Ease yourself in gently, go through your preparatory rituals. Pick a really good hand to play first – and raise with it. Now, you've got off to the best possible start.

40 Don't Try to Bluff Poor Players

This is a very important tip because it probably contradicts your instincts: that a poor player will be easy to fool. Many weaker players believe that their opponents are constantly bluffing them, trying to steal pots and generally hoodwinking them out of their money. For this reason – and also natural, but costly curiosity – they tend to call down hands much more than an average or good player would think of doing. What this results in is that the game becomes simpler – the best hand wins at the showdown – but, equally, unless you hit some hands, it leaves you with very few manoeuvres in order for you to exert your superiority. This type of situation is quite standard in low-limit online games:

You hold: A♣ Q♣ and, one from the button, you raise. An early-to-act opponent, who has previously just called, calls you on A♦ 5♠. The flop comes:

Your opponent checks and you make a continuation bet of two-thirds of the pot. Your opponent calls. The turn comes:

Your opponent checks; you decide to bet again, because you suspect your opponent might be on a heart flush draw or that you might take him off the hand. Your opponent calls, and the river comes:

Your opponent checks yet again. What can you do now? If you bet, it is almost certain that your opponent will call; if you check, you lose the showdown. Maybe going all-in will work, but I've been called in this spot before, by both great players and complete duds. The fact is, against really weak opponents, the fold equity of a continuation bet is usually greatly reduced because, if they have hit anything, anything at all, they will call you down.

So, what's the solution? Firstly, tighten up a little and play only very good or premium hands. The subtle advice is to tighten up so that you are just the tightest player at the table. If the table is ultra-loose, you can play a loose style also, just so long as it is less loose than everyone else. Lastly, vary your play: make your bets and raises smaller or much bigger or, best of all, take down a couple of big pots early on and show them that, when you bet, you mean business.

41 Don't Expect your Superiority to Show Quickly

This is linked somewhat to the tip above and it is of great significance to all players, but particularly online players who may, at any stake, suddenly encounter what they consider their 'dream table'.

The problem here is expectation: specifically, your own. When you find a table full of calling stations, fish and mad people, you instinctively expect a feast. The problem is that your superiority may take a while to reflect itself in the relative sizes of your chips' stacks. In fact, it may take so long that your opponents have won your money and left the table. This situation then leads to resentment and ultimately tilt – and from there, your chips disappear ever more quickly.

Online players may encounter such tables at cash games, Sit & Gos and in Multi-table Tournaments. Indeed, as discussed earlier, some poker search engines are designed to seek out tables just such as these. The key is to remain patient. You will have a significant skill advantage and, if you stayed at this table long enough, you would win all the chips. However, that superiority may get a chance to be aired only on a very few hands out of the hundreds that you play.

As you see from the above tip, bluffing may not be a weapon at your disposal and nor may the subtleties of betting size. Generally, but by no means always, a check-raise does strike fear into the hearts of less experienced players – they've been told that it shows great strength and they tend to believe it. However, since checking and calling are the hallmarks of optimistic fish, you may find that your planned check-raise turns into a free card for your opponent when he checks also.

The worst scenario of all is when you face a table of weak players who seem to be in league against you. You raise with your premium hand and then, one by one, almost everyone at the table calls you. This has the effect of devaluing your hand considerably and making it very likely that at least one opponent will hit a very good flop and perhaps overtake you. Some players think the solution to those types of game is to increase your bet size and try to drive people off the hand by force. However, if you are playing a low-stake game, this often doesn't work*. The real solution is to switch tables to where you can play each hand against two opponents, or, better still, just the one opponent.

42 Don't Make Bad Cards Worse

Poker can be a really dull game sometimes; your cards can be dead and everyone else at the table is whooping it up and having fun. To be a long-term winner, you must accept that this is part of the life of a serious poker player. At least, you should reflect, you are losing only the blinds.

Let's imagine you are playing for eight hours and you scarcely see a playable hand. What will that cost you? Assuming that you are at a nine/ten player $1/$2 table, playing 30–40 hands per hour, maybe $100. That's nothing – you could win that back on one single hand. It's boring, sure, but it's not really that detrimental to your bankroll. But . . . if you start to play marginal hands, begin to call raises on speculative starting cards, run bluffs against otherwise disciplined players . . . if you keep yourself entertained . . . then you *will* lose more – perhaps, lots more. So, what do you want: entertainment or success?

It's fine to play poker just for fun, not worrying about whether you win or lose. In fact, there's a game in every

---

* Particularly online, but also in live games, just because someone is playing in a very low-stake game doesn't mean that they couldn't afford – if they so chose – to play in a very high-stake game. I know a dollar billionaire who plays poker for fun, but only for low stakes. The fact that he sometimes re-buys a dozen times in a session is of absolutely no importance to him, but it might be to you. If you have $70 in front of you and you push all-in to a $35 pot, don't expect a weak opponent to be impressed that you have just bet double the pot. He may be thinking: it's only seventy bucks, I can't resist seeing what he has. And, then, if you were bluffing, you'll get busted. The fact is that inexperienced players just don't see poker in the same way we do: we want to play correctly; they want to have fun, make sure that they don't get bluffed, and find a story to tell all their buddies.

town in every country of the world just waiting for you, but don't whine when you end the year a loser. You made your choice, and you opted for fun, not profit. The blunt truth is that poker is rarely both fun and profitable (when it is, it's almost as wonderful as being in love – that heady, slightly woozy, everything's-going-my-way feeling), so learn to enjoy the atmosphere of the table, the card room or casino, to use the time to observe your opponents, learn from the better players, spot the tells that could guide you to a big pot later, or save you from betting into the stone-cold nuts another time.

And another thing: what you and I think are bad cards are probably just ordinary cards. Imagine that you are an online player. You sit down for a four-hour session of $1/$2 NL Hold 'Em, playing about 60 hands per hour (or a live game for eight hours). On average, how many premium hands do you expect to see? Come up with a number for each of the following before checking the answers:

AA
AK suited or not
KK
Mid-pairs QQ–88
Low pairs 77–22
Ace-high

I wonder what your figures were . . . When I first did this test before running the computer simulations, I didn't guess well. On average, this is what you would expect to see:

AA: one. Yes, just the one . . . and we all know how, having waited for hours to see bullets, some fool calls us with QJ off and hits a 1098 flop!

AKs or AK: four. It's always nice to see a Big Slick, but if you are at a loose table where continuation/follow-up bets are not respected and several players call you down to the end, you'll need to hit a flop to feel confident.

KK: one. Again, just a single appearance is expected.

QQ–88: seven. Bear in mind that the power of these hands is largely dependent upon the position in which you find yourself when you pick them up and how many callers come with you and then, the minor matter of the flop texture.

77–22: eight. These hands can cost you money and, unless you are prepared to raise with them, their success is entirely flop-dependent.

Ace-high: forty. A great figure, but a dangerous one, since ace-high hands can end up costing you a bundle of chips. Remember that the general advice for these hands is to limp in when they are suited and hope to pick up a cheap nut flush draw, or flop two pair or trips. Otherwise, unless you are looking at AQ, let these hands go to raises both pre-flop and post-flop.

So, perhaps, like me, your expectations of decent cards were a little optimistic. Even if you were spot on (in which case, well done), watch out for the marginal hands that we so often like to play when we feel that the going has been really bad. KQ, KJ, K10, QJ, Q10, J10, J9 – suited or not – these can all cost you dearly and should be played with great care and attention to your position, the flop and the reaction of your opponents.

Above all, remember that marginal hands played lamely or out of position will cost you, day in, day out, for the rest of your poker-playing lives. Resist the jibes of your opponents, your own urge for an adrenalin rush – just muck those hands. Remember that playing those types of hands is exactly what you want your opponents to do and, by doing so, they are giving you an easy route to success. Don't fall into that trap. If the session continues without your seeing any hands, accept a small loss; the next time you play, it may just be your day.

43 Use All-in Moves Sparingly

No-Limit action is certainly exciting but don't let the fact that you can go all-in persuade you to make that move too often. You need an opponent to get lucky only once for you to lose everything.

Even if you find that the players at your table are calling bets and raises too loosely and they are then hitting their draws, don't be tempted to push all-in just to try to make a point. If they are that loose, they'll call you anyway (better players may put you on a semi-bluff and call you too), and you really don't want to be all-in on 50–50 or even 70–30 chances too often: you'll win in the long run, but you may have to re-buy dozens of times in one session if one or more opponents are hitting everything in sight.

This is a situation you'll see in online play quite frequently. As I have learnt to my cost, taking out your frustration on your own stacks can be a big losing strategy:

You hold: K♣ K♦. You raise four times the big blind and get called by one player. The flop comes:

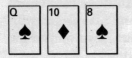

You bet two thirds of the pot and you get called. The turn comes:

You are very concerned by this card: it completes both flush and straight draws. You are really ahead now only if your opponent called you on a queen. You decide to find out if your opponent has you beat so you bet half the pot and get called. It seems like he's hit his draw yet again. The river comes:

You check, he bets – and, reluctantly, you fold.

One round later, you raise on A♥ K♣ and the same guy calls you. The flop comes:

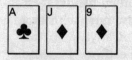

You're not going to be outdrawn a second (or third, fifth or tenth) time, so you stick in all your chips. Your opponent calls you and shows:

The turn and river offer no help and you are broke.

Yes, you have been unlucky; your opponent called you on a marginal hand and hit the flop beautifully, but you could – and should – have continued to make exploratory bets and raises. It looks like you are reacting to previous hands negatively, instead of absorbing the pain and not letting it affect your play or betting judgment.

Clearly, you are being cold-decked, but you do have the chance to lose the minimum rather than the maximum – and that is something which distinguishes the good players from the average: the ability to avoid going broke when the rest of us would.

Hopefully, you don't think like this when playing online (or at any time) but, just in case you are tempted, beware!

44 If you Fight Without Weapons, At Least Look Tough

Weaker players call raises consistently with marginal hands – and often with downright terrible hands. They might (and against me, they probably will) hit a miracle flop. However, mostly they don't and they lose their call and, perhaps, further bets too.

The point is that to call raises is a reactive, passive move and their success depends entirely upon what the board brings. If you must play marginal and bad hands, then at least play them positively and strongly: raise with them. Let's look at an example:

You hold: J♠ 8♠ and decide to call pre-flop. The player on the button raises with K♥ 10♥ and you call. Even if you hit a decent flop, you are out of position and playing the rest of the hand will be tough.

What would have happened if you had raised with this hand? Almost certainly the button player would have passed and you would have taken down the blinds. Even if that button player calls and you hit part of your hand, a continuation bet should end his aspirations for his modest cards. Even if you don't hit the flop, a continuation bet sees him off . . . so, to raise gives you masses of extra potential; to call is feeble and deserves its likely fate: loss.

45 Most of The Time, Players Have What they Say

It is easy to become convinced that everyone is out to get you (mentally, they should be), bluffing and stealing all the time but, in truth, most of the time people are betting their hands reasonably obviously.

If someone check-raises you, they are usually strong; if they call and then check, they are usually weak.

This may seem obvious, but I see so many chances go begging, it is worth repetition. For example:

You hold: 3♥ 3♣. An opponent in mid-position raises and receives two calls to you. You decide to make a speculative call. The flop comes:

The raiser bets half the pot and the two callers before you both pass. Rightly, or wrongly, you decide to call. The turn comes:

Your opponent checks. What does this mean?

He might be trapping but, far more likely – way more likely – he has nothing. He tried an aggressive continuation bet after the flop and removed two opponents, but now he's worried that you have a queen. This is the time to make a decent bet. In all probability, your opponent will sigh and muck his cards.

I've seen so many examples, especially online, of players checking in your position here and then finding that the river brings an overcard which makes your opponent's hand. Trapping here, if you are that confident, may not even bring you more chips. Your opponent has more or less given up on the hand now so, unless he tries a big bluff – which won't be pleasant to call anyway – you won't get any more chips out of him. Make your value bet and take down the pot (or learn that you are beaten and get out).

46 *Free Cards*

To see another card on the board without paying is always a bonus when they are given to you, but you must be equally alert to avoid providing them to your opponents. Inexperienced players give far too many free cards – usually through disinterest. These two examples are regular occurrences at friendly tournaments:

Example 1
Player A holds: K♠ K♥ and raises, receiving four callers. The flop comes:

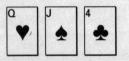

Correctly, he bets and all but one player fold. The turn comes:

And now Player A checks! The opponent checks also and the river comes:

Now, Player A wakes up again and bets. His opponent raises and he calls. The opponent shows: J♣ 8♦, and takes down the pot with two pair.

Hopefully, you are disgusted by Player A's play (as well as, possibly, by that of his opponent) but this kind of play is routine for some players. Weak players often call one bet or raise, but fold if their opponent musters a second bet. If you'd tell me that Player A's check on the turn was a trap, then I'd answer that he shouldn't be trapping against a weak player. The fact is that, against weak opponents, just bet out your hands.

Example 2

This is more subtle but just as important and it occurs regularly in home games, club games and friendly tournaments:

There are two callers to you on the button. You hold: K♣ 8♠ and decide to limp in. The small blind folds and the big blind checks. The flop comes:

Everyone checks to you and you decide to check yourself. The turn comes:

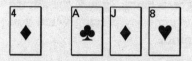

Everyone checks to you again. You must bet. Even if you don't have the best hand, a player with a jack may debate calling you. The chances are, the first to bet takes the pot, and you have had the luxury of seeing everyone check twice in front of you. If you check, the river might come:

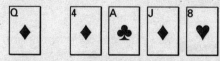

And now, someone will bet and you will be beaten.

To check on the turn here is sheer laziness. Many players would have bet the flop when everyone checked to them, but if you check the turn also, then why play the hand at all?

Again, you should be reading this and saying to yourself that you would never play like Player A in these examples but, if you play low-limit games online or in a local club, you will see these plays – just don't make them.

Five Times Never to Play Poker

47 *When you Are Tired*

It's simple: you want other players to be tired when you play against them, so that you can profit from their mistakes.

48 *When you Feel Impatient or Frustrated*

These are precisely the opposite of the correct feelings you should be experiencing when you play poker. Calm, patient, disciplined, in-the-zone: this is the state you want to be in when you sit at the green baize. Ignore the advice by all means, but you will lose money playing when you are in the wrong frame of mind.

49 *When you Are Feeling Paranoid*

If you feel that the world is out to get you (it is!), the last thing you need is a bad beat, or even seven or eight. Anything negative (and there is much of this in poker) will reinforce your mood.

50 *When you Are Drunk*

Obviously . . . yet, over and over again, I see players unable to focus on their cards, let alone form rational, logical thoughts.

I am a great believer that, to succeed at poker, you have to exploit the weaknesses of others – it's a rough, tough game. However, draw the line at encouraging drunks into your game. That isn't poker. And, besides, drunks aren't good news at the table. They are unreadable, slow down the game, spill stuff (drinks, pretzels, their stomach contents) and lack any social graces whatsoever.

51 When There Is Nothing Else in This World you Would Rather Do Than Win A Poker Hand

In other words, if winning is more important to you than playing your cards correctly. Ultimately, in poker, there is only one priority: playing every hand correctly – even if that means folding for four hours straight, or ducking out of a mammoth pot. It also means taking time to select your game and your table, hunkering down quietly and picking a premium hand with which to begin: all actions requiring patience and a calm, logical demeanour.

52 Adjust Quickly to Short-handed Play

Both in tournaments – MTT and Sit & Go – and in ring games, there will be times when the table becomes short-handed (six players or fewer). You must be ready to 'change gears' to adjust to the new style of game. If you continue playing your full-table tight style, you will find that the blinds begin to bite. Instead, be aware that:

- Hand values increase.
- Aggression is even more effective.
- Draws become poorer value (because pots are likely to be smaller).
- Blind stealing and bluffing opportunities increase.
- Winning-hand values fall.

As well as incorporating these factors into your thinking, you must be aware that your opponents will have adjusted their games also. It is common to see weaker players left behind when a game becomes short-handed. Above all, calling speculatively becomes much poorer value because there are fewer chips in the pot. This example, from a televised tournament, is a good one:

   Six players remaining; blinds high
   In second position, Player A raises three times the big blind
   Player B, to his right, calls
   On the button, you hold: 7♣ 7♥.
   What action do you take?

With a couple of other callers, you might justify a call, but with just two, your options are limited. Unless you spike a third seven on the flop (which will occur only about 12 per cent of the time), you won't be able to call any further bets.

   Your two viable options are to fold – which is perfectly reasonable, since you would far rather be raising with this hand than calling lamely; or to re-raise. This latter play is certainly recommended at tournament play (unless you have a good read on your opponents). The chances are that your opponents have lowered their raising requirements and are trying to pressurize you. You want to turn that aggression and shove it right back in their faces. Your position is perfect and that will increase the fold equity of such a move.

   On the actual deal, Player A held: A♣ 9♠ and Player B: J♠ 10♠.

   The player in your position did re-raise and took down the pot. Imagine a call against those two hands: the chances are huge that one of them will hit something.

Be aware that, if you have demonstrated a tight, disciplined image up to the point that the table becomes short-handed, your switch to greater aggression will carry extra weight: you can expect more of your raises and re-raises to be shown respect. Conversely, a looser early image limits the effect of your gear change and lessens your power at the crucial stage of a tournament (or late on in a shrinking ring game). In that situation, your raises are less likely to be respected and you must be prepared to scrap it out.

53 Be Aware of Image and Precedent, and React Logically

This is a two-way tip, because it refers both to your opponents' actions and your own.

Clearly, if a player is ultra-aggressive and you find that he raises pre-flop and receives only your call, if he then checks the flop, this is suspicious, because his modus operandi to this point has been to bet out aggressively. A two-handed confrontation is the ideal one in which to slow-play and he may well use this as an opportunity to be seen to mix up his play a little.

Similarly, if you raise and the tightest player at the table calls, or even raises you, then he is very likely to have a big hand. If the loosest player takes that action, it may mean nothing.

When you are playing at a decent standard, you must also be aware of the image that you yourself have projected, because decent players will have noticed and will be adapting their play accordingly.

For example, you are a tight/aggressive player, playing only a few hands. You raise in second position and a good player re-raises you. Accept that he has a very powerful hand. You, as a tight player, have made an early position raise – this shows a very good hand; your opponent knows this and he has no reason not to take you seriously. Therefore, logically, the vast majority of the time, he thinks he has you beat. Respect his respect of you and lay down anything marginal.

This next example still stings, but I reveal my weaknesses to you in the hope that you can avoid making the same errors:

After hours of cold-deck action, I call to play a three-way pot holding: A♠ J♠. The flop comes:

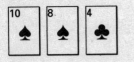

There are two checks to me and I bet two-thirds of the pot. The first caller passes, but the second raises. I decide to call. The turn comes:

My opponent checks and so do I. The river comes:

At last, I've hit a hand. It's been two hours. My opponent bets the pot, and I happily raise him. He goes all-in. I'm not letting this go, obviously, so I call. He turns over: 9♠ 7♠!

I've lost my entire stack. I can't believe it. How unlucky is that?

I log off and think about it. I could have played the hand much better. My opponent was the best player at the table by far – I'd noted as much. In fact, I'd rated

him very highly: tight, aggressive, selective and patient.
He probably saw me in a similar vein, despite my miserable session up to that moment. The point is, I think
that I should have got away from the hand. My big raise
at the end is clearly showing that I've hit the flush. If he
had hit one too, he could just have called. To raise, he
had to believe that he had my nut flush beaten. No matter
that I never put him on 9♠ 7♠, that I didn't think that
he'd be the first caller into the pot with that hand.
Because he was a good player and the betting told me
something I couldn't know until that moment, I should
have acknowledged it and made a great lay down. But I
didn't . . .

54 Watch your Opponents, Not The Flop

A truly golden rule, and one ignored by the vast majority
of average and less experienced players. Even quite decent
players give away information as the flop hits: shoulders
slump, players sit back, they sit up, they hold their breath,
they stare at the flop . . . all of these usually indicate
interest or disappointment – and that information can
make and save you a lot of chips.

Read all about these various tells in the Tells Extra
chapter.

Similar attention should be paid on the turn and river.
Keep your head up and scanning the table rather than
down in your lap.

55 You Want Bad Beats

I'm not joking. If you don't get bad beaten a few times
each session, you're probably not playing correctly. Unless you are a naturally brilliant player, in order to win,
you require your opponents to make mistakes. You should

want them to call you with ridiculously poor cards, come fishing each time you bet out, and commit themselves all-in on a draw. Of course, from time to time, they'll hit their 30 per cent chances, make trips on the river and hit runner-runner draws to suck you out, but the majority of the time, they will lose to you. If you are winning anything near your percentage, then your wins will over-take your losses in the long run.

Think of bad beats as how a casino views a big winning punter: an anomaly, a reasonably rare occurrence. It doesn't hurt the casino because their 2 per cent and 3 per cent edges always bring home the bacon in the long run. And so it is with poker: if you really do have a small skill advantage over other players, that will eventually convert into profit. Even casinos have bad runs: players who win ten sessions of Roulette on the trot; players who take a big win at Craps but, because of the size of their bankrolls, the casino bosses don't panic – in fact, finan-cially, they hardly notice them at all.

And therein lies the moral to the tale: you need a big bankroll to prevent a series of unexpected losses from upsetting you, affecting the way you play. Every top poker pro has been broke sometime in their careers, sometimes for long periods. Expect huge variance and accept it as part of the game. If you are playing your best, you will win in the long run.

Here are two online hands (at $2/$4 NL Hold 'Em) which almost finished me off:

I raise with AA and get called by one player on 5♣ 4♣. The board comes:

That cost me several bets and a raise at the end.

Fifteen minutes later, against the same opponent, I pick up: A♥ K♥ and I raise, only to be called again by exactly the same hand: 5♣ 4♣

This time, the board comes:

Nice. This time, he hits his flush and I'm down to barely enough to last another couple of rounds of blinds.

Does this make it right to call early-position raises with 5♣ 4♣? Of course not. To call with such a hand has a significant negative expectation, but that isn't any consolation when it smacks you in the gob twice in a row.

If you let this get to you, you could rationalize that you may not play against this opponent again and he has got the better of you twice but, equally, you know that any minute now, you will get called by someone else on something sub-standard and the next time your premium hand will stand up. Just take a deep breath and keep hoping that they keeping calling . . . because in that game, eventually, you are going to get rich.

56 Bet Out When you Flop Trips

Many players think that they have a lock on the hand when they flop trips, but this very pleasant development is still subject to being overtaken by draws and, when the opposition hit, it's tough to lay down your hand and, like all good second-best hands, it costs you a bundle of chips.

The best policy is usually to bet straight out – or raise/re-raise. Despite this, you will often get called just when you want to be, because players automatically think that you won't be betting so strongly with trips.

Against a single opponent, with a non-threatening flop, you might slow-play but, even then, you may end up being paid more by betting out.

One successful low-stake No-limit Hold 'Em online player told me that he frequently went all-in when he flopped trips and, thinking he was on some kind of semi-bluff, opponents called 50 per cent of the time and he won almost all of them. Maybe this is a bit extreme, but it demonstrates how a value bet (or even an over-bet) works so well with trips – and protects your hand against the marauding loose draw-callers.

57 Beware Online Short-Stack Buy-Ins

When playing cash games online, you will frequently encounter players buying in for the minimum amount, or some small odd figure (suggesting that this is all they have left in their online account). Beware attacking these players as you would a short-stack in a tournament, because you will find that they may be quick to fire the all-in trigger, pressurizing you to hand them your raise, or call for a gamble. You can spend an hour adding 50 per cent to your starting stack through careful play and then lose it all when you lose two 50–50 or 65–35 gambles to a reckless, perhaps desperate, short-stack.

When these short-stack players arrive, wait a few hands to ascertain how keen they are to gamble. Judge your raises carefully to avoid pot commitment on marginal hands and raise robustly only when you are prepared to go all the way with an all-in re-raise. Time your play correctly, and you can wipe out multiple short-stacks in a short time; misjudge their mood and a little poor luck can cost you dear.

58 Beware Playing Immediately After Watching Poker on Television

This is a big money-saving tip based on accounts from countless poker buddies, particularly students and less experienced players. Poker on television has revolutionized our game, popularizing and glamorizing it. However, there is a significant danger here: poker on television is almost entirely tournament play, with a structure that requires excessive aggression, features huge pots, joke starting cards, tight big-money decisions, dramatic bluffs and action, action and yet more action. There are no table passes to the big blind, no single raise causing everyone to fold; everything you see is entertainment. The problem is that to play successful poker is usually not entertaining: it is slow, patient, hard graft. Passing twenty hands in a row, folding marginal hands to raises and resisting the temptation to bluff every time you miss the flop is not glamorous, not dramatic, and certainly not sexy – but it will lead to profit.

The chasm between seeing the high-octane, never-ending action of television poker and the reality of an online cash game or casino ring game is just too great for many players to appreciate. Watching late-night poker broadcasts, feeling inspired, ready to take on the world, usually leads you to log on to your online poker room, click on the first available table (often at a higher stake than you might usually play), and steam your way through the first few hands, raising on garbage, bluffing your way to a few early pots. However, you're playing out of your comfort zone, probably tired, maybe tanked up, and soon your chips will get eroded, slowly but surely, by the grinders who have seen it all before and get your number far quicker than you might imagine. Next, you tighten up, and the game gets boring: now, tilt can set in, and all your chips disappear.

I've heard so many stories of this scenario, I offer it up to you now to convince you not to confuse a television producer's idea of drama with money-winning poker. Enjoy the entertainment, but remember that you don't see the other 99 per cent of the story: dull, disciplined folding, careful value bets and diligent observation of betting patterns that account for so much of an expert's long road to consistent profit.

59 Don't Chase Losses to A Particular Opponent or Table

It is tempting to wage war at the poker table; our game is a combative one. However, if you find that your cards are dead, your opponents keep getting lucky, or one opponent has become a nemesis, don't feel wedded to your table, or the need to take personal revenge on a player who you think has stolen your chips. Sigh and stand up, take a breath of fresh air, and return later, perhaps to a new table, with new opposition and none of the pervasive atmosphere of doomed loss-chasing that sometimes characterizes poker games.

Online, it takes only one click of the mouse to leave the game, and there are a thousand others just moments away where, perhaps, your big blind doesn't get raised every single time, your AK raises hit a flop just occasionally and some fool doesn't keep hitting full houses with his 83 off-suit call under the gun.

It boils down to ego, of course, with so much being psychological in poker. Swallow your pride, realize that it doesn't matter to whom you lose, nor from whom you win your chips. All poker players know the feeling that they are swimming through treacle, against the tide – and we all seek those wonderful tables where everything we do is right, feels right and our opponents know it. So, why stay at the unpleasant table rather than seek our Elysian Fields? The desire to save face; to take revenge? Those emotions have no place in your poker game. Eliminate them, remain flexible, and seek success wherever you may find it!

60 Be Stronger to Call a Raise Than to Make One

The 'Gap Concept', popularized by the fascinating poker writer David Sklansky, explains that you must be stronger to call a raise than you would normally be to make one in such a position.

It makes sense because, when you call, you have no fold equity. An opponent isn't going to say:

Oh golly, he's called my raise, I'm giving up the hand.

But, opponents do pass hands when you raise them. That is why it is so dangerous to call raises on marginal hands, just because you have position over the raiser. The cult of calling on a middle ace (say, A8 or A9) seems to be growing and, for me, that's great news, because I rarely raise on hands which are behind those.

Of course, there are times when to call a raise speculatively feels right to you. Many tournament players find that suited connectors can hit a flop in a big way and wipe out an opponent, but your timing must be right – and the odds on offer very tempting.

61 Reject 50/50 Chances in Tournament Play

Your level of aggression in any tournament will be governed by a number of different elements: the timescale of the event, the size of your stack, the size and speed of the blinds, your knowledge of, and position over, your opponents.

However, since your number-one rule in tournaments is stack protection, you should be wary of too willingly entering into coin-toss races. Many top pros will tell you that they reject these offers, and even early all-in situations where they consider that they might be 60 per cent or 65 per cent on to win the hand, because they recognize one important factor: if you go all-in and lose, you're out.

To triumph in a tournament, you will almost certainly have to win several coin tosses, possibly bad beat an opponent or two, and certainly hit your draws and have opponents miss theirs. The key is that when you do go all-in, you should be making the move. At least, you have the extra chance of your opponent folding to add to the chances of your hitting (or their missing) your hand.

62 Take A Stand (Early On)

If you are playing a home game, or you are at a card club where there is only one table likely to form, you will be spending your entire session at the same table with, largely, the same opponents. In this scenario, it may well be worth making a statement of intent early on, by taking a stand, to prevent your opponents gaining momentum over you.

One situation might be if the player two places to your right consistently raises you when you are the big blind. You may need to pick a decent hand and take him on, perhaps re-raising. Even if you lose this encounter, you have still made it clear that you will take on your opponent with anything half-decent. Often, this decreases the frequency of the button's raises.

Another time when you may need to take a stand is when facing a bet-bet-bet type of player. If you suspect that you are being bullied off hands, you may decide to call down the aggressor. If you expose him as being overeager, you will certainly dent his confidence but, again, even if you lose these bets, you have laid down a marker that you will not be taken off a hand without good reason; that you do have the guts to call him down.

Don't let the cost of these positions outweigh their overall value in the scheme of the game. You may find that a few dollars spent early in these situation can equate to hundreds saved in the long term as opponents decide that you are the wrong opponent to try to push around.

Finally, don't seek to act too early in these situations as you may simply be encountering a rush on the part of these opponents but, once you feel a tone may be set, and it's not your tone, it's time to put a stop to it!

63 Take a Stand (before The End)

There comes a point in almost every tournament, whether it is a one-hour Sit & Go or a five-day tournament, when you are almost down and out, but you have just enough ammo for one more fight. The key is to use this ammunition wisely, since it may be your last battle.

The moment that you get so far down that you need three double throughs to return to average chip count, you need to act. The chance of making those three double throughs is roughly 1 in 8; leave it any later and you'll have to double through four times just to get even – and that takes the odds out to 1 in 16.

Seek position, feel for the moment when no one is exuding strength and put all your chips in. If you steal the blinds and loose calls, you have bought yourself some more time to pick a better hand; if you get a caller, you are likely to be behind now, but there are five cards to come.

If you try to wait for a premium hand, you may indeed see it, but with so few chips that the double through becomes worthless.

The old saying about chip and chair is all very well, and an inspiration to short-stacks the world over, but the odds against recovery are enormous. A few chips, doubled through before they have shrunk to nothing, is a much better proposition.

64 Don't Have Pre-Set Time Limits

Set yourself limits, definitely, just don't set them in advance without knowing what playing conditions you'll discover when you reach your venue. A great skill, required by all winning players, is to quit when the signs are clear: cards go cold; stronger players replace weak ones; you feel tired, angry, frustrated; or your mind is wandering back to land-based responsibilities.

However, to have pre-set times can be destructive. You may be having a terrible session and you just want to get up and go home. You may be having an amazing session and your table is filling up with rich, passive players. In either case, you want to set your own limits and not be influenced by external concerns.

This type of problem sometimes manifests itself in very destructive practices: winning, you may try to push way too hard to make the most of a situation before you have to leave and end up handing back most of your profit to very weak players; when losing, the value you place on your remaining chips may be devalued. You might think: I've lost $300 tonight, so what if it's $500? I might double through my remaining $200 twice and go home with a profit. Well, you might, but your attitude will be dead wrong and you will be relying on luck. That's not poker – that's just lack of discipline.

Try to avoid also:

- Being dependent on friends for transport (their games may last much longer than yours or they may want to leave hours before you).

- Having a non-playing friend in tow. He/she will find you far less attractive if you keep them waiting. Besides, the sound of their sucking their teeth in your ear will probably disturb you.
- Playing online tournaments without sufficient time before you have to leave the house. (You see this happening amazingly frequently online.)

65 If you Are Improving your Game, Don't Exclusively Play Tournament Poker

Although there are significant changes in style required for a move between cash games and tournaments, if you are trying to improve your poker, it is a good idea to play both. Some parts of the style of each game will benefit you in the other.

In terms of winning money, tournament play is much more luck-orientated, especially online where the blinds tend to get very high, very quickly in relation to the stack sizes. This leads to more coin-toss situations and, often, increased frustration.

Although to make money consistently in tournament play is not impossible, it is very difficult and time-consuming. To play cash games, even at low limits, is more likely to help you to develop the patient discipline of good long-term strategy – and without this experience costing you too much money.

I'm a big fan of Sit & Go events online: they offer a great chance to practise final table-style conditions and you get to play lots of hands pretty quickly. Indeed, I find that Sit & Go tournaments can be a profitable enterprise, especially if you can find a site where a relatively small group of impatient, loose players regularly enter the Sit & Gos at your price level. However, just as with cash games, and MTTs, the decks can run cold for long periods and, when they do, it is important to remain attentive and observant: if you are going to lose, at least gain some information about your opponents for future confrontations.

66 Change Online Identities

Every few months, I change identity. Online, it is simple to open extra accounts or change screen names. If you are a winning player online (or even if you want to hide the fact that you have been losing consistently while you've been learning the game), then to change identities can be helpful to you. Players who have attached online notes to your old persona have no idea who this new character might be; players who use search engines to scrutinize your results will not be able to find you; you can even use your change of identity as a clean sheet: to resolve to play in a more focused, disciplined way.

Changing identity is, ultimately, another way of mixing up your play to keep your opposition guessing.

67 They Don't Know What you Have . . .

Weaker players do not even consider what their opponents might be holding; they just play their cards.

Intermediate players may try to put you on a hand, or even a range of hands but, unless your betting is very predictable, they really don't have much idea.

Experts are experts because they are first-rate at putting their opponent on a hand – and guessing what hand their opponent thinks he's up against. However, unless you are exposing your cards, they don't *know* what you have – they are simply making an educated guess. So, when you hear Phil Hellmuth Jr saying: 'I can see into your soul', treat it for what it is: an amusing titbit of gamesmanship.

68 . . . But you Know What they Have

Experts gain a vast edge over their less experienced opponents by being able to read their cards. It is the part of the game on which, if you are not naturally gifted, you have to work the hardest.

For every deal you witness at your table, try to put the combatants on a hand; whenever there is a showdown, compare it to your own estimate. The more that you practise, the greater your accuracy becomes.

When you do put an opponent on a hand, and that hand is revealed at the showdown, it can be incredibly rewarding to find that you did know your opponent's cards on that deal.

For less experienced players, putting a player on a hand is an almost unfathomable concept. How can you possibly know what your opponent is holding since he could have bet on anything? The fact is that for most of the time, players have what they say they have. So, if Player A, who you have noted seems to play normally, raises in first position, you can, at least, put him on a range of hands:

AA, KK, QQ, AK . . . maybe JJ or 1010.

Then, when the flop comes and there is further betting, you can then adapt and adjust your initial estimate, usually narrowing the range of possibilities. Let's look at a very simple example, for less experienced players:

8-player table, NL Hold 'Em. Player A, in second position, raises three-and-a-half times the big blind. You put him on one of the five or six hands above and decide to call. The flop comes:

Your opponent checks. What does this mean?

At higher levels of the game, it could mean one of many things, but at a modest level, it suggests that the raiser has a big pair and he is checking, hoping to raise you when you put in a bet (maybe hoping he has missed). You might put him on AA, KK or QQ here.

A largish bet here suggests pressure on you, perhaps because he has missed, holding AK or AQs, or possibly to protect a vulnerable overpair, like: JJ, 1010, 99.

As you become more experienced and attuned to your opponents' general styles, you may be able to pinpoint the precise hand.

Bear in mind that online, players in low-stake games may have just about anything for any of their bets, and reading becomes close on impossible. However, if you maintain your tight/aggressive image, you will make so much money through their mistakes that you can survive without good reads on opponents' hands.

Five Good Times to Play Poker

69 You've Come Back, Slowly and Steadily, from A Lengthy Losing Streak

You've gone through a bad patch, but you have got back to winning ways through patient, solid play. Now is the time to continue the good work but to show actual profit from it. You will be feeling quietly content, eager to make the right decisions. This is a good frame of mind to be in for poker. Two warnings:

- Don't press for profits, nor loosen your starting requirements, just because you have a positive bankroll.
- Don't let a quick reversal of fortune throw you. You are definitely on the way to long-term profit, but you may have some bumpy periods before you feel financially secure.

70 You Have The Day Off, All to Yourself

You have decided to enjoy a day of poker, and you've taken time to prepare yourself mentally:

Patience
Discipline
Concentration
Calm, considered guts

You have no time restraint, nor conflicting responsibilities. To play well, you must enter the poker world and leave everything else outside. This is the way that you become attuned to all the subtle changes that occur throughout a session. If you can spot them quickly, you will be ahead of everyone else at your table.

71 When you Have Qualified for A Big Tournament

When you have qualified for an event, perhaps in a satellite, you are primed for what is to come. You have a chance to make a basic game plan and develop your starting strategy. Because you have qualified for the event, rather than having paid an entry fee, you may feel freed up to take a few extra risks; this, in tournament play, is likely to be the right attitude. Finally, you know that you are on good form because, if you have qualified by winning, or placing high, in a satellite, then you have proved to yourself that you can be a winner.

Playing in satellites, especially online, is highly recommended, since you can win the chance to play in some big money events, against the best players and, possibly, take home a big-prize purse. However, before entering satellite events, check that you are available to play in the big event if you happen to qualify.

72 *You Feel in The Mood to Learn*

To improve at poker, you must truly want to improve. Much of this improvement comes from immersing yourself in the atmosphere of the game, your table, your opponents and their changing moods. The effort involved in doing this is quite great, but it will pay dividends over time.

Learning at poker may involve losing. If you can train yourself not to mind losing provided you are learning something, always to concentrate on trying to play the hands as well as possible, then you will achieve your goals far more quickly.

Whilst you observe, try to resist the temptation to be critical of other players' methods, and focus instead on the positive elements of the winners' games. Sometimes, when your cards are dead and the game is boring for you, it is easy to become cynical and dismissive but those feelings do nothing to improve your game and should be resisted.

You also learn from observing the play of other successful players and, almost by a process of osmosis, absorb new ideas and skills.

73 *When your Luck Is in*

However unscientific it may be, all gamblers will tell you that there are times when they feel positive and lucky – and they usually win, and other times when their feelings of negativity and ill fortune ooze out of every pore and soon become a self-fulfilling prophecy. The simple solution is to heed those innate, dire warnings and steer clear of the card room or casino. Mind you, any gambler will tell you that this is easier said than done.

When you are on a roll in life generally, everything seems better at the green baize. Beware allowing over-confidence to drain you of chips. Use that confidence internally and it will work for you.

At least, when playing poker, if you are feeling down, use that as a warning to play carefully: tight and positive. Better still, leave the game alone for the day and return refreshed another time.

74 *Pause Before Laying Down your Hand*

If you bet and then, when your opponent raises you, you muck your cards immediately, you give away that you did not have a real hand. Anyone watching now knows what you look like, how and when you bet when you are trying to steal.

There are two other reasons why you should pause before mucking your hand.

Firstly, you might consider re-raising. If you judge your opponent is testing you, you can ramp up the pressure by re-testing him; you might also choose to call if the potential pot odds (implied pot odds) warrant it.

Secondly, there is a psychological reason, particularly apt for live games but not irrelevant online too. If you fold quickly, you lose the opportunity to observe your opponent while you are pretending to think. You give him an easy time, and it becomes engrained. Your opponent starts to think: if I raise, he folds, and I take the chips – easy.

But, if you think for a while, consider your options and then fold, your opponent will have been holding his breath all that time. He'll feel a little drained. He won't put raising you and having an easy time together so readily the next time. Maybe, searching for a quiet life, the next time he'll just call, or fold.

75 *Stick to Poker*

For casinos, poker isn't much of a money maker; they could use the card-room space for slots and make ten times more. They are hoping that you'll be distracted on your way to and from your table, by the lure of Blackjack, Craps and Roulette. When you have played a patient game for eight hours, you may tempted to seek an adrenalin fix. I urge you to resist.

There are many people living in abject misery in Las Vegas, but none so sad as the skilful poker player who has just lost all his day's profits, expertly accrued, on ten minutes of Blackjack.

Even the online poker rooms have cottoned on to the fact that distractions can be a major leak in a poker player's bankroll and a leak to the house too. So, in have come the buttons that you click to take you to a Blackjack game or into their main casino software. In the time it takes to play out a hand you're not involved in, you could have played five hands of Blackjack. Resist.

By the way, in my years of research, I have identified at least one major online Blackjack program as not random and adjusted in a way to benefit the casino. It is still in operation and I don't believe that it has cleaned up its act. For this reason, I do not recommend playing Blackjack online on any site.

76 *Ignore Casino Poker Games*

Casino poker games are not really poker. They are table games based around a few of the rules of poker but with a significant house edge built in. The three main casino poker table games are:

- Caribbean Stud Poker
- Let 'Em Ride Poker
- Three-Card Poker

These have amongst the highest house edges of any casino game and are a gold mine for the casinos (and therefore terrible for the players). There are best strategies for each, but you have to be lucky to make a profit, even a short-term one.

Caribbean Stud Poker might be worth playing when there is a huge progressive for picking up a Royal Flush. However, even then, since you have to play the basic game in addition to the top-hand bonuses, you are likely to lose too much to justify play.

Three-Card Poker is based, as the name suggests, just on three cards. In this game, the likelihood of a flush is greater than a straight and so the value of these hands is reversed.

Let 'Em Ride Poker has the worst odds of any of these games. If you must play, go for the lowest possible stake.

Video Poker has been around for a long time now and remains one of the most popular casino games. Skilful play on certain machines can produce a tiny edge to the player, but such an edge would require hundreds of thousands of hands perfectly played to yield anything worth talking about. However, if you dare not grace the poker tables on your next visit to Vegas or Atlantic City, but you crave some poker action, at least you get a decent bang for your buck with Video Poker, since if you play decently, the house edge is pretty low.

By the way, most casinos will sell you booklets showing you the optimum way to play each poker machine and these are usually worth the investment. Books on expert Video Poker can also be found online and in decent bookshops.

The only poker game which presents the chance to play with a positive expectation of success, based on skill, is poker. Stick to that or, at the very least, keep your poker bankroll separate from any other gambling.

Five Things to Do When Playing Online

77 *Turn Off The Online Chat*

It's such a bad idea to chat while trying to play poker. It distracts you from your observations, encourages protracted bad-beat stories and childish argument, and provides opportunities to reveal information you should keep secret.

There are some excellent poker forums where the game is dicussed in great detail by true devotees. However, join one of those at times when you are not actually playing.

78 *Eat and Drink Regularly*

It sounds obvious; it is obvious, but many of us forget to do it. To maintain concentration it is important to keep well fed and watered. If you are thinking you are thirsty, or you are craving a big, fat sandwich, your mind really isn't on your game.

79 *Stretch your Legs*

This is beginning to sound like a public information film, I know, but these tips for online play will save you, and make you, money. It's as simple as that.

Not only does this prevent cramps and aches and general discomfort, but it rests your back, your eyes and your hands at the same time. Schedule, as part of your leg stretch, a comfort break, or a visit to the kitchen. Try to structure such a break into your games every hour or so (at the very least, every two hours). Remaining alert and relaxed will add to your bankroll for certain.

80 When you Hit Tilt, Leave The Room

This is a major advantage over live play. In a home
game, or a card room or casino, to leave the table when
you feel indignant and aggrieved, when you are affected
by a horrible bad beat, can be awkward. You might lose
your seat; you might be taunted; it takes an effort. At
home, you can stand up, leave the room which contains
your computer, and take some nice deep theatrical
breaths.

When you've calmed down – you've accepted that this is
your lot, as a poker player, to suffer humiliation at the
hands of idiots – you can return to your game and continue
playing.

Adherence to this tip will save you money; that's guaranteed.

81 Cut Communications with The Outside World

Turn that horrible, filthy intrusive mobile phone off . . .
and set your home phone to answer-service. Answering
phone calls has cost me thousands of dollars. I'm done
with that now. I advise you to do the same.

82 Leave The Mascots at Home

I know that Amarillo Slim wears his stetson with a dead
snake as a hatband and Johnnie Chan rubbed his 'Lucky
Orange' to win one World Series and nearly rubbed his
way to a second the next year but those poker greats used
them to intimidate, not to reassure themselves.

Poker is a thinking (wo)man's game of logic, deduction
and skill. To demonstrate that you believe it is about
anything else is a bit silly.

You really don't need a pointless artefact to bring you luck; less still, to comfort you when you misplay the hands. Forget luck having anything to do with it – it evens out over a long period of time – just concentrate on playing your hands correctly. I know of no mascot which can help you to do that.

83 It's A Lottery

One of the finest players ever, Doyle Brunson, has famously commented along these lines: A No-Limit Texas Hold 'Em tournament is a lottery. The best players hold more tickets, but they still have to win a lottery.

Thought of in this way, you can explain why even very good players rarely win tournaments. The fields are so enormous, the standard of play rising and the luck factor so significant, that your skill provides only extra chances – not a guaranteed route to the final table.

As you play tournaments, use them for experience and for exploring different styles of play, do not be dispirited that you are not finishing in the money regularly. What you will find is that you more regularly make it into the stages of the event where you have a chance to make it to the last few tables. Slowly, you'll find yourself making more money finishes and, when your skills are honed and fortune is with you, you'll see your chance to make the final table. It is a slow and uncertain path to tread, but it can be done incrementally; and you still have to be lucky.

84 Don't Slow-play Multiple Opponents

Slow-playing is a dangerous business, not only because an opponent may overtake you when you provide cheap access to further board cards, but also because it is that much harder to lay down a hand when you know that it was winning only moments ago.

Unless you hold the absolute, stone-cold nuts, avoid attempting to slow-play more than one opponent since you have to be very adept at post-flop play and you will find it very hard to find out where you are later on. In any case, for the vast majority of the time, betting out with the best hand remains the most effective way of maximizing the potential of any winning hand.

85 Bullying Short-Stacks

The chances of a short-stacked player picking up a premium starting hand in the last gasps of their tournament are very remote. If you give them enough time, however, they may just hit what they need for their last stand. To that end, prevent short-stacked players from calling cheaply for a flop, by raising whenever you hold a decent hand in position.

As you do this, decide whether you will call an all-in re-raise from a short-stack. If the answer is yes, you can raise slightly more than average; if the answer is no, you might scale down your raise, so that you can escape inexpensively if re-raised. Obviously, you will mix up your raises, but this would be a good default position to hold.

When you are in a tournament approaching a bubble (either the payout bubble or the Final-Table bubble), you should also concentrate on players who, if left to their own devices, might fold their way past the bubble (to qualify for the money or the Final-Table accolades) but who, when challenged with a raise, may be tempted to protect their almost safe position by folding tamely. Often, these players are more reluctant to risk an all-in than the actual short-stacked player and therefore your raises carry greater fold equity against them. In this way, you can build your own stacks quite safely, improving your position and building a bigger barrier between you and elimination.

86 If you Keep Being Raised, Change Tables

Because of the combative nature of poker, it is easy to become locked in personal battles against individuals. However, if you encounter consistent raising from a specific opponent or just generally, there is no requirement for you to continue fighting this particular battle. It is not a matter of honour that you remain at the table. To re-raise usually requires a very good or premium hand and you may simply not wish to take on an opponent who seems hell-bent on ramping up the size of every pot at every opportunity.

Online, to change your table is easy and there are always hundreds available from which to choose. Unlike in tournament poker or in a home game, you do have a choice of tables when you play cash games in a card room or casino. Although it may seem like an effort to stand up, add your name to the waiting list for the next suitable table and hang around wasting your valuable playing time, to sit there playing in unsuitable conditions is plain idiotic. If the greatest exertion you have to perform to succeed at poker is to move tables, you'll be lucky. So, no excuses, don't fight unnecessary battles.

87 Trust – Indeed, Nurture – your Gut Feelings

What you sense at the poker table, how you feel, what your gut tells you – these are not ethereal emotions. These feelings should be linked to your growing understanding of the game, your knowledge of your opponents: observation of their betting styles, physical tells, their clear and

apparent interest (or otherwise) in the hand, the atmosphere at the table, the underlying history between you
and certain opponents, the results to date in the current
session. All these factors will, to a greater or lesser extent,
influence your view of your opponents' actions and lead
you to feel differently about various situations. All of this,
combined with the simple fact that for the vast majority of
the time a player's betting is his strongest tell, may lead
you to feel instinctively that you are beaten (or, better still,
that your hand is winning).

The purpose of this tip is to reassure you that to have
such feelings is not only normal, but highly desirable. Far
from dismissing them as 'intuition' (often considered to be
illogical and unscientific), these feelings should be em-
braced and encouraged, because it is these which, as your
experience is developed, will help you to win key big pots
and to get yourself out of, potentially, even bigger ones.

Let's look at a quick, simple example:

A player raises in fourth position and you, holding: 5♣
5♦, decide to call. The flop comes:

The raiser bets out and you decide to call. The turn comes:

The raiser bets again, and you decide to call. The river
comes:

The raiser now goes all-in. You call. The raiser shows: A♠ Q♠. You take down the pot. What happened here?

Assuming that you are not a calling-station, there will have been a combination of reasons you decided to play this hand the way you did. Perhaps you knew (or remembered) that your opponent had only one gear; that once he started betting, he kept betting. Perhaps you sensed that he had missed the flop and turn, and that the river was meaningless to him. Perhaps you felt that, with a good hand, normally he would slow-play or check-raise. Perhaps you sensed that his all-in bet at the end was a sure sign of desperation . . .

Normally, a re-raise, perhaps on the flop or turn, would sort out the situation more clearly for you, but to call down the occasional hand shows that you cannot be bullied off the pot. Whatever the reason for your choice of calling here, it was based on a positive feeling – that your opponent had nothing.

Doubtless, there will be comments and reactions to your play. Maybe, you cannot fully explain (even to yourself) why you decided to call him down in the face of four raises. However, your play was right and, somewhere deep inside you, you strongly suspected that it was right.

The feelings in your gut are sometimes the most primitive and honest emotions you experience. Trust them.

88 Don't Complain; Never Explain

Originally a business tycoon's motto, this is one of the all-time great poker tips.

Because of the nature of odds, you will frequently be disappointed. Try to resist moaning and bitching. Not only do such actions reveal you to be a rank amateur, they also reinforce your own feelings of paranoia and lucklessness.

If you win a pot through good play, or sheer damned luck, and your opponent(s), kibitzers and disinterested parties all start asking you how you could have played that hand in the way you did, ignore them. You should be self-aware enough to know that either you got lucky (and you probably shouldn't be repeating your play) or that you played the hand perfectly and your opponents simply don't get it. Either way, keep your own counsel.

This tip is especially appropriate for online players. There, players frequently taunt and goad each other using online chat. To waste time berating opponents, or explaining your line of play, is exactly what any decent player should want you to do. If you are a good player, don't give free lessons; if you are learning the game, you'll learn little from table talk and far more through observation.

In any case, you should have online chat switched *off* when you play! It is one of the very worst elements of an online game for inexperienced players.

89 If you Are Losing, Don't Discount Being Outplayed as A Reason

Because so much of poker, in the short term, is based on luck, it is easy to blame your losses solely on that element of the game. Strangely, players rarely credit good luck as the reason they won so much in the previous session. For them, their skill was the sole defining feature of their success.

So, you can see the point of this tip immediately: if you are losing, it may well be because your cards are dead, or because your opponents keep catching key cards on the river. But, equally (in fact, more likely), it may be because you are:

- Outclassed by two or three key opponents, who are making your life nigh on impossible.
- You are not as good as you think you are.
- You are playing at a stake so high that it inhibits the correct actions on your part – perhaps you are reluctant to raise or re-raise when this would be the best play.
- You are not focused on the job in hand.
- Your sense of entitlement is not being met by the cards you are receiving or the respect you are being (or not being) shown; your game deteriorates as a result.

If you can review your game accurately and honestly, you may discover that there is more to your poor form than merely luck. To adjust your stake downwards, to remain positive and disciplined, not to compromise on starting hands and to focus on playing every hand as correctly as you can manage: these are the things you can do. Luck, if that is the true cause of your slump, is beyond your control.

90 The Fewer The Players at your Table, The Bigger your Cards Become

Is Q♠ 8♥ playable?

It will depend on the variation of Hold 'Em you are playing: cash game, Sit & Go, MTT, position, style of game you play and, importantly, how many players there are at your table.

Personally speaking, Q8 isn't usually a hand which gladdens my heart when I see it but, if I'm heads-up, or on the button in a three- or four-player game, it might well be playable, even worth a raise.

The key to successful Sit & Go play, final-table tactics and short-handed ring-game play is to recognize that the fewer the players, the more valuable your cards become.

This is not only because they actually do become more valuable – the chances of one or two opponents holding better, or making better after a flop, are lessened – but also because you must appreciate the need for aggression in short-handed games and, if you raise, or re-raise, feeling that your cards are strong, that often reveals itself to your opponents through increased confidence in your betting. Once you can get your opponents on their back feet, worried that you are picking up consistently good cards, unable ever to play back at you without a premium hand, you are on your way to wearing them down before they know what to do.

Five Things Not to Do at The Poker Club

91 Slowroll your Winning Hand

If you want to provoke controversy and become the villain, slowroll. It's the height of bad manners and will provoke anyone who sees you do this. To slowroll is to turn over your cards slowly, as you see the supposed experts do in movies. It's just rude. If you've won the hand, show it, gather in your chips and then gloat.

The real downside, for you, of slowrolling, is that it will make your opponents mad and harder to read. Keep everyone chugging along in the same old way and their play, and their tells, will be predictable.

92 Splash your Chips

To splash your bet is to throw your chips carelessly into the pot. When you make a bet, the dealer (or other players) must see that it matches the required amount. Place or push your bet in a pile in front of you towards the pot, but not into it. That way, your bet can be verified. Once everyone has called, then the chips go into the pot.

93 Comment On A Hand In Which you Are Not Involved

Don't get involved in arguments, disputes, or debates about poker knowledge. Apart from the fact that it disturbs your concentration, you will also affect the perception players have of you, and this may alter their play in a fashion that is hard for you to interpret. Avoid commenting on bad beats, ridiculous plays or dumb luck; some casinos ban players for being critical or aggressive at the table (especially low-limit games). Stay quiet and focused and bow out of any debate at the table.

Incidentally, the excellent Irish player, Andrew Black, did get involved in a now infamous incident at the most prestigious tournament of all, the Big One at the WSOP. Most of the players there disagreed with him, but I think he was absolutely right:

Down to the last couple of tables, a meal break is called – but the length of the break is not made clear to everyone. Almost everyone reappears to restart the crucial, tense play leading up to the Final-Table bubble. To reach that hallowed spot at the WSOP can be a once-in-a-lifetime event and everyone who plays poker dreams of making it. However, at Andrew's table, one player has failed to appear. The game recommences, but Andrew is unhappy that no one is calling for this missing player. He tries to have play halted but, to his astonishment, most people want to play faster – to wear down the missing player's stack with the enormous blinds. Andrew protests and then the fights begin.

To me, this is a clear case to get involved. You want to win, but to win fairly – up against the best anyone can throw at you.

94 Stay Glued to a Lousy Seat

If you decide that you don't like your seat for whatever reason: the opponent to your left keeps raising; your right-hand opponent is breaking wind; you are under the air-conditioning duct; you can't see the board cards properly; your chair wobbles; you are not in line with your feng shui desires – ask to change your seat or leave the table.

Anything which is putting you off your game, however small, will cost you money, so either put it out of your mind, or do something about it. Don't just sit there.

95 Hold your Cards under The Table

You need to keep your cards above the table so that the cameras (or your friends) can see that you are not swapping cards in your lap. Also, if the dealer can't see your cards, he/she does not know that you are still in the hand and the action may hurry past you before you have had a chance to act.

A further, bonus, tip here is: remember to give your cards back to the dealer when you have won a hand. Hang on to them until the dealer indicates that you have won and then give them back. I know several absent-minded players who hang on to their winning hands until the next hand is dealt and then, to the dismay of the table, the hand has to be re-dealt.

Oh, and another thing. However much you love your home-game buddies, whenever there's money involved, there's temptation. I'm used to a pack of cards – my relative dexterity is down to a misspent youth – so when it was my turn to deal one evening, I felt that the pack was a few cards short. I counted them out and, sure enough, three cards were missing – never to be found. They were there when we started; I always count the pack. Where did they go?

96 Enjoy The Entire Poker-Winning Process

To play poker in a disciplined, patient and aggressive fashion can prove testing even to the most dedicated. One of the ways I like to enhance my enjoyment of the game is to reflect upon all the enjoyment I derive from the battle in its entirety.

If you visit Las Vegas or any other major casino city, you must do so knowing that everyone there is determined to part you from every last cent you have about your person. However friendly, however generous they may appear, a casino's job is to win your money. However, if you gamble sensibly, following the best strategies, cash in on complimentaries and special offers, and enjoy the battle between you and the casinos, then you are far more likely to win and, even if you don't, you will enjoy the mental challenge of trying to get the better of your enemy.

So it should be with poker. Your table selection, your seat choice, whom you choose to play against at what stakes: all this should be part of your plan and part of the pleasure of settling down to a session of poker.

As mentioned throughout this book, the playing of poker itself is just one part – the best part certainly – of winning at poker. All the peripherals are of utmost importance to your likely success and therefore, if you can enjoy those processes, you will enjoy your session even more.

Above all, let's face it, to win is usually the most enjoyable feeling of all.

Here's your before-play checklist:

- Assess your own mood accurately: are you feeling alert, positive, optimistic, confident, awake, sober? If you don't feel all of these things, consider not playing.

- Ensure you have a long, uninterrupted session available to you (this may be two hours, six hours, or 24 hours).
- Find table(s) at the right stake for you. Never move up stakes just because there is no game available at your usual stake, nor simply because you have been winning in the short-term. If necessary, move down stakes – if you can beat a higher-stake table, you should be able to beat a lower-stake table also (but be aware of strategy changes which may be required).
- Before starting to play at/logging on to your chosen table, review what information you have about your opponents.
- Accept/choose a seat only if it's where it benefits you most (ideally with stronger/aggressive players to your right; weaker/passive players to your left).
- Promise yourself that you will take a break/leave the club if you feel frustrated, bitter, negative, heading towards tilt.

If you follow these basic pre-poker rules, you will reduce losses, increase winnings and enjoy your game more. The question is: can you resist the temptation to play fast and loose at the first table that becomes free? If you can't, you're doomed.

97 Make your Online Poker Room Comfortable

There are many advantages to online play but, possibly, my very favourite is that you are at home, comfortable and with everything you could want around you.

Ensure that you are not going to be disturbed; online poker is not a good game to play whilst you are doing something else. It requires all your concentration and that comes best when you are rested and comfortable.

Make sure that you have a comfortable, supportive chair – you're gonna be in it for long periods of time. Ensure that you have fresh air coming into your room and schedule breaks for stretching and mixing up your heart rate a little.

Make sure that you drink plenty of water or other soft drinks of your choice. If you can't resist a beer, alternate it with something soft.

Food-wise, try to avoid beer lunches, cocktail and nachos dinners and stick instead to fruit, salad, cheese, even some chocolate; these proteins will keep your mind alert and your body happy.

You may think that changing your eating and drinking habits for poker is a step too far but, when you feel well, you play better; when you remain alert, you keep your chips rather than dribbling them away.

A friend of mine, who started playing online poker quite seriously, used the first few months of his poker winnings to pay for a drinks fridge, an ergonomic chair and some funky casino-style lights in his study. Now, he says that he feels relaxed and refreshed and that he wins even more money; he's seriously thinking about giving up work for a year and seeing how he gets on as an online poker pro.

98 Feel in Control

Because your default playing style should be tight/aggressive, you want to remain aggressive and positive even when you have poor cards. This keeps open the possibility of blind stealing and bluffing. Refrain from sighing, shrugging or slumping when you see yet another lousy unsuited 73 or 92. Fold your hands positively; ignore taunting and backchat designed to get you involved when you shouldn't be. Every time that you play with a marginal hand, you are giving money away. That is what good players want you to do – it makes life much easier for them.

Ideally, when you enter a pot, you want it to be with a very strong or premium hand, or in position with a potentially strong hand. Entering the action by raising, or even re-raising, will immediately wrest control from your opponents. Every time you are in a pot, you want them to feel uncertain, fearful; you want them to be looking to you to set the action, to be waiting for your actions, and not taking positive steps themselves.

If you cannot achieve these moments and (sometimes, when things are going well) periods of domination, then your task will be far harder and you should consider changing table, tightening your starting-hand require-ments even further, or even quitting the poker session for that day – it may be that, mentally, you are unready for the tasks ahead.

It is no coincidence that so many top professional poker players come across as arrogant, opinionated and supre-mely self-confident; to be at the top of any game or sport, you need great self-belief, an almost over-the-top faith that you are the best player out there, that everyone else is just lining up to see if they can measure up to your skill. But, I'll let you into a secret: at any given moment, only a fraction of those great players actually *feel* the way their outward persona might suggest. However, being pros, they keep up the bravado and front of resolute confidence because they know that, at some point, they will need it in order to assume control of their table.

So, let the pros be your guide. Feel in control; appear in control. When your opponents respect your actions, they'll do what you want them to do – and you will win.

99 *Make your Opponents' Decisions Marginal*

You can start thinking about this only once you have mastered putting an opponent on a hand (not getting it right all the time, but at least making an educated guess). Once you can do that, you have a new variable to add to your betting: how do I give my opponent a problem?

Most poker decisions are quite simple: you have a good hand so you raise; your opponent has bet and you have nothing so you fold. You have a 20 per cent chance of making your flush on the final card and it will cost you only 10 per cent of the pot to call, so you call. Only very poor players get these decisions wrong.

The time when even a good player will make the wrong decision is when you give him a close decision and external factors – such as impatience, frustration, ego – persuade him to make a costly mistake.

Let's look at a simple example:

You hold: K♠ 10♠ and the flop and turn have come:

You put your opponent on an ace, possibly two pair, and it's your turn to bet.

If he is on two pair, then he has only four cards which can make him his full house. He may suspect that you hold a made hand so he'll be reluctant to call for much more. With 100 chips in the pot, how much, as an example, should you bet?

If you bet 100 chips now, your opponent will probably fold quickly; if you check, he'll take the free card happily. Either of those actions does not give him a problem. Let's bet 25 chips. That still means he'll have to call 20 per cent of the pot for only an 8 per cent chance of overtaking you.

That gives him a temptation – and a chance to exaggerate the potential pot odds – to call and see the river. It's statistically wrong to do so but it's still a reasonable chance. That is where you, as a good player, can lure other good players into the pot.

Incidentally, once that third spade appeared on the board, perhaps any bet will cause him to fold; perhaps he just made a lower flush and will call down anything. Indeed, depending upon the style of your opponent and your history together, maybe another size of bet altogether would work better here. However, in principle, I hope you see the idea of giving your opponent some kind of deal to think about, rather than making the wrong bet and giving him no problem.

100 Luck Is A Cruel Mistress

In *Casino Royale*, Ian Fleming's first James Bond novel, his character muses on the nature of lady luck. Bond, of course, wants to seduce her, take her roughly, enjoy her but he acknowledges that she is fickle.

There are periods in every player's life when he will feel as if luck has deserted him utterly. The depths of misery this brings can be almost beyond description. Far from merely reflecting an integral element of gambling, instead these feelings are transferred into our real lives. I have known players make themselves seriously ill through depression and disappointment at the poker table.

I know, personally, an intense bitterness at being cheated by luck because she has ruined my favourite game and failed to reward skill and study and dedication over idiocy.

However, luck is cyclical and, however miserable it may make you one day (week, month or year), it can revive your spirits by its almost inevitable return.

My advice during spells of appalling luck is this: slow down. Don't stop playing, but play less. Take time to read books on specific elements of the game, reread basic texts such as this one. Reconnect yourself with why you are playing poker and, preferably, that you value playing your cards correctly over short-, or even medium-term, luck. If you can do that, you will find the side effects of bad luck are lessened.

If you can remind yourself that, over a lifetime of poker, your luck will be pretty-much average, then the bad times might even herald the onset of the good times. Perhaps, above all, enjoy the whole poker experience, even if you are only watching and absorbing information rather than playing lots of hands. If you simply enjoy the atmosphere, you lessen the pressure which builds on you to play marginal – that is, losing – hands when you should not.

Finally, Nick-the-Greek, the renowned high-stake gambler, famously said:

'The best thing in life is gambling and winning . . . and the second best is gambling and losing.'

If you love poker enough, luck becomes irrelevant. Only the game, and the playing of the game as best you possibly can, is important.

TABLES AND STATISTICS

Completing Hands on Turn and River

This table shows you the likelihood (in exact percentage odds) of hitting your out cards on the turn and river.

Number of Outs	2 cards to come (%)	1 card to come (%)
20	67.5	43.5
19	65	41.3
18	62.4	39.1
17	59.8	37
16	57	34.8
15	54.1	32.6
14	51.2	30.4
13	48.1	28.3
12	45	26.1
11	41.7	23.9
10	38.4	21.7
9	35	19.6
8	31.5	17.4
7	27.8	15.2
6	24.1	13
5	20.4	10.9
4	16.5	8.7
3	12.5	6.5
2	8.4	4.3
1	4.3	2.2

Key Statistics You Should Understand

When holding four cards to a flush, you have nine possible out cards to complete your flush. With two cards remaining this is a 35 per cent chance; with one card to come, less than 20 per cent. If/when you make your flush by calling bets, players are less likely to bet into you or call your bets since players are always 'afraid of the flush'; if you have raised, as a semi-bluff, you may confuse your opponent and it is more likely that they will call your final bet.

When holding four cards to an open-ended straight, you have eight possible out cards to complete your straight. With two cards remaining this is a 31.5 per cent chance; with one card to come, just under 17.5 per cent. Note also that some open-ended straights offer other players opportunities to make higher straights.

Gut-draw straights (where you require a single card) are *very* poor propositions: 16.5 per cent with two cards to come; a paltry 8.7 per cent with one card to come; avoid them.

To convert a pair to trips: with two cards to come: 8.4 per cent; with one card to come: 4.3 per cent

To convert two pair to a full house: with two cards to come: 24.1 per cent; with one card to come: 13 per cent

Additional to the existing pot value, the likely value of the pot (potential pot odds) must also be assessed in the event of you making your hand: will your opponent(s) bet again or call your bets. If you assess that this is likely, you may/should be more ambitious than the simple pot odds suggest.

Principle of Two-and-Four

A simpler, quicker method of calculating odds – though less accurate – is the principle of Two-and-Four:

With one card to come, take the number of out cards you believe you have (to give you the winning hand), and multiply this figure by *two*.

With two cards to come, take the number of out cards you believe you have (to give you the winning hand), and multiply this figure by *four*.

If you compare these figures to the accurate percentages in the table, you will see that this method provides a quick, reasonably accurate method of calculating odds.

Likelihood of Being Dealt Each Five-Card Poker Hand

This is the same as the likelihood of seeing this hand after the flop. That is to say: your two hole cards, plus the three board cards brought by the flop. The chances of seeing at least one pair are quite high.

The significance is how likely it is that opponents at a full table (nine or ten players) hold better than you. Together with betting, hard reading and your own actions, you have a decent chance of working out where you stand after the flop has appeared.

royal flush	1 / 649,740
straight flush	1 / 72,192
4-of-a-kind	1 / 4,164
full house	1 / 693
flush	1 / 508
straight	1 / 254
3-of-a-kind	1 / 46
2-pair	1 / 20
1-pair	1 / 1
no hand	Evens

Comparative Hand Statistics

This is a set of statistics to illustrate how likely it is that your hand is beaten pre-flop. Assuming a full table of nine players, these are the key results:

If you hold   The chances of an opponent holding better

KK   4% chance that an opponent holds AA

AK   4% chance that an opponent holds AA or KK

QQ   10% chance that an opponent holds AA or KK

JJ   14% chance that an opponent holds AA, KK or QQ

1010   20% chance that an opponent holds AA, KK, QQ or JJ

This shows why it is usually wrong not to play AK or KK, since the chances of your being dominated are very small. Experts may talk about folding these hands pre-flop – a brilliant thing to do – but, in real life, very few do pass these hands and rightly so.

Basic Chances of Receiving Key Hole Cards

How likely is it that you will be dealt premium hole cards? Not very likely, as these statistics show:

AA   0.45%   or, roughly, once in 220 deals

KK   0.45%   once in 200 deals

Any pair has an equal chance of being dealt to you, since all pairs require two cards of the same numerical value. If you are being dealt plenty of 44 or 77 pairs but no AA or KK pairs, that is just short-term poor luck.

AKs   0.3%   or, roughly, once in 333 deals

Despite the fact that suited hole cards provide only a 3% advantage to the player, you are three times more likely to be dealt unsuited cards. In the case of AKs, this rare hand seems far nicer than it really is.

AK   0.9%   or, roughly, once in 111 deals

Statistics for Ace-High Poker

Many players, especially online, raise aggressively pre-flop with almost any ace. In short-handed games (say, 5 players), this policy is certainly aggressive but, combined with the fold equity of such raising, is probably a winning strategy. In full games (say, 9 players), the chances are simply too high that another player will hold an ace. In these circumstances, your kicker, and what you hit on the flop, will prove crucial. However, playing ace-high poker runs the risk of your holding the second-best hand and those are the most costly hands in poker.

Situation	Full Table	Short-Handed Table
	(9 players)	(5 players)
No one holds an ace	17%	41%
No one *but you* holds an ace	30%	59%

This also illustrates why, particularly in a full game, to call raises with ace-rag is really dangerous. There is a 70% chance that another player holds an ace and, if you are out-kickered, you are really playing only your low card against your opponent's higher card, that is, you are dominated.

Top 20 Hands in Hold 'Em

When you run computer simulations of the most profitable hands (those with the highest earning power) for Texas Hold 'Em, the results are intrinsically affected by: how the hands are played; how many players are at the table; what standard the game might be; the decisions you, as the holder of the hand, choose to take. However, the following list gives you a good idea of the hands you should be most confident about playing. Note that those lower on the list will require your judgment about position and the style in which you choose to play your hole cards.

s = suited
1   AA
2   KK
3   QQ
4   JJ
5   AKs
6   1010
7   AK
8   AQs
9   KQs
10 AJs
11 A10s
12 AQ
13 99
14 KJs
15 KQ
16 K10s
17 A9s
18 AJ
19 88
20 QJs

TELLS EXTRA

This section contains a wealth of information on tells – those inadvertent physical signs – which, if you are watching, can make a vital difference to your decision-making in a live game.

The true experts of this game make mental notes on everyone against whom they play, knowing that, sometime down the line, be it the following hand, the next session, the next tournament, they will encounter you again and use their information to read how you are playing your cards.

For most players, this seems an impossible task. At the very least, however, notes should be made online and, if you are playing in a fairly consistent school, you should spend five minutes after the game, jotting down any observations you may have made during the last session. Over time, this information can be reviewed to build up a good picture of your regular opponents' game. In case you are wondering why you would bother to do this, the answer is simple: knowledge equals power and that equates to profit. Do you want to win, or do you just want to play? It all comes back to that question.

Observation

Observation of your opponents will lead to fast identification of their standard style: tight/aggressive; tight/passive; loose/aggressive; loose/passive. You may also begin to notice tells which will guide you to call bluffs and set those of your own.

How best to observe? Unobtrusively, your head angled slightly towards the players you are watching. Ideally, with a look of supreme boredom and indifference on your face, as if you are not watching them at all. In fact, you can even stifle a yawn or two.

To stare at a player becomes something else since, once a player knows that he is being watched, he may well tighten up his defences or attempt to mislead you with a false tell. Indeed, a stare is really an intimidation technique, an attempt to learn about a player's hand, but in a different way. By staring, you are trying to scare your opponent into revealing weakness.

1) First Fifteen Minutes

This time is vital to establish your opponents' standard styles, assess your position in terms of suitability for your style of action – and seek to move seats, or even tables, if you discover you are unfavourably positioned. Try to identify weaker players and seek to pressurize them.

2) The Deal

Do not look at your own hole cards until it is time for you to act. Instead, watch for reactions from opponents as they look at their cards. No matter how disciplined the player, it is difficult to tough out a very lean spell of cards, and often sighing, frowning, and shoulder slumping can be observed. A stiffening of the body upon seeing hole cards usually means strength.

3) The Flop

Train yourself never to watch the flop. This is one of the greatest failings amongst weaker players: to watch the flop is to waste a prime opportunity to gather information. It's a great time to observe opponents; they will be focused on the appearance of the board and often pay no attention to their own reactions. Even at quite high stakes, I have seen players smiling, nodding – more often, grimacing, sighing, shrugging – and knowledge of these inadvertent physical tells can quite simply transform a hand to your benefit.

4) The Turn and The River

Usually you will have an idea whether or not an opponent has hit a draw but, once again, you may be given help if you are watching to take advantage of it. Players sometimes remember to adjust their poker faces as the hand develops, particularly if they see you observing them. This is why observation of your opponents on the flop is so important. However, in lower-stake games, there are plenty who, having failed to obscure their emotional reaction to the flop, fail just the same on the turn or river.

5) When you Are Not in The Hand

This is prime viewing time since the protagonists are unlikely to be paying you any attention. Watch at all the above times but also after a big uncalled bet on the river. If this is a bluff and the proponent succeeds in stealing the pot, less experienced players often show the bluff, either literally or by their reaction to their own success: a stray comment here, a smirk there – you must not miss these sources of information.

6) When you Are in The Hand and Someone Not in it Makes A Comment

This is a rare, but significant, time when you can gain extra information. Players not in the hand frequently react to a flop, almost always because they have folded a hand which would have fitted it perfectly. Listen for snorts of frustration, watch for rolling eyes and clenched fists – you will see them all. Although they should never do this, players also speak when they see the flop, telling everyone what cards they held. In the midst of an important hand, it is easy to miss these gestures and comments, but they can help you.

For example, you might decide only to call a first-position raise when you hold AK, and the flop comes:

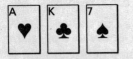

And, just about audible to you is an opponent's whisper to his neighbour:

'I folded A7 there.'

Now, you know that your opponent does not hold AA and is unlikely to hold KK: your hand looks rock-solid in the face of whatever is bet at you.

Basic Tells

Much has been written about tells and the art of reading them accurately and, if you are to progress to a very high level in poker, you cannot read too much about the game.

Here are just a few basic tells of which every poker player should have an understanding. It is quite likely that, if you watch closely enough, you will see all these in your very next game. However, over a few sessions, you will definitely see most of them and, having seen them, you won't believe how much your opponents are inadvertently revealing to you.

Folding, Checking and Betting

This is the most reliable tell of all, since it is accurate (depending upon the game) up to almost 99 per cent. For the sake of a figure, let's just say that when people bet, at least 75 per cent of the time they are showing strength; when they check, at least 75 per cent of the time they are showing weakness. Amidst all the turmoil of a poker hand – trying to remember what to be watching, what to be doing, how to play the hand – this information is often overlooked.

The folding bit was a joke. If you can't read that tell, you are in serious trouble.

Strong Is Weak – Weak Is Strong

For less experienced players, this is the basic understanding of how to hide your hand. Usually, it's very obvious and, unless you know that your opponent is a much stronger player than average, applying this simple interpretation of whatever they do is likely to give you a decent read.

The two main tells you seek are signs of strength or weakness. This is a checklist of what you should be looking for.

Tells Which Suggest Strength

Change of Demeanour

Like a policeman at a crime scene, you should be looking for anything unusual. A previously noisy player who falls quiet usually has a decent hand – and, strangely, vice versa also. A slumped player who sits up, a tired guy who wakes up, a player with a relaxed facial expression who suddenly tightens up – all these almost always indicate interest in the hand and, usually, interest equates to strength.

Shaking Hands

This occurs very frequently. A player who places a bet with shaking hands is almost always strong. Strangely, most people can control external physical tells if they are focused on doing so – as you would be if you were bluffing – but people find it much harder to conceal excitement when strong.

Breathing Hard

Particularly on the flop, rising and falling of the chest indicates strength: why be so excited if you have missed the flop? You will see this occur frequently because most people aren't thinking about breathing when they are doing other things – it just takes care of itself. For this reason, it is easily influenced by emotional and psychological changes in the brain. Best of all, many players are not even aware of this change and do nothing to try to control it.

Sighing and Shrugging in The Spotlight

A player who shrugs or sighs when he is not the player about to act, may be revealing weakness or uncertainty, but a player on whom everyone's eyes have now fallen will not give an honest tell. Sighing and shrugging here is a clear sign of overacting – the player is strong.

Vocal Reluctance in The Spotlight

Unless the player has shown strong table-talking skills throughout, a quiet aside when in the spotlight is usually a weak attempt to occlude strength. Players who mutter:

'Well, it's probably time to go home'

or

'Well, I guess I'll call'

or

'I don't think I should be calling this'

are usually strong and know exactly what they are doing.

Eye Movement towards Chips

If the player knows he is being watched, this could be a false tell, as could reaching for his stacks before you have even made a move. However, in most cases, eyes move down to chips because the brain is telling them that shortly they must decide how much to bet.

Hand Movement towards Chips

If observed without the knowledge of the player, this is almost a physical tick; the hand moves towards the chips because the brain is telling it to prepare for that action. Beware players who reach obviously for their chips while you are deciding how to act – this is usually an intimidation move and those are almost always signs of weakness.

Tells Which Suggest Weakness

Holding Breath

This is another good tell, usually accompanying a bluffing bet. Players who are betting with the best of it are usually pretty relaxed. After all, what is there to worry about?

Intimidation Moves

If you have the best hand, why would you want to put pressure on to your opponent? It will prove far more effective, and profitable, to appear ineffectual rather than aggressive. Therefore, the following tend to suggest weakness:

Staring at an opponent whose turn it is to act;
Forcible placement of chips into the pot;
Placing of chips in the direction of an opponent (sometimes called a 'directed bet');
Visible disappointment that you might fold.

Instant Calls

If you are certain that you have the best of it, you would take time to assess how best to approach your betting on this deal. To call a bet instantly is an attempt to display strength and therefore usually indicates weakness. Incidentally, an instant call is also a poor player's way of making a semi-bluff into a draw. The quick call replaces the raise – but it should make it obvious to you.

Some further tells occur after the hand is completed, but before the next deal:

Tells between Hands

Flashing of One Hole Card

Players who bet or raise, take down a pot, and then flash one hole card are usually revealing that their other card was weak. Many players in these situations flash an ace: if they were really strong and wanted to show it, they could flash both their hole cards – or, better still, neither. To show one is an attempt to represent strength.

Reaction to Opponent's Fold

An obvious sign of displeasure or frustration usually means that the bettor/raiser did not want to contest the hand any further and is relieved to have taken down the pot.

Silence and/or introspective looks suggest greater strength and a genuine displeasure that the hand was passed without further contribution to the pot.

Revelation of The Nuts
Players who show their solidly-bet nut hand at the end when they are not required to do so are advertising their honesty. Thus, they are plotting to be dishonest in the near future. Watch out for a raise in the next hand or two: this is more likely than usual to be a bluff.

Finally, there are some tells which suggest a player's intentions mid-hand (usually on the flop):

Tells during A Hand

Staring at The Flop
A player staring at a flop is unlikely to be strong: you would prefer to occlude that with a neutral approach. Equally, he is unlikely to have missed the flop altogether, since it is more natural to slump in such circumstances. Most often, a pronounced staring at the flop suggests a hand which has caught part of the flop. The brain is processing the chances of converting a low pair into trips, or straight or flush draw odds, and the eyes keep staring.

Players who have stared at the flop and then raise are more likely than usual to be semi-bluffing into a draw.

Checking Hole Cards after Flop
Rarely do players forget their hole cards and if they hit the flop they pay careful attention not to look at their hole cards. When players do so, it is usually for the reasons above: they have hit part of the flop. Further betting is more likely than usual to be based on a draw.

Long Betting Time before Calling
Unless renowned for their acting prowess, players who appear to be considering pot odds and draw possibilities usually are. This is particularly true when they are staring

longingly at the pot itself and their subsequent action is to call.

Aggressive action on the next round is probably required to remove them from the hand.

Interpretation of Tells

As you improve, it will be your job to decide which of these tells comes from inexperience and lack of self-awareness, and which might be the product of a devious mind. As a general rule, my interpretation of tells is as follows:

Any tell which you pick up when the player is unaware that you are watching him is likely to be accurate. Such action is usually a solid one, but is not emphasized in any way.

Any tell which you observe when the player in question knows that he is being watched (either specifically by you, or because he is about to act), is much less likely to be accurate – it is performance. These actions are usually emphasized and slightly exaggerated to ensure that even the unobservant might pick up on them.

Layers of Understanding

The more consistently you play within a single group of players, the more about your game they know. This is where layers of understanding begin to play a bigger part in the proceedings.

Imagine that you notice that you are being watched by a certain player. You decide to send him a false tell: when the flop hits you perfectly, you slump your shoulders just a tiny bit, almost like a movie star would just hint at a facial expression, knowing that they are in close-up. He picks up on this and when you check, he bets and perhaps you call reluctantly. You run this uncertain attitude to the end and then reveal the nuts. Your opponent knows that he's been duped. You know that he knows, and he knows that you know that he knows. That's just the first layer . . .

A fortnight later, you notice that he's watching you again and, once again, you try to mislead him. How he reacts to this will be based on his knowledge of your playing history and what he detects on this very hand. What's more, you know this, he knows you know, and you know that he knows that you know. You see how the layers start to develop?

True experts remember each and every battle: their decisions when playing against one another may seem to the viewer (on a televised Final Table perhaps) to be madness. Yet, they are based on all the information that has been accumulated over what could be years of playing against one another. That is why, at the highest level of the game, a bluff is never just a bluff. It is a bet based on a lifetime of poker histories.

BAD BEATS EXTRA

This is a brief section to read when you are having a truly lousy time at the poker table. Sadly, it is almost inevitable that this will happen to you on a regular basis, since misery at the green baize is just part of the kaleidoscope of emotions which you will enjoy or endure over the course of a number of sessions.

The world's greatest players all recount how they have had to suffer appalling sessions, losing to players who, by comparison, know virtually nothing about the game. This should not be a surprise in a game that relies heavily (especially in the short term) on luck.

Bad Cards

There is nothing unusual or surprising about suffering an hour or two of bad cards. It is only marginally less surprising if you suffer a whole eight-hour session of predominantly unplayable cards. To find that you hold terrible cards for three or four sessions is not unusual; it is commonplace to hear that someone (reliable) has held appalling cards for several weeks.

None of these occurrences is, in any way, noteworthy, other than to reflect that if they did not occur, that *would* be remarkable. In other words, far from defying the odds, these dry spells are to be expected.

The key to surviving these spells is to limit your losses to a minimum. In simple terms, this can be achieved by playing very few hands. That is deeply boring, of course, but it is not hard to do. Indeed, if you focus on observing rather than playing the poker at your table, you may find that you enjoy yourself more than you imagine and learn a good deal about the game and your opponents. You might decide to leave the card room or casino early: that is frustrating and disappointing, but it is not a tragedy. You might even give up poker for a couple of weeks and return to it refreshed and maybe better read. Again, an annoying interlude in your pastime, but not a prison sentence.

Finally, it is worth mentioning that, whilst you fold hand after hand in a disciplined, sensible way, you will observe appallingly weak players betting on all kinds of rubbish and having lots of fun and winning. You will yearn for them to be punished for their looseness and stupidity. In a just world, they would be. But this is gambling, and there is nothing just about the way luck sprays the unworthy with gold dust and punishes the prudent, knowledgeable and disciplined. Learn to ignore the taunts of lady luck and focus entirely on using every minute at the poker table to increase your knowledge and prepare yourself for the time when the cards do come your way.

Cold Decks

To be cold-decked is to find that the board never helps you or, worse still, it helps you just fine, but helps your opponents even more. For example:

You hold: 10♥ 10♣. You raise and receive one caller. The flop comes:

This is a great flop for you. You make a big bet to protect your hand and your opponent sticks in all his chips. Deciding that he is bluffing you because he thinks you have just made a continuation bet, you decide to call. He shows 3♣ 3♦. The turn and river bring no help.

You reflect that, had the board brought even one over-card, you might have got away from the hand but, as it was, you couldn't lay down your tens. Drawing dead a third ten on the board gives your opponent a full house – you are virtually drawing dead.

You hold: K♥ J♣. On the button, you raise and the big blind calls you.

The flop comes:

The big blind bets, you raise, and you are re-raised all-in. You decide to call and your opponent turns over Q♣ 10♥. The turn and river do not transform your hand into a full house.

You raise with A♠ K♥ and receive one caller. The flop comes:

You bet and you are raised all-in. You decide to call. Your opponent shows Q♠ 4♠. The turn and river bring no more spades. What the heck was he doing calling with Q4 suited?

Each time you hit a great flop for you: a flop which, realistically, made laying down your hand to the re-raise almost impossible. Each time you were cold-decked – your opponent held cards which destroyed your excellent hands.

By the way, these weren't random examples. These three occurred within a few minutes of each other at an online table where the opponents were loose and foolish.

Note: although I was convinced I was jinxed, the most unlucky man in the entire world, I did stay focused and positive and I did win back those lost pots and more besides because, eventually, luck turns and loose calling gets what it deserves.

To be cold-decked from time to time is routine. To be cold-decked for a session is not unusual; to be cold-decked for an entire week happens from time to time. In an ideal world, when you had a good hand, you'd get paid; when you had a poor hand, it would cost you. This isn't an ideal world – not even close.

Bad Beats

There is no end to the misery bad beats can bring. To play a hand perfectly and be overtaken on the river by a player who should never have been in the hand in the first place, nor called on the flop, nor called on the turn, is beyond frustrating: it is depressing, demoralizing, disheartening, energy-sapping, unfair, unjust and immoral.

I have lost every last cent of the hundreds of dollars won through eight hours of good play on just one hand where an opponent over-bets, misplays and then hits a miracle card at the end. The sense of waste, of pointlessness, to your discipline, skill and correct play is almost a mortal wound. It makes me want to give up the game forever. What point is there, I ask myself over and over again, in improving my game if any old fool can come in and take all my chips?

I have cried and wailed and moaned and sulked. I have smashed more than one computer mouse, knocked over drinks and sworn at the heavens. I have truly felt that I was cursed or jinxed and that the bad beats would never end.

The problem for poker players is that every single one of them has experienced these feelings on multiple occasions and everyone thinks that their run of bad beats must be the worst ever known to man. Even more frustratingly, right now, as you read these paragraphs, there is some poor, blighted soul, suffering far worse than you.

There are some reassurances, as hollow as they may seem when you read them in the midst of the mists of misery:

- You couldn't suffer bad beats if your opponents weren't making mistakes (or you weren't playing outstandingly well). You *need* your opponents to misplay hands because, in the long run, this will be a major source of your profits. In other words, you've found the right table, with the right opponents: you just have to be patient to cash in on your advantage.
- The worse the player to whom you have lost a big hand, the more likely it is that you will win back your money later and, probably, some more besides. You don't need to be winning all through the race, as long as you are ahead at the finishing post.
- Once you are genuinely beating your regular game, despite the terrible bad beats, you will still find yourself in profit most of the time. Without the bad beats, you might think you would have a far bigger profit. How-

ever, this is wrong: without the bad beats, and your opponents' bad play, you would have smaller profits. You need those bad beats to prove how bad your opponents are compared to you.

- The pain lessens over time.
- One of the most annoying, provoking and downright disgusting sayings is this:

'Adversity is an opportunity to display courage.'

Unfortunately, it's also true, especially at poker.

If you can pick yourself up from the bad beat, retain control and focus and then play well immediately afterwards, that courage will translate into smaller losses and bigger profits – the precise profile of a winning poker player. What's more, the reaction becomes habitual and the emotional affect of a bad beat will transform from an overwhelming feeling of grief, loss and frustration to a mere pinprick of annoyance.

Tilt

If you allow bad cards, cold decks or bad beats to adversely affect your play, particularly in a manner which results in loose, wild play and the squandering of chips, this is said to be going on tilt. I mentioned in an earlier book that:

'In my experience, more money is lost due to a player's reaction to a bad beat than to the bad beat itself.'

I was amazed by the reaction to this statement. I received so many e-mails and comments from players agreeing that this was the case. Agreeing that, when they looked at their statistics and histories, this was exactly what they found.

I shouldn't have been surprised, because the opinion was based on my own personal experience in my early days of playing poker, and later when I played online. So often the bad beat cost me, say, a quarter of my stack at the table, but the resulting tilt cost the remainder of it. So, when you feel yourself thrown off kilter by a bad beat, and put off your game in a way that your mind wanders to subjects such as injustice, revenge and paranoia, I urge you to do one of the following. And I'm urging you to *do* these, not just to read them:

- *Stop playing* (possibly just for a moment or two; possibly for the rest of the day).
- Stand up and go to the restroom or go outside for some fresh air. You will miss only a couple of hands and your opponents will respect you for your discipline (whatever they may say).
- Online, leave the room in which your computer sits, get some fresh air. Perhaps leave the table at which you are playing and spend five minutes or so researching your next game.
- If you must keep playing – if you really must – tighten up your starting-hand requirements to very good or premium only, in any position, for at least the next ten hands.
- Do not fixate on revenge against the player who perpetrated such a miserable, disgusting bad beat on you. If you do that, you will miss many other chances to win money from your other opponents.
- Ignore the player who finally ends up with the chips which some lucky idiot unfairly won from you; it's usually not you.

Remember that there is no limit to the depths of misery that bad beats, cold decks and lousy cards can inflict upon you. Chances as low as 5 per cent can come in hand after hand against you. Then a 2 per cent out can be hit . . . and another. It is statistically likely that this will happen occasionally: it is not defying the odds.

The key is that if you can cope with these miserable occasions cheaply, then you will show bigger – much bigger – profits at the end of the year. To put it another way: any fool can cope with success, but only the strong can deal with failure and bad luck and misery. Prove your strength to yourself and you will be rewarded.

To conclude, I want you to consider a very brief case study. Let's say, for the sake of argument, that poker is 95 per cent luck. That means that 5 per cent of the game is down to skill and judgment and your ability to play well. This low percentage doesn't sound much and, in the short term, odds like that can be overtaken without breaking sweat. A few sessions of bad beats, cold decks and lousy cards can render your skill worthless and the value of sheer dumb luck very high.

Now, think of the Las Vegas strip, with its billion-dollar-casino resorts. Think of the high rollers' suites and villas, the de luxe rooms with their wide-screen televisions, the free meals and the millions of free beers given to players. How do they pay for all that?

By having an edge over the opposition: you, the punter. And how big is that edge? Well, at Blackjack, Baccarat or Craps, it might be 1 or 2 per cent; at Roulette and casino poker games, perhaps 3–5 per cent; slots and video poker, anything from 1 per cent to about 10 per cent.

So, the casino's edge is, on average, maybe 3 or 4 per cent and, at the end of each month, they've made millions of dollars in profits. How do they do it?

The answer is that they have many punters, betting over and over again and, every time they play a hand, shoot the dice, pull the handle, statistically the casino makes its profit. Of course, that's not to say that the players don't win sometimes. I've won fourteen sessions of Craps in a row. That sounds odds-defying, but really it's to be expected at some point. That's because, in the short term, anything can happen. In the long term, however many reversals of fortune the casino suffers along the way, the edge relentlessly battles on behalf of the house and can never be beaten.

So it is with poker. If you can genuinely claim that you have a 5 per cent edge in terms of superiority at your table, then if you sit there long enough, you *will* win, quite definitely, however many times other players get lucky against you in the short term. The next time you suffer a terrible bad beat, just think of it as a punter in a casino who puts one coin in a slot machine and wins one thousand coins. It's a terrible loss now, but it will be made up and the machine will turn a profit – for sure. All you have to do is be there – playing right.

GLOSSARY OF POKER TERMS

add-on in a tournament, you may be offered the opportunity to add to your chips by buying extra chips after the first session of play

advertising the act of showing one or more of your hole cards to show that you have a strong hand when you say you do; done probably to mislead subsequently; occasionally, the showing of a bluff to encourage more action from opponents

aggressive a tendency to bet out and raise/re-raise rather than just to call or check

all-in to place all your remaining chips into the pot

ante bet made before the cards are dealt on each hand

ATM a mildly abusive description applied to a player who appears to be dispensing cash to anyone who cares to call

bad beat a hand which you lose to a player against the expected odds

bad-beat story a lengthy dissertation of a supposedly very unlucky occurrence when the 'expert' storyteller has been beaten by a mindless fool who has hit miracle cards to beat him; usually not that bad a beat; always much less interesting to the listener than to the storyteller

bet   to make the first movement of chips on any betting round

big blind   the bigger of the two ante-bets placed before each hand of Texas Hold 'Em

big slick   slang term for AK in the hole

bluff   to attempt to steal the pot by representing a hand stronger than the one actually held

board   the table; the community cards showing on the table

boat   a full house

bubble   the position in a tournament that is one off the money – the worst place to be eliminated

burn   to discard; the dealer 'burns' the top card before dealing the 'flop', 'turn' and 'river'

button   the dealer button which denotes the position of the dealer; also sometimes referring to the player in that seat

buy-in   the exchange of cash for chips; the amount required to sit at a given table

call   to match the highest bet made to date

calling station   like an ATM, a loose, forever-calling player

cap   the limit some casinos and card rooms put on the number of raises per round permitted in Limit games

cash in   to leave the table and exchange your chips for cash

check   when no other player has bet, to check is to make no bet at that stage (sometimes indicated by tapping the table)

check-raise   a play that you are usually strong; to check at first and then, once an opponent bets, to raise him

chips   also known as 'checks', these are circular, plastic or clay discs which represent different financial values and which are used instead of cash in almost all poker games

community cards the flop, turn and river cards dealt face up in the middle of the table

continuation bet a follow-up bet by a pre-flop raiser once the flop has appeared – designed to re-enforce the appearance of great strength

dead money a disparaging description of those competitors in a tournament whom you consider to have no chance of winning, who are therefore contributing to the overall prize pot generously

dealer the player who deals (or for whom a paid dealer deals) the deck, before this honour moves on to the next player in a clockwise direction

deuce a two

dog short for underdog

donkey a poor player

down cards your 'hole' or 'pocket' cards

draw to improve your hand with the community cards

early position the two or three players immediately to the left of the dealer; the first players to decide what to do

fifth street the fifth and final community card, also known as 'the river'

final table the last table of ten players (sometimes eight or nine) in a tournament when all other players have been eliminated

fish a player who stays in pots hoping to catch the right cards to create a winning hand – but against the odds

flop the first-three community cards

flush five cards of the same suit

flush draw when you have four cards of the same suit and you are hoping that your subsequent card(s) will produce a fifth card to complete the flush

fold to throw away, or muck, one's cards

fold equity the extra value a big bet carries because of the chance that the opponent(s) may fold rather than continue to contest the pot

fourth street   the fourth community card, also known as 'the turn'

free card   to allow the turn or river card to appear without there having been any betting and calling

gut-shot draw   a straight draw that can be filled by only one card: you might hold QJ and the flop comes 982; only a 10 can make your straight

heads-up   head-to-head play at a table containing only two players, or when only two players contest a pot

high roller   a player who competes for very high stakes

hole cards   the player's two secret cards, dealt face down

home game   poker played at home

HORSE   a style of poker game where five variations are played in succession: Hold 'Em, Omaha, Razz, Seven-Card Stud, Seven-Card Stud Hi/Lo Eights or better

house   the casino or club in which you are playing

implied pot odds   the potential pot odds given that the chips currently in the pot are likely to be boosted by further action; there will be further betting and therefore more chips in the pot by the end of the hand

in the hole   the player's two secret cards, dealt face down

kicker   card or cards not involved in the formation of a poker combination, but still part of the five-card poker hand

late position   player(s) immediately to the dealer's right, last to act on each round of the betting

lay down   to concede or give in; often a good play in poker if you feel you that are beaten

leak   a small, but consistent error which, over time, leads to repeated losses

limp in   to call a small bet in 'late position' when you are unlikely to be raised

loose a player likely to play too many hands, remain in pots for too long and make speculative plays which will result in chips being lost

mid-position in the middle of the table between the big blind and the dealer

MTT Multi-Table Tournament; an event featuring more than one table of action in simultaneous play

muck to fold, or discard

no-limit a game with no maximum limits on the amount which can be bet

nut, nuts the best possible hand; a 'nut' flush would be an ace-high flush, with no chance of a straight flush

off, off-suit cards of different suits

out, outs card or cards which will complete your hand and improve it, usually to winning status

overcard card, or cards, which are higher than those showing amongst the community cards

palooka an inexperienced card player

passive a player who tends to check and call as opposed to betting and raising

pigeon similar to donkey, palooka and fish

pocket rockets AA 'in the hole'

position a player's location at the table, measured in terms of the order in which action must be taken on each round of the betting

pot the collection of chips (sometimes cash) which will be awarded to the winner of the hand

premium hands the best cards possible as starting hands (in Hold 'Em: AA)

quads four of a kind

rainbow board cards which are all of different suits, offering no flush draw possibilities

raise increase the size of the biggest bet at the table

rake the amount, usually a small percentage, taken out of each pot by the casino, card club or online poker site as payment for hosting the game; there should be no rake in home games

re-buy in a tournament, when you lose all your chips early on, you may be offered the opportunity to pay the entry fee again for another chance and another set of starting chips

represent to give the impression of a very strong hand from all your betting actions

re-raise as above, once a player has already raised; considered a very strong, intimidating move

respect on the basis of his powerful betting actions, to believe that your opponent has a good hand and acting accordingly

river the fifth and final community card

rock a player who chooses only the best hands with which to enter the action and bets only when he is sure that he holds the best hand

rush to be on a roll, a sequence of successful plays

satellite a qualifying event for a big poker tournament

school a regular poker game, acknowledging that you never stop learning: a poker school

semi-bluff a bet or raise made without currently holding the best hand but with the potential to improve to the best hand if a successful draw is made

set 3-of-a-kind, 'trips'

side pot a secondary (sometimes tertiary) pot, formed because one player is all-in and cannot bet any more into the main pot, contested by the remaining players

Sit & Go a one-table tournament (occasionally more) most often played online, which begins the moment the required number of players are signed up

short-handed a poker game containing five players or fewer; the value of hands often changes as a result of having fewer players at the table

short-stack when you have less than the average amount of chips in front of you

showdown   when a bet (or bets) is called after the river card, all players must show their hole cards; the best hand wins

slow-play   to give the impression of weakness or uncertainty by checking or calling bets rather than raising them

slowrolling   to turn over a winning hand slowly after another player believes that he has won; poor form at the poker table

smooth call   to call, rather than to raise, with a strong hand which, at a later date, you intend to raise your opponent; a trapping call to disguise strength, possibly to induce further callers into the pot

stack   a player's chips, either literally or, online, metaphorically

stealing   to bet or raise when opponents have shown comparative weakness in the hope of taking down the pot there and then; often used in the context of a button raise in an attempt 'to steal the blinds'

straight   five cards of mixed suits in sequence

suited   of the same suit

super-satellite   a satellite event from which the winner(s) can gain a seat in a satellite

table image   the personality that you have displayed in order to create an image of your style of play; may well be misleading designed to trap opponents into misjudging your future actions

take down   win (the pot)

tell   a physical indication, often subconscious or unrecognized by the player himself, by which other players may gain an insight into the strength of a player's hand

tight   likely to enter only a few pots with very good or premium hands; opposite of loose

tilt   usually a sign of frustration or anger, a player may go 'on tilt' by playing too many hands of poor quality and subsequently showering opponents with chips

trap   to mislead an opponent into believing that you have a weak hand – perhaps by checking or calling when a bet or raise would normally be called for

treys   pocket threes

trips   a 'set'; 3-of-a-kind

turn   the fourth community card; sometimes known as 'fourth street'

under-bet   a bet which, considering the size of the pot and the preceding action, appears too small

under the gun (UTG)   the first player to act after the blinds in Hold 'Em

value bet   to bet a hand you believe to be winning to extract the best value from your opponent; a bet made at the end of a hand which, over time, will lead to profit

WSOP   the World Series of Poker – the world championships of the game, held each summer in Las Vegas